NAMING THE ANTICHRIST

NAMING THE ANTICHRIST

The History of an American Obsession

ROBERT C. FULLER

OXFORD UNIVERSITY PRESS
New York   Oxford

Oxford University Press

Oxford   New York
Athens   Auckland   Bangkok   Bombay
Calcutta   Cape Town   Dar es Salaam   Delhi
Florence   Hong Kong   Istanbul   Karachi
Kuala Lumpur   Madras   Madrid   Melbourne
Mexico City   Nairobi   Paris   Singapore
Taipei   Tokyo   Toronto

and associated companies in
Berlin   Ibadan

Library of Congress Cataloging-in-Publication Data
Fuller, Robert C., 1952–
Naming the Antichrist : the hisory of an American obsession
Robert C. Fuller.
p.   cm.   Includes bibliographical references and index.
ISBN 0-19-508244-3
ISBN 0-19-510979-1 (Pbk.)
1. Antichrist—History of doctrines.
2. United States—Church history.
3. United States—Intellectual Life.
4. Good and evil—History of doctrines.
I. Title.   BT985.F85   1995   236—dc20
94-18602

1 3 5 7 9 10 8 6 4 2

Printed in the United States of America

Acknowledgments

The idea for this book came during a lunch-time run with my colleague Peter Dusenbery. Peter was curious about how undergraduate students typically respond to the types of questions and insights that arise in the academic study of religion. I laughed and confessed that some must surely view me as the Antichrist owing to my insistence that religion can and should be made the subject of intellectual inquiry. Over the next few miles we had a good time recalling various people and ideas that at one time or another had been called the Antichrist. We returned from our run a bit late for a faculty curriculum committee at which I sat uncharacteristically silent. Hoping that my colleagues would assume I was fervently recording their lofty comments, I managed to finish transcribing Peter's and my earlier conversation into a detailed outline for this book.

Peter is not the only one to whom I owe thanks for the insights and material that helped me complete this project. Several noted scholars offered bibliographical suggestions. John Corrigan of the Arizona State University and Ron Numbers of the University of Wisconsin were particularly generous, as was Martin Marty of the University of Chicago. Paul Boyer, also of the University of Wisconsin, directed me to his immensely helpful discussion of apocalyptic thinking entitled *When Time Shall Be No More*. Perhaps the most assistance came from Stephen O'Leary of the University of Southern California. His continuing advice and bibliographical suggestions have been greatly appreciated.

Interlibrary loan service has made it possible for me to conduct the research for seven books while rarely leaving Peoria, Illinois. Bradley University's library staff, particularly Marina Savoie, has worked very hard to keep me supplied with research materials and I am grateful. Debbie Doering has patiently printed draft after draft, and diplomatically ignored the mood swings that accompanied my work on this book. I would also like to acknowledge my appreciation for the administrative competence of my long-time colleagues Kal Goldberg and Claire Etaugh. Their willingness to step forward from faculty rank to perform so professionally the most difficult tasks of academe surely deserves recogniton.

Finally, I would like to thank Oxford University Press's Cynthia Read for her confidence in this project since its inception. I have been fortunate to have had her able advice and assistance on three projects now, and am envious of her professional skills.

Contents

NAMING THE ANTICHRIST

Introduction

The term Antichrist barely appears in scripture. Only two minor epistles, 1 John and 2 John, actually use the term, and its meaning even there is fairly obscure. Yet, from the earliest times, the concept of the Antichrist has captured the popular Christian imagination. The Antichrist represents the ultimate enemy of Christ who will appear in the final chapter of history to lead the forces of Satan in one last desperate battle against the forces of God. This notion of the incarnation of ultimate evil has mingled with other apocalyptic imagery like that found in the books of Daniel and Revelation. These biblical sources portray a rebellious "beast" who will tyrannize the faithful before he is finally vanquished by Christ at the dawn of the long-awaited millennium. The Antichrist is therefore the most dreaded of the obstacles standing between believers and the fulfillment of Christian hopes. Even though the Antichrist's tyranny and deceit are to be feared, the prospect of his imminent appearance is also a source of hope and even jubilation, for it is the appearance of the Antichrist that will initiate the sequence of actions culminating in the creation of the Kingdom of God on earth.

Christians have been remarkably unwilling to let biblically prophesied "end times" come to pass on their own. Instead, for nearly two thousand years they have anticipated the final phase of history by trying to identify or name the Antichrist in advance of the actual world calamities that would reveal his identity beyond doubt. In the early days of the church, first Emperor Nero and then Caligula were identified as the ultimate enemy of Christ. Subsequent centuries have witnessed a parade of candidates for this infamous designation: whereas many Protestants have identified the pope as the Antichrist, others have looked to political figures such as Napoleon Bonaparte, Adolf Hitler, Henry Kissinger, Mikhail Gorbachev, and, most recently, Saddam Hussein.

Much of this history of the concept of the Antichrist has been chronicled. For example, the early history of this persistent symbol of humanity's most vile enemy can be found in Bernard McGinn's study of medieval apocalypticism, *Visions of the End*.[1] In addition, J. Burton Russell's history of the devil, *The Prince of Darkness*, Richard Emmerson's *Antichrist in the Middle Ages*, and Christopher Hill's *Antichrist in Seventeenth-Century England* describe important stages in the evolution of Christianity's attitudes toward its archenemy.[2] Yet there has been surprisingly little attention given to what might be called "the American Antichrist," the distinctive treatment of the Antichrist throughout American religious and cultural history. But there is a fascinating story concerning this dark side of the American religious psyche. The history of the Antichrist reveals Americans' historical obsession with understanding themselves—and their enemies—in the mythic context of the struggle between absolute good and absolute evil.

As we approach the year 2000, the story of the American Antichrist is especially timely, and the dawning millennium is already stirring up speculation about the end of the world. A special issue of *Time* magazine entitled "Beyond the Year 2000: What to Expect in the New Millennium" asserts that 53 percent of adult Americans expect the imminent return of Jesus Christ, accompanied by the fulfillment of biblical prophecies concerning the cataclysmic destruction of all that is wicked.[3] Television evangelists, itinerant revivalists, and local pastors alike are offering chronologies of these latter days, but ironically, their tales of impending disaster are intended to comfort their audiences. Indeed, true believers are assured that their faith has already secured them a place among the righteous remnant to be spared by Christ and to be invited to assist him in ruling over a sanctified earth. As the *Time* survey indicates, millions of Americans share an apocalyptic worldview that makes them look forward to the sequence of events leading to their final triumph over scoffers and unbelievers. It is thus no fluke that Hal Lindsey's *The Late Great Planet Earth* has sold over nineteen million copies since its release in 1970. Lindsey, who warns that the "prophetic countdown" has already begun and that we now live in "the era of the Antichrist," has struck a responsive chord in American thought. He and his readers share a common theological vocabulary that makes it possible to see in the "signs of the times" a continuous gathering of the Antichrist's forces of evil. The approaching millennium thus will certainly have great psychological power in popular culture. Although for some it promises a bold new age of human achievement, for others it means redoubled vigilance for discerning, however camouflaged, the beast who will seize this moment in history to make his final assault.

The symbol of the Antichrist has played a surprisingly significant role in shaping Americans' self-understanding. Because they tend to view their nation as uniquely blessed by God, they have been especially prone to demonize their enemies. Throughout their nation's history, they have suspected that those who oppose the American way must be in league with the Antichrist's confederation of evil. Their attempts to "name the Antichrist" consequently reveal much about their culture's latent hopes and fears. Americans in the colonial era, for example, were certain that the Antichrist held special power over the Native Americans, whose pagan ways and prior ownership of the land threatened the successful completion of their efforts to build a new Zion in the west. Later in the colonial era, when nationalist sentiment grew stronger, it became clear that both the church and the king of England wielded the Antichrist's tyrannical power and so must be opposed at all costs.

Over the last two hundred years, the Antichrist has been repeatedly identified with such "threats" as modernism, Roman Catholicism, Jews, socialism, and the Soviet Union. Today, fundamentalist Christian writers see the Antichrist in such enemies as the Muslim world, feminism, rock music, and secular humanism. The threat of the Antichrist's imminent takeover of the world's economy has also been traced to the formation of the European Economic Community, the Susan B. Anthony dollar, the fiber optics used in our television sets, and the introduction of universal product codes. In and through such efforts to name the Antichrist, there is an intriguing story of how many Americans go about establishing the symbolic boundaries that separate all that is holy and good from the powers of chaos that continually threaten to engulf them.

The history of Americans' obsession with naming the Antichrist draws attention to their almost limitless capacity for mythologizing life. With the help of biblical metaphors, many Americans are able to mythologize life by "seeing" that there are deeper powers at work behind the surface appearance of worldly events. Everyday life is viewed against a cosmic background in which the forces of good are continually embattled by the forces of evil. The problems and confusions that Americans face consequently can never be reduced to political, social, or economic causes. Instead, these are guerrilla tactics employed by Satan in his never-ending war against the people of God.

The Antichrist has generally been understood to be Satan's chief disciple or agent for deceiving humanity in the final days, and for this reason the symbolism surrounding these two mythic creatures overlaps a great deal. As we shall see in Chapter 1, the Antichrist's relationship to Satan is traditionally conceived in an analogy to the relationship between Christ and God: the incarnation into the human world of a son or mediating agent whose purpose is to secure—or thwart—the salvation of souls. Just as Christ works through the church and other historical agencies to promote God's will on earth, the Antichrist assists Satan by working through various persons and social movements to spread chaos and to thwart the redemption of souls. Perhaps the most distinctive feature of the lore surrounding the Antichrist, as distinct from

Satan, is the relatively greater attention given to his presence in those ideas or events that threaten to seduce members of the believing community into adopting heretical beliefs or lifestyles. The Antichrist is most vividly present in those moments when otherwise faithful persons are attracted to ideas that would gradually lead them to abandon unqestioning commitment to group orthodoxy. The efforts of various persons to name the Antichrist thus tend to mirror the internal struggles of individuals and communities to ward off doubt or ambiguity.

The symbolism of the Antichrist receives its sense of overriding urgency from its close association with what are referred to as *apocalyptic* or *millenarian* beliefs. From the time of Jesus, Christianity has been concerned with the expectation of the "end times" (often known as eschatology from the Greek work *eschaton*, which means "the end"). Jesus' message was unabashedly eschatological in that he announced that the Kingdom of God was at hand and that we must therefore waste no time before repenting our sins and preparing ourselves for the final judgment. Jesus' references to the imminent end of the world as we know it were fairly straightforward pronouncements like those generally associated with the great Hebrew prophets who also called on us to repent our sins. The Hebrew Book of Daniel and the Christian Book of Revelation, however, add much more mystery to their predictions of the impending judgment. These and similar texts from the biblical era are referred to as *apocalyptic* in nature (the word *apocalypse* comes from the Greek *apokalypsis*, which means "an unveiling or uncovering of truths that are ordinarily hidden"). The authors of these texts claim to have received special revelations that provide "inside information" concerning God's timetable and game plan for his final confrontation with Satan. Apocalyptic texts are usually filled with highly cryptic, indeed downright confusing, references to dragons, beasts, false prophets, angels, and other supernatural entities, all of whom have precise roles in the cataclysmic cycle of events through which God will move history to completion.

In Chapter One we trace the origins of apocalyptic thought in the Judeo-Christian tradition and the subsequent development of apocalyptic beliefs up to present-day Christian fundamentalism. According to contemporary fundamentalism, the final sequence of events will be triggered by what is called "the Rapture."[4] The term *Rapture*, not found in the Bible, refers to a passage in 1 Thessalonians describing "the catching up" of believers just before the onset of the great tribulations destined to beset the earth: "For the Lord Himself shall descend from heaven with a shout, with the voice of the archangel, and with the trumpet of God. And the dead in Christ shall rise first; then we who are alive and remain shall be caught up together with them in the clouds to meet the Lord in the air" (4:16–17). This Rapture will spare all who have previously embraced Christ as their Savior from the seven years of catastrophic events that beset on all those left behind on earth. It is predicted that these tribulations will begin with the rise to prominence of the Antichrist, who will be the leader of a ten-nation confederation. The Antichrist will at first be embraced as a man of peace and spirituality (owing to his great powers of deception). He will begin his demonic reign by seeming to be an ally of Israel in its political struggles with Russia and other northern nations. But after a period of three and a half years, he will withdraw his support from Israel and will enter the temple of Jerusalem and make it his political headquarters. In the meantime, 144,000 Jews and a large number of Gentiles will have realized the error of their ways and will accept Jesus as their savior. Nonetheless, these new converts will, unfortunately, have to face the full brunt of the Antichrist's persecution and torture.

Amid stupendous natural disasters such as floods, fires, plagues, and earthquakes, the Antichrist will gain total control over the earth's entire population and require that every person wear a mark or number in order to participate in the new world economy. It is prophesied that anyone who accepts this mark of the beast (usually thought to be the number 666) will receive eternal damnation. During these tumultuous events, Christ will appear in the heavens and return to earth in all his glory. He will lead the forces of good into the climactic Battle of Armageddon in which he will slay the Antichrist and cast him into a lake of fire. It will then be Christ's privileged act to bind Satan and to throw him into a bottomless pit where he will remain for a thousand years. This thousand-year period during which Satan is bound constitutes the glorious millennium, from which the term *millennial faith* is derived as a synonym for Christian apocalyptic belief. It is described as an age in which the faithful will enjoy ageless bodies and inhabit a world of peace and plenty. For reasons that are unclear, God will permit Satan to be "loosed" at the end of this thousand-year period for one last desperate effort to lure unfaithful souls. After tolerating this final gasp of blasphemy and perdition, God will cast Satan into the lake of fire with the Antichrist, where they will be tormented for the rest of eternity. At this point the earth will be purified by fire and replaced by a "new heaven and a new earth" in which the redeemed will enjoy the glories of eternity.

This apocalyptic worldview is based on a style of thinking that is wholly alien to the scientific spirit of modern intellectual thought. Apocalyptic belief, for example, presupposes a literal interpretation of ancient biblical writings and postulates an overtly supranaturalist vision of reality in which angelic beings are expected to intervene in worldly events. Those who believe in the imminent threat posed by the Antichrist are thus in a "cognitive minority." Although perhaps not a minority in a statistical sense, they are certainly swimming against the mainstream of twentieth-century cultural and intellectual developments. This is, of course, precisely their point and helps us understand their obsession with seeking out invisible enemies. Under assault from secularist culture, fundamentalist Christian groups are forced to demarcate the boundaries separating them from their modernist adversaries. The community of believers must be helped to avoid temptations to cross over into more ambiguous intellectual territory, by understanding the dire consequences of apostasy. To this extent, fundamentalism requires believing in a treacherous enemy whose existence gives these boundary-setting behaviors a sense of urgency. As historians Martin Marty and R. Scott Appleby observed, it is critical to the survival of fundamentalist groups that they continually "name, dramatize, and even mythologize their enemies."[5] Millennial beliefs are especially helpful in this regard. The biblical prophecies concerning the Antichrist "provide fundamentalists with a cosmic enemy, imbue fundamentalist boundary-setting and purity-preserving activities with an apocalyptic urgency, and foster a crisis mentality that serves both to intensify missionary efforts and to justify extremism."[6]

A history of the American Antichrist therefore must be alert to how the "crisis mentality" fostered by apocalyptic belief helps believers maintain their purity and identity. Certain psychological and cultural functions are served by a worldview that encourages people to see themselves as actors in a "dramatic eschatology," an eschatological drama unfolding in the mind of God and assuring them of final victory over those who would oppose or even differ from them. Michael Barkun, for example, argued that apocalyptic thought emerges as an attempt to explain and understand the meaning of disasters, both natural and human made.[7] David Aberle focused on how the belief that the end is near (and that the tables will soon be turned, ensuring that the last will become first and the first will become last) helps people deal with economic or social deprivation.[8] Stephen O'Leary examined how apocalyptic discourse is intended to solve the problem of evil by explaining its cosmic origins and assuring believers of the ultimate triumph of good over evil.[9] Perhaps the most striking interpretation of apocalyptic thought is Norman Cohn's contention that obsession with battling cosmic enemies can be likened to a form of paranoia:

> The megalomaniac view of oneself as the elect, wholly good, abominably persecuted yet assured of ultimate triumph; the attribution of gigantic and demonic powers to the adversary; the refusal to accept the ineluctable limitations and imperfections of human existence, such as transience, dissension, conflict, fallibility whether intellectual or moral; the obsession with inerrable prophecies—these attitudes are symptoms which together constitute the unmistakable syndrome of paranoia. But a paranoiac delusion does not cease to be so because it is shared by so many individuals, nor yet because those individuals have real and ample grounds for regarding themselves as victims of oppression.[10]

Cohn's somewhat cavalier attribution of paranoia to those who stand vigil against the Antichrist has been criticized for interpreting historical data in terms of modern psychological thought. Nonetheless, his views are shared by many.[11] Richard Hofstadter, for example, also finds apocalyptic thought to be associated with extreme forms of individual and group paranoia. In his *The Paranoid Style in American Politics*, Hofstadter examines a continuing subculture in American life that views conspiracy as the motive force of history. The distinctive feature of the paranoid outlook is that it views history as "a conspiracy, set in motion by demonic forces. . . . The paranoid sees the fate of this conspiracy in apocalyptic terms—he traffics in the birth and death of whole worlds, whole political orders, whole systems of human values."[12] Apocalyptic thought aids and abets the paranoid style by showing the "enemy" to be not simply a human adversary but, rather, the very incarnation of cosmic evil. What is at stake in the conflict with this enemy is the final confrontation between absolute good and absolute evil. Hence there can be no compromise, no retreat. Yet as Hofstadter perceptively notes regarding the paranoid style, this "enemy seems to be on many counts a projection of the self: both the ideal and the unacceptable aspects of the self are attributed to him."[13] Indeed, the naming of the American Antichrist reveals a great deal about how Americans—from Cotton Mather to Hal Lindsey—have projected their own unacknowledged doubts, shame, and guilt on a worthy cosmic adversary. The Antichrist, it seems, almost invariably embodies those alluring traits and qualities that at a deeper level threaten to seduce even the "true believer" into apostasy.

As Cohn's and Hofstadter's assessments of apocalyptic thought make clear, any attempt to interpet Americans' portrayals of the Antichrist will reflect the author's own assumptions about historical interpretation, human nature, and social–historical change. It is, therefore, important that my readers understand that I regard intellectual history as a discipline that must alternate between two distinct but complementary modes of interpretation. First, intellectual history must appreciate the way in which ideas and texts come to have a life of their own. That is, we cannot overlook the fact that belief in the Antichrist is part of a literary and theological tradition that is itself capable of influencing a person's or even a historical epoch's self-understanding. This tradition is, moreover, transmitted through a variety of cultural institutions that are relatively immune to the kinds of social or economic forces that a Cohn or a Hofstadter insist on seeing as central to an explanation of why individuals are "driven" to apocalyptic belief.

Apocalyptic belief has attracted adherents for more than two thousand years and in almost every kind of cultural context imaginable. Concern with the Antichrist has existed in periods of both relative tranquillity and social upheaval, in persons who have paranoid tendencies and in those with stable personalities, in people with great hostility toward minorities or foreigners and in people who welcome cultural diversity. Intellectual historians cannot overlook the autonomous power of scriptural texts to structure Americans' thoughts about the world. For example, many Americans whose anti-Semitic prejudices would otherwise make them political opponents of Jews have instead become ardent supporters of Israel, principally because of Israel's ostensible role in "Bible prophecy." Similarly, many ultraconservative Protestants went to great lengths to argue that the Soviet Union was not the Antichrist but, rather, the biblical "Gog" who will arise and battle the Antichrist in the final stages of world history. Biblical passages put hard and fast limitations on the kinds of inferences that can be made about the nature and activity of the feared agent of Satan. For this reason, intellectual history must be careful not to overlook the most obvious factor responsible for various acts of "naming the Antichrist."

A second task of intellectual history is to be alert to what might be called the *sociology of knowledge*. As a humanistic discipline, historical analysis assumes that all cultural phenomena, including religion, are the expressions of humanity's efforts to construct an intelligible system of ideas and meanings. An important goal of intellectual history is thus to shed some light on the ways in which various sociological, economic, and psychological conditions prompt us to accept some ideas as palpably true while rejecting others as either irrelevant or sheer nonsense. Developed by such theorists as Max Weber, Karl Mannheim, and Peter Berger, the sociological approach to the history of ideas illustrates how beliefs and ideas can explain, correct, or complete otherwise unmet sociological or psychological needs. These are important considerations when trying to understand why belief in the Antichrist becomes more prominent in one period of history than in another. They also help us understand how the Antichrist's identity keeps changing from generation to generation and why there is so much urgency associated with efforts to warn others of the Antichrist's presence, even though the logic of scripture dictates a more resigned attitude toward the inevitable fulfillment of divine providence. Sociological and psychological perspectives assist us in discerning why beliefs about the Antichrist's efforts to seduce people into apostasy so often mirror a person's or community's internal struggles with belief. We should remind ourselves that what distinguishes the humanities as academic disciplines is their interest in interpretation. The whole point of humanistic inquiry, particularly historical inquiry, is to explicate meanings that are not overtly present in a text, a historical event, or a person's self-awareness. A judicious use of social, economic, and psychological perspectives that make such an explication possible is thus an indispensable part of the interpretive process.

Readers should be warned that this book is not intended to be an encyclopedic cataloging of every mention of the Antichrist by an American author or lecturer. It is instead a narrative history of the American obsession with mythologizing life in apocalyptic terms. Topics and authors have been selected for treatment largely for their ability to illuminate the human drama entailed in efforts to "name the Antichrist." This volume, then, is less concerned with providing an exhaustive set of Antichrist citations than with interpreting the broader significance of this enduring American obsession.

The first chapter discusses the origins and development of the Antichrist legend in Western intellectual history. The letters 1 and 2 John were written by a person (or persons) who envisaged his readers as threatened by a heresy. What made this false teaching so dangerous was that it was promulgated by a group of charismatic Christians whose spiritual enthusiasm was drawing many to their heretical views. Calling them the Antichrists, this biblical author(s) provided a term that would soon symbolize the ultimate enemy of the true church. This term, moreover, had clear connections with the developing apocalyptic tradition whose major homiletic function was to encourage audiences to remain faithful despite temptations to embrace unorthodox ideas or morals. In this chapter we trace how the symbol of Antichrist emerged as central to this apocalyptic tradition and how it was elaborated upon from the earliest days of Christianity through the Middle Ages.

Chapter Two describes the migration of the Antichrist legend across the Atlantic. Convinced that salvation history was moving from east to west, the early American colonists knew themselves to be on God's "errand into the wilderness." The purpose of this errand, as Cotton Mather explained, was to engage in "the last conflict with anti-christ" by establishing a holy commonwealth against which the forces of evil could not prevail. As fate had it, however, this errand repeatedly fell on hard times. The first legions of the Antichrist to be reckoned with were the pagan Native Americans and the Catholic French. This fiendish power of iniquity later attacked the very heart of this community of saints by inspiring internal discord in the form of such self-styled dissenters as Anne Hutchison, Roger Williams, and the infamous witches of Salem. No sooner were these threats dispatched than the colonists began to discover that both the Church of England and the whole institution of monarchy were merely the instruments through which the Antichrist sought to exercise his tyranny over the fledgling new Zion in the west. Apocalyptic rhetoric from influential clergy provided a religious imperative for colonists to sever their ties with England and launch themselves headstrong into the building of a new nation under God.

At the dawn of the nineteenth century, Protestant Americans were largely in accord that the power of divine providence was with them. The third chapter discusses what is often referred to as "the Second Great Awakening," in which popular opinion was galvanized around the belief that moral resolve alone is sufficient to bring about salvation and the regeneration of society. White Anglo-Saxon Protestants confidently set about the task of constructing an empire that they believed would in and of itself inaugurate the millennium. This view, known as *post-millennialism*, touts the power of concerted human effort to perfect the earth in expectation of—and prior to—Christ's final return. Those in the consensus culture knew full well what agencies of the Antichrist still stood in their way: non-Protestants, immigrants, intemperance, the city, and—at least to Northerners—the institution of slavery. Members of the Protestant establishment largely eschewed apocalyptic imagery and rhetoric and instead sought to rid their nation of these final blights through a variety of social reform movements. Yet even as the Protestant mainstream forged ahead in its crusade for a Christian commonwealth, new religious voices were championing the premillennial form of apocalyptic thought, in which Christ was expected to return to earth in order to defeat the Antichrist personally. The Mormons and Millerites (later to emerge as the Seventh-Day Adventists) appeared on the American religious scene as forerunners of the revival of premillennial and apocalyptic understandings of the Antichrist tradition.

Chapter Four takes up the growth of premillennial thought in the fundamentalist movement of the twentieth century. By the late 1800s, modernism had hit full stride. Rapid advances in the natural sciences, the emergence of the social sciences such as psychology and sociology, and the startling discoveries of biblical scholarship combined to create a new intellectual climate that fostered secular humanism. Many conservative Christians, however, were quick to recognize the work of the Prince of Apostasy in these seductive teachings. By 1920 a new coalition of premillennial Protestants emerged with a fully articulated and biblically based chronology for the end times. Known as *fundamentalists*, they were called upon to do "battle royal" for Christ in his urgent quest to eradicate the modernist, secularist, and humanistic forms in which the Antichrist proudly paraded across American intellectual life. Chapter Five follows the development of this crusade as it extended beyond modernism to battle the confederacy of social, economic, and racial forces that seemingly was aimed at the dissolution of God's chosen America. The 1930s and 1940s witnessed a new intensification of efforts to name the Antichrist as Americans vented their latent fears and prejudices in relentless displays of anti-Semitism, anti-Catholicism, and anti-socialism. Hate mongers like Gerald L. K. Smith, Carl McIntire, Gerald Winrod, and the Ku Klux Klansmen all used apocalyptic imagery to identify the diabolic nature of the many enemies who conspired against the glorious culture forged by God-loving Protestants.

The kinds of ethnic hatred and pious hyperpatriotism that surfaced in the Antichrist rhetoric of the 1920s, 1930s, and 1940s have certainly stayed with us. Ronald Reagan's and Pat Robertson's references to the

Soviet Union as the Evil Empire and Protestant clergy's recent denunciation of Muslim leaders such as Saddam Hussein are ready examples of the continuing popular appeal of Antichrist imagery in American thought. Chapter Six examines these and other contemporary efforts to find the camouflaged conspirators plotting the overthrow of Christian civilization. The creation of the modern state of Israel in 1948 and the formation of the European Economic Community strike many evangelicals as indisputable fulfillments of biblical prophecy concerning the end days. If the end is indeed so near, the Antichrist—or at least his allied conspirators who are preparing the way—must already be among us. And, it seems, he is in the form of the United Nations, ecumenical religious bodies such as the National Council of Churches, feminism, rock music, secular humanism, New Age religions, universal product codes, and the fiber optics in our television sets sending live signals from our living rooms directly to the Antichrist's headquarters.

The story of the American Antichrist is varied and fascinating. It reveals a legacy of powerful religious emotion directed toward those persons or social forces that challenge the boundaries of theological orthodoxy. This book concludes by inquiring into the nature and meaning of this historical obsession. Americans' enduring tendency to mythologize life in the categories of apocalyptic thought is, as our narrative will show, laden with social and psychological significance. By projecting Americans' doubts and uncertainties onto a demonic "other," the act of naming the Antichrist protects their personal and collective sensibilities from the frailties of human existence.

One

Antichrist: The History of an Idea

Children, it is the last hour; and as you have heard that antichrist is coming, so now many antichrists have come; therefore we know that it is the last hour.

1 John 2:18

❧

The New Testament letters known as 1, 2, and 3 John rank among the shortest and most obscure of all the books in the Bible. We do not know with any certainty just who wrote them, when, or where. But their conviction that the end of the world was near and that Christians must fend off the feared Antichrist soon earned them an authoritative place in Christian thought. These letters are striking in their depiction of the urgency felt by early Christians as they prepared for the final judgment. The author was alert to the anxieties aroused by the expectation that Christ would return at any moment to pronounce this final judgment. It was imperative that someone define Christian faith clearly so that believers might be careful not to stray accidentally into heresy and thereby cost themselves eternal salvation. Both 1 and 2 John respond to this need for erecting definite theological boundaries and warn their audiences against adopting beliefs that, however popular or alluring, would lead them into heresy just as they approached the final hour. In particular, these letters condemn the beliefs and spirituality espoused by a relatively affluent group of Christians who had separated from the main community. It was imperative that others not be led astray by these renegade Christians, who appeared to be genuinely inspired by God but whom the author knew to be guilty of the gravest heresies. Both 1 and 2 John tell their readers that these false prophets were empowered by "the spirit of the antichrist." And in so doing, these otherwise obscure New Testament epistles gave form and clarity to the supernatural face behind all that oppose Christians as they approach the day of judgment.

Boundary Setting in the Johannine Epistles

The letters 1, 2, and 3 John are examples of written communications passing among different Christian groups around the turn of the first century. It is clear from these letters that at this time there was a great deal of confusion about what could and could not be considered part of Christian faith. There is, however, no consensus among scholars as to who wrote these pastoral letters. According to church tradition, all three were written in Ephesus by the apostle John, who is also said to have written the Gospel of John. This is, however, almost certainly not the case.[1] Scholarly analysis of the texts indicates that 1, 2, and 3 John were written by at least two different persons, neither of whom was the author of the Gospel of John.[2] The distinctive structures and patterns of 1 John, for example, bear little resemblance to the Gospel of John. In addition, stylistic differences in 1 John strongly suggest that it is the work of at least two different writers, and it also seems probable that 2 and 3 John were written by yet another author. All three letters seem to be familiar with the contents of the Gospel of John, and their author(s) apparently used the familiar practice of adopting the pseudonym of John to garner authority for their writings and to show their commitment to what is often called the Johannine doctrinal tradition.

Kenneth Grayston gives us a plausible reconstruction of the situation that elicited these early Christian writings.[3] A sizable group of well-to-do members had withdrawn their support from the larger Christian community, apparently having disagreed with the "orthodox" community's decision to separate themselves from the world. The dissident group insisted instead on participating fully in the world about them and argued that holiness did not require withdrawing from the affairs of the world. It is also clear that this group possessed a great deal of spiritual charisma. Their prophetic gifts had already brought them some degree of popularity ("the world listens to them"), and in all likelihood their bold spirituality aroused the jealousy of the larger community. The dissidents further claimed to have been anointed by the Spirit, just as Jesus had been. The implication, then, was that they lived in the light and directly participated in divine nature. Because they believed that they had direct and unmediated access to God, they rejected the emerging Christian doctrine that only Jesus could mediate between humans and God. Indeed, the historical Jesus was more or less irrelevant to their version of Christianity, which put the major emphasis on each person undergoing the experience of being directly anointed by the Spirit. As a consequence they no longer felt bound by the doctrines or structured fellowship that the author(s) of these letters believed were central to Christian faith.

The first letter of John addresses the embattled community with a comforting reminder of Jesus' role in mediating the forgiveness of their sins: "My little children, I am writing this to you so that you may not sin; but if any one does sin, we have an advocate with the Father, Jesus Christ the righteous; and he is the expiation for our sins. . . . And by this [belief] we may be sure that we know him" (2:1–3). The author of 1 John thus makes it clear that there are distinct doctrinal boundaries beyond which one cannot stray and remain a Christian. Those who do stray beyond these boundaries no longer belong to the world of God. He then proceeds to the issue at hand and explains why these former members of the community must be shunned despite their alluring lifestyle, their inspiring spirituality, and their attractive theological notions. They are nonconformists, they are the antichrists. Their beliefs reveal that they were never true Christians in the first place ("They went out from us, but they were not of us; for if they had been of us, they would have continued with us."). The author reminds his readers that even though these renegades will try to deceive them, they must be secure in the knowledge that the time of judgment is at hand and that steadfast faith will be rewarded. "Children," he warns, "it is the last hour; and as you have heard that antichrist is coming, so now many antichrists have come; therefore we know that it is the last hour" (2:18).

The author here is alluding to a tradition concerning the appearance of the Antichrist, with which he assumes his readers are familiar. We will never know, however, precisely what tradition he had in mind. Subsequent generations of readers have assumed that he was referring to the dreaded figures mentioned in other biblical materials, such as Daniel or Revelation. These apocalyptic texts use the imagery of beasts, dragons, or monsters to describe the ultimate eschatological adversary that must be defeated by the Son of Man before the establishment of the millennium. But this is supposition, and no such references are explicit in the text. On the contrary: The term *antichristos* lacks the definite article that would designate *the* well-known or widely anticipated figure. The word *antichrist* is used three times in 1 John and once in 2 John and nowhere else in scripture. In addition, the author not only refers to the Antichrist as *an* opponent of Christ (rather than *the* opponent) but also uses the word in the plural, by designating all the dissenting members of the community as antichrists. We thus should be skeptical of the customary assumption that the Johannine antichrist is simply one variant of the long-established, widespread expectation of an intensely evil adversary such as is found in Revelation and believed in by later

Christians. The Johannine antichrist refers to apostate humans rather than a supernatural beast, such as was common in ancient myths depicting a dragon of chaos that opposes the creative deity. It "names" not an evil supernatural entity but humans whose manifest spirituality and growing popularity are causing resentment and jealousy. If the author who first used the term *antichrist* had any mythic figure in mind, he certainly did not develop it any further. Rather, his principal concern was to attack those who were undermining the community's theological purity.

According to 1 John, what is to be dreaded about the Antichrist is not the unleashing of awesome destruction but the fomenting of heresy. This heresy, moreover, did not come from unconverted Jews or Gentiles but from Christians themselves! For this reason, the author of 1 John warns his readers to test all beliefs, even those of persons who claim that the Spirit abides in them. He is consequently not concerned with measuring alleged inner spirituality but with testing consistency of belief with the emerging tradition. The test, we are told, is a doctrinal one. Its purpose is to identify and separate out those who do not conform to the community's doctrinal standards: "This is the antichrist, he who denies the Father and the Son" (2:22). The word *antichrist* is not found elsewhere in or out of Christian circles and may well have been invented by the author to dramatize the apostasy of diverging theological beliefs. In Greek, to be "anti" something indicates a claim to be in opposition to it, to be equivalent to it, or to be a substitute for it.[4] The author of 1 John seeks to establish the "anti" or oppositional nature of the views held by the dissident members of the community, by explaining that all who truly are of God will proclaim that Jesus is the Christ and that he has come in the flesh. This was an important theological point at the time because it counteracted the so-called docetic heresy according to which Jesus was actually a spirit and had only appeared to take on an actual human body. The dissident community seems to have held this view. The author's third reference to the antichrist develops this point:

> Beloved, do not believe every spirit, but test the spirits to see whether they are of God; for many false prophets have gone out into the world. By this you know the Spirit of God: every spirit which confesses that Jesus Christ has come in the flesh is of God, and every spirit which does not confess Jesus is not of God. This is the spirit of antichrist, of which you heard that it was coming, and now it is in the world already. (4:1–3)

The author of 1 John was thus not looking to the appearance of some supernatural being in the prophesied future. Instead, the antichrists were already about him in the form of persons who had been members of the believing community but had left it in order to teach doctrines that now threatened to seduce others into leaving as well. The closest biblical parallels to this development of the Antichrist are Mark 13:22, which claims, "False christs and false prophets will arise and show signs and wonders, to lead astray, if possible the elect," or Peter 2:1, which warns of false teachers in the community who "bring in destructive heresies, even denying the Master who brought them." Indeed, the fourth and final use of the term *antichrist* in the New Testament comes in 2 John, which continues this point by warning us that "many deceivers have gone out into the world, men who will not acknowledge the coming of Jesus Christ in the flesh; such a one is the deceiver and the antichrist" (1:7).

As Charles Erdman pointed out, what made these "false teachers" all the more dangerous was the fact that they moved in the best circles of society and were of pleasing personality—and were all of this while claiming to be Christians.[5] The community with which they disagreed, however, had withdrawn from the world so as to be separate, pure, and unambiguously righteous while awaiting the moment of judgment. The heresy they represented was thus both theological and communal; they threatened to seduce even more members into a mode of thinking and living that was "of the world" rather than of separatist faith. To prevent his readers from straying closer to this alluring boundary, 1 John sharply contrasts the regions of God with those of "the world": "Little children, you are of God, and have overcome them; for he who is in you is greater than he who is in the world. They are of the world, therefore what they say is of the world, and the world listens to them. We are of God. Whoever knows God listens to us, and he who is not of God does not listen to us. By this we know the spirit of truth and the spirit of errors" (4: 4–6).

The message is clear. Christians should not listen to the reasoning or wisdom of the world, no matter how tempting it may be to do so; they should instead listen only to God. At stake is the promise of salvation. Immediately after warning of the deceptions of the Antichrist, the author of 2 John cautions his readers to "look to yourselves, that you may not lose what you have worked for, but may win a full reward. Any one who goes ahead and does not abide in the doctrine of Christ does not have God; he who abides in the doctrine has both the Father and the Son" (1:8–9). Christians are therefore wise to shun all those who might lure them into apostasy. The more tightly the boundaries are monitored, the safer they are: "If any one comes to you and does not bring this doctrine, do not receive him into the house or give him any greeting; for he who greets him shares his wicked work" (1:10–11).

The Johannine antichrist thus served the early Christian community by helping identify who was of God and who was not, who could be trusted and who could with whom one could safely have fellowship and with whom one could not. The letters 1 and 2 John provide a litmus test to identify the antichrists seeking to deceive Christians and thus rob them of the salvation they have won. In this case, it is a theological litmus test and mandates professing the belief that it is not Christians who are anointed by the Spirit, but Christ and Christ alone. Those who teach otherwise exist outside the community's symbolic boundaries and should be shunned at all costs.

The Antichrist in an Apocalyptic Context

Christianity was born of eschatological hope and expectation. The excitement that Jesus generated among his followers stemmed largely from his assurance that they lived in the final hour. The first generation of Christians lived in constant anticipation of Christ's imminent return to inaugurate the promised Kingdom of God. But when it became apparent that Christ's return was delayed, interest shifted to the Antichrist and things associated with the enemies responsible for postponing Christians' final victory.[6] Christians fervently believed that they were already in the last hour, yet all around them life was continuing as usual. The discrepancy between belief and outer appearances created a great deal of cognitive dissonance, but this dissonance could be reduced by interpreting world events against the background of apocalyptic myth.[7] That is, the cryptic and evasive symbols associated with apocalyptic belief made it possible to see the "signs of the times" being fulfilled and therefore gave reassurance that the divine timetable—no matter how intricate and beyond full understanding—was nonetheless right on schedule. The symbol of the Antichrist, by providing a deceptive enemy against whom the believers could rally, made it possible for the early church to refashion existing apocalyptic traditions into a new and distinctively Christian form.

It was thus all but destined that the term *antichrist* would absorb the apocalyptic elements of early Christian belief. It is, of course, possible that both 1 and 2 John were referring to these apocalyptic expectations all along, as most Christian writers have maintained over the years. For example, it is possible to argue that the epistolary author knew the mythological expectations of final opposition by a single evil being but merely reinterpreted these traditions as part of his polemic against the secessionists in order to associate them with ultimate evil.[8] Christian scholars who are committed to the inerrancy of biblical texts often explain that what 1 and 2 John "really meant" was that the dissident members of the community were forerunners of a single dreaded antichrist who has yet to appear. Countless Christian writers over the centuries have used this reasoning to "name" the precursors and colleagues of the Antichrist, whom they see about them spreading his malicious spirit while adhering to a more expressly apocalyptic (i.e., drawn from Daniel and Revelation) interpretation of the actual Antichrist who will be personally defeated by Christ in the cataclysmic battle at the end of the world. Whatever the case and whatever the author of 1 John may have had in mind by the remark that "you have hear that antichrist is coming," it is certain that expectations of Antichrist's appearance combined in different ways with the apoclyptic beliefs prevalent in the Jewish world at the time of Jesus. The history of the idea of the Antichrist is the history of these apocalyptic beliefs.

The Greek word *apokalypsis* means an unveiling, an uncovering, a revealing of what is normally hidden. As applied to biblical writings, it means the disclosure of a dimension of human events that is ordinarily closed to human view. Biblical writers claim to have been the recipients of special revelations that describe how every last detail of human history is controlled by cosmic powers (i.e., God and Satan) who are contending with each other as they seek to move history toward its final destination. Apocalyptic literature describes these revelations and hence provides secret or mystical information concerning how events in our world are implicated in God's plan—or Satan's counterplan—for creation. A flood of such literature appeared from the third century B.C.E. to the end of the first century C.E. The most famous examples of apocalyptic writing are the biblical books of Daniel and Revelation, although several other texts from this era such as 1 and 2 Enoch, 2 Esdras, or 2 and 3 Baruch also adhere to the apocalyptic pattern. Usually referred to as the apocrypha or pseudepigrapha, these texts were not placed in the Hebrew scriptural canon but nonetheless give us a great deal of insight into the religious thought that dominated popular culture in the intertestamental period.

Central to the apocalyptic orientation to life are the convictions that (1) the world is sharply divided into the forces of good and those of evil; (2) the conflict between these two powers is about to be joined decisively, after which the world will be transformed and the children of light will enter into their inheritance on a purified earth; and (3) the duty of the faithful community is to wait in confidence and quietness for God to bring all of this to pass.[9] It should be pointed out that the apocalyptic worldview grows naturally out of, and is continuous with, the entire range of prophetic literature in the bible. Paul Hanson drew attention to the fact that the prophetic witness found in Isaiah, Zechariah, and Ezekiel shades imperceptibly into an apocalyptic outlook.[10] Both apocalyptic and prophetic thought provide a religious perspective of how God will act in history to restore purity and holiness among his people. The difference between the two is how much emphasis or confidence should be placed on the ability of humans to participate in bringing about this redemption. *Prophetic eschatology* focuses on God's providential action in plain history, real politics, and human actions. *Apocalyptic eschatology*, on the other hand, expresses a more pessimistic view of the human condition and consequently emphasizes that human history can be improved only when God (or God's agents) actively intervenes. We should be careful, however, not to draw too great a line between the apocalyptic and prophetic perspectives, as the two overlap and combine together throughout Western religious history.

Apocalyptic literature has several distinguishing characteristics.[11] First, the word *apocalypse* means a "revelation" and thus implies that it has been mediated to the author by an angel or other supernatural being. Second, apocalyptic writings interpret every event on earth, including the persecution of the righteous, as part of a cosmic drama designed and orchestrated by beings who exist in a transcendental reality. From this perspective it becomes obvious that humanity is divided into two opposing camps of intrinsically different ethical quality: those who have aligned themselves with the forces of God and those who are instruments for the forces of evil. Also common to apocalyptic writings is their tendency to be pseudonymous, to use mythic imagery, and to build on a series of narrative "cycles" that repeatedly describe and resolve the community's spiritual turmoils.[12]

David Hellholm insists that regardless of the precise mix of these formal characteristics, we should keep in mind that apocalyptic thought is "intended for a group in crisis with the purpose of exhortation and/ or consolation by means of divine authority."[13] Sociological studies indicate that apocalyptic writing commonly originates during times of crisis and tension. It appears to be a cultural response to severe persecution, a threat to the group's welfare, a decline in religious enthusiasm, or a growing awareness of the discrepancy between the group's eschatological expectations and current sociopolitical realities. Apocalyptic thinking helps the believing community by locating its problems in a transcendental or mythic context in which a victorious outcome is assured. Its purpose is to show that people can and must endure such crises, secure in the knowledge that their tribulations are part of God's plan for the final triumph over evil. The promised day of the Lord is thus still at hand, regardless of how bleak the prospects of victory may seem. When evil is at its height, he will come to defeat the wicked and return worldly power to his people. This message of consolation and exhortation can, as John Collins explains, be applied to almost every sort of problem:

> An apocalypse can provide support in the face of persecution (e.g. Daniel); reassurance in the face of culture shock (possibly the Book of the Watchers) or social powerlessness (the Similitudes of Enoch); reorientation in the wake of historical trauma (2 Baruch, 3 Baruch), consolation for the dismal fate of humanity (4 Ezra) or comfort for the inevitability of death (the Testament of Abraham). The constant factor is that the problem is put in perspective by the otherworldly revelation of a transcendent world and eschatological judgment.[14]

What is important to understand about apocalyptic writings is that their language is not descriptive or denotative but, rather, is the expres-

sive language of poetry. It is the art of apocalyptic writing to use symbols and imagery to convey a particular sense or feeling about the
world.[15] Their value does not lie in the pseudoinformation they provide about future history but in their ability to affirm belief in a transcendent world that will complete or correct the shortcomings of this
world. Apocalyptic thought helps us penetrate life's mysteries and am-
biguities so as to see the divine plan in which all of our sufferings and
privations have a definite meaning. In this way apocalyptic writing
inspires its readers to commit themselves to a system of beliefs that will
shape their actions and attitudes in light of the community's shared
values.

It is against this background that we can begin to appreciate the
tenacious hold that the Book of Daniel, with its description of a ten-
headed beast, has had on the thinking of those who anxiously await
the end of the world.[16] The author remains unknown to us. We know
only that he lived in Judea in the second century B.C.E. during a protracted struggle between the Jews and the king of Syria, Antiochus IV.
Antiochus, it seems, had plundered the temple in Jerusalem in order
to finance a campaign against Egypt. Then, as was the custom for roy-
alty, he appointed his own priest to preside over the temple. The Jews,
however, challenged his authority over religious matters and orchestrated a number of heated riots. In retaliation for the assault on his
authority, Antiochus issued an edict forbidding circumcision and worship on the Sabbath under penalty of death. He then ordered that shrines
to a number of non-Jewish gods be erected throughout Judea and that
pigs be sacrificed on these shrines instead of the lamb customary to
Hebrew observance. Violence erupted in protest over these actions, and
Antiochus, in turn, intensified his persecution of those who challenged
him. Because Jews were consequently under siege by an overpower-
ing enemy, their spirits began to falter. It was at this juncture, probably
in 165 B.C.E., that this unknown author produced the apocalyptic mas-
terpiece that fueled, at least in Christian circles, religious commitment
and strident opposition to the Antichrist, even to this day.

The author of Daniel wove his plot around a legendary figure, Daniel,
who had lived four centuries earlier when Israel had been taken into
captivity and its faith had come under the threat of extinction. Setting
the tale four centuries earlier helped the writer accomplish two closely
related purposes. First, it permitted him to show his contemporaries that
their ancestors had faced similar tribulations and, with faith and courage,
had triumphed. Second, it helped him demonstrate that such events
had not occurred by accident, nor was there reason for despair. All the
insults and hardships that Antiochus had hurled at the Jews were parts
of a divine plan about which every detail was foreknown and foreordained by God. Behind every historical enemy there were cosmic
powers at work, the leaders of the forces of darkness and evil conspir-

ing against the faithful people of God. The point, then, was that every tribulation Antioch heaped on them was part of God's majestic plan and that the moment was near when he would act decisively to turn the tables. Yahweh, the Lord of all nations, was about to cleanse the world of abominations such as Antiochus, and so the faithful had only a short time to wait until the last day would dawn.

The Book of Daniel skillfully employs every tool of the apocalyptic trade. Its hero, Daniel, is the recipient of mysterious visions and is said to be more adept at the occult arts of divination and dream interpretation than even the keenest magician, astrologer, or enchanter. Blessed with these powers, Daniel had a dream that revealed God's plan for overcoming evil and establishing a kingdom of righteousness on earth. Yet God's will was so intricate and beyond the ken of ordinary humans that even Daniel was forced to ask an angel for assistance in deciphering the full scope and significance of his vision. In the seventh chapter Daniel relates his dream in which "four great beasts came up out of the sea." The first was like a lion and had eagle's wings. The second was like a bear, and the third was like a leopard with four wings on his back. The fourth was by far the most dreadful. It was exceedingly strong, had great iron teeth, and—most terrifying of all—had ten horns. While beholding these horns Daniel saw yet another tiny horn with eyes and a mouth. This tiny horn, a thinly veiled allusion to Antiochus IV, continued to grow and uproot other horns that got in its way: "This horn made war with the saints, and prevailed over them."

But even as evil reached its zenith, the ultimate triumph of good was assured. Daniel learned that a mysterious figure of awesome power, "the Ancient of Days," would appear and destroy the beasts. Then from the clouds of heaven there would come one like a "son of man" to whom would be given dominion and glory and kingdom that shall not be destroyed. Thus despite the terrible persecutions that Jews were suffering at the hands of the four beasts (i.e., four worldly kingdoms whose policies pit them against the people of Yahweh), the Book of Daniel was able to promise that "the saints of the Most High shall receive the kingdom, and possess the kingdom for ever, for ever and ever."

Daniel finally offered a complex chronology that would signal this decisive turning point in history. He revealed that he overheard an angel explain that they must wait "for two thousand and three hundred evenings and mornings; then the sanctuary shall be restored to its rightful state." Daniel's chronology was intended to forecast the time between the first desecration of the temple and the triumph of the Macabees, an event that had already taken place when the author wrote this work. By setting his tale four hundred years earlier, the author was able to "predict" historical events with astonishing accuracy and thereby give his work the aura of inspired prophecy.

Interestingly, many Bible readers closer to our own day have read

the Book of Daniel from the perspective that it contains specific information about events that will soon transpire in our own age. More specifically, Daniel is frequently believed to predict the emergence of a ten-
nation confederacy that will be ruled by the Antichrist who, in the final
minutes of world history, will be defeated by Christ as he returns to pronounce judgment on the living and the dead. A Vermont farmer by the
name of William Miller, for example, took up the habit of Bible reading shortly after his conversion early in the nineteenth century. His Bible
guide dated the events of Daniel in 457 B.C.E. Assuming that 2,300 days
of God are actually 2,300 years for humans, Miller's arithmetic led him
to the stunning realization that Christ would return in about 1843. Miller
soon had thousands of Americans so whipped up into a frenzy over the
Second Coming that many sold all of their possessions and congregated
on hilltops in expectancy. The disappointment generated by this and
other such paroxysms of "Bible prophecy" have failed to dampen enthusiasm for such interpretive efforts. After all, in other passages
Daniel also cryptically refers to "seventy weeks of years" and "one thousand three hundred and thirty-five days." When put in conjunction with
other, and equally vague, chronologies found throughout the Bible,
much is still to be deciphered by new generations of prophecy pundits.

Apocalypticism like that in Daniel grew rampant in the Jewish world
just before the dawn of Christianity. The Dead Sea Scrolls provide vivid
testimony to the grip that such thought had over small religious communities like the one at Qumran. The scrolls were the scriptural possessions of an "apocalyptic community" that awaited a conflict of cosmic forces, the Sons of Light against the Sons of Darkness. In anticipation
of this conflict, the Qumran community withdrew from the main Jewish settlements to await the Messiah. Here, in seclusion, they could preserve a level of holiness that would ensure them of salvation at the time
of final judgment.

Similar impulses to live apart from the distractions of secular life
animated early Christianity. Jesus' proclamation that the reign of God
would irrupt at any moment brought new attention to apocalyptic expectations. Expectations of Christ's return for the final victory over evil
so enveloped the early Christian church's theology that the predominant title for Jesus was the apocalyptic title Son of Man. The early Christian understanding of the nature of Christ was thus filtered directly
through the apocalyptic tradition of Daniel and others who had awaited
the arrival of a supramundane, preexistent being who would come down
from heaven to hold judgment and bring salvation in the final days.[17]

The Son of Man must have a worthy adversary, and the early "soldiers for Christ" needed an enemy. Christian writers responded to this
need by adapting Jewish apocalyptic traditions to the new social and
political contexts of the early church. For example, in his second letter
to the Thessalonians, Paul wrote about the "son of perdition" or the "law-

less one" who opposes and exalts himself against all that is of God. Paul cautioned the Thessalonians that Christ could not return until the lawless one—identified by later Christians as the Antichrist—had begun his work of tyranny and deceit. "The coming of the lawless one by the activity of Satan will be with all power and with pretended signs and wonders, and with all wicked deception for those who are to perish, because they refused to love the truth and so be saved." For Paul, then, the "lawless one" is an integral part of God's foreordained plan—a Pied Piper of delusion in charge of leading the unrighteous into such obvious apostasy that no one can doubt the justice of their final destruction. Christ will then "slay him with the breath of his mouth and destroy him by his appearing and his coming . . . [while] inflicting vengeance upon those who do not know God and upon those who do not obey the gospel of our Lord Jesus."

The decisive Christianizing of the Jewish apocalyptic tradition had not yet taken place, however, in the form of the Apocalypse or Revelation of John.

Revelation and the Beast from the Sea

No portion of the Bible can rival Revelation for its hold on the religious imaginations of contemporary Americans. Biblical fundamentalists are certain that its elaborate and often confusing narrative refers not to the time of the biblical writers themselves but to the late twentieth century. Its coded messages provide vigilant believers with "insider information" concerning Jesus' plans to establish his thousand-year reign on earth. Modern apocalyptists approach the Book of Revelation with the belief that it provides exact references of events that will soon separate those whose names are written in the Lamb's Book of Life from those who can expect to suffer for their indifference. It is also believed that Revelation contains much information about the Antichrist, who will emerge as a "beast from the sea" to be Satan's ally in a last, desperate assault on Christ and his church. This beast will take control of the world economy "so that no one can buy or sell unless he has the mark, that is, the name of the beast or the number of its name." The "number of its name," 666, supplies contemporary purveyors of apocalyptic zeal with an all-important clue concerning the beast's identity. Such hints about the identity of the awaited beast have prompted generations of Christians to view the Book of Revelation as God's authorized instruction manual for naming the Antichrist. In recent years these apocalyptic clues have helped Bible prophecy experts to find the beast at work in such previously unsuspected persons as Jimmy Carter and King Juan Carlos of Spain, or in such otherwise innocent places as fiber optics, grocery store bar codes, and the Susan B. Anthony dollar.

From a scholarly perspective, the Book of Revelation was written not to predict a far-distant future but to give the Christians of its own day the courage to withstand their hour of crisis. The author borrowed freely from existing apocalyptic legends, most notably Daniel and several ancient "dragon myths," and reshaped them to address current issues. Debates still rage as to just who this writer was. In about 135 c.e., Justin Martyr stated that it was written by John, one of the original apostles of Jesus. The early church father Irenaeus decided that it was written by John, son of Zebedee, who he alleged also wrote the Gospel of John. Almost no twentieth-century scholars agree with these ancient assessments.[18] The long period of time between Jesus' death and Revelation's composition (probably between 95 and 100 c.e.) makes it unlikely that the author was one of Jesus' apostles. Nor do the literary styles or theological terms used in Revelation support any connection with either an original apostle or the author of the Gospel of John. Some scholars argue that the text is pseudonymous and that the name John was attached for the purpose of linking its message with the emerging and influential "Johannine school" of Christian thought.

Although complete certainty about these matters eludes us, sound judgment indicates that the text was written by a Jewish and Palestinian man named John who is otherwise unknown to us. He was obviously self-conscious about his role as a seer and prophet. The tale he spun, originally intended to persuade his contemporaries to shun all doubts and temptations to join the world about them, continues to this day to inspire apocalyptic fervor with an intensity matched by no other book in world history.

Christians of the late first century found themselves a beleaguered group. Their public status was dismal. They were in continual conflict with Jews, who found their apocalypticism irritating. The Romans likewise viewed them with disdain. Christians, like Jews, resisted Roman culture and were openly anarchical. They withdrew from public life secure in the knowledge that next week or next month the King of Kings would return to reverse the tables; the first would become last, and the last would become first. Christians were, moreover, social pariahs, for the most part poor and socially disenfranchised. Their low socioeconomic status caused them to resent the fact that so many Jews and Gentiles among them openly cooperated with the Roman system—and profited both economically and socially from such cooperation. From the Christian point of view, such worldly riches would prove tragically ephemeral, fating those with ill-gained wealth to eternal damnation at the time of final judgment. Christians, on the other hand, would receive their eternal reward if they could hold out and sustain their exclusivist, world-renouncing stance toward life just a little longer. One among them, John, sensed the doubts and wavering commitments, and he was able to portray the contemporary situation in a mythic, apocalyptic framework. His aim was to show that the conflicts and tensions felt by his fellow Christians had cosmic significance. At stake in each person's decision to remain faithful was nothing less than his or her eternal destiny. John was also shrewd enough to realize that nothing so unites a community as having a common enemy. His book, known as the Apocalypse or the Revelation to John, vividly depicted just such an enemy—Satan's ally—the Antichrist.

Anyone who has tried to read John's Revelation can sympathize with George Bernard Shaw's remark that it is "a curious record of the visions of a drug addict."[19] There is such a profusion of images and such an apparent lack of structure that even the most conscientious of readers cannot help but be bewildered. Indeed, John's references to seven messages, seven seals, seven trumpets, seven bowls, and seven unnumbered visions merge together to lead the reader into hopeless confusion. With repeated readings, however, it becomes clear that there is a pattern running through each series of John's visions. The cyclical or repetitive pattern is characteristic of apocalyptic language and is an indication that the book's "message" is the overall structure of the events rather than the particular details of any one story or image. Each sequence of events recapitulates a threefold pattern of (1) persecution, (2) punishment of the persecutors, and (3) salvation of the faithful accompanied by the triumph of the Lamb over the Dragon and Beast.[20] In this sense, Revelation functions in the same fashion as do countless other "combat myths" in which order (God) triumphs over the dragon of chaos. Revelation activates this mythic structure to reinforce resistance to Rome and to inspire willingness for martyrdom. Its use of apocalyptic forms and imagery reassures readers about the ultimate resolution of the conflict in which they are involved. Even though evil seems to be gaining strength all about them, God is firmly in control of world destiny and even now is commencing the decisive actions that will secure their salvation and bring crushing defeat to their adversaries.

The opening sentence makes clear the apocalyptic nature of the message that is to follow: "The revelation of Jesus Christ, which God gave him to show to his servants what must soon take place; and he made it known by sending his angel to his servant John." Mystery follows mystery as the angel gives John visions of seven messages, seven seals, seven trumpets, seven bowls, and finally seven visions (the number seven indicating fullness and completion). In Chapter 12 we learn that a great and final war is arising in heaven between the angels and Satan, who is described as a great red dragon with seven heads and ten horns. Adela Yarbro Collins points out that a Jew reading about a dragon in the first century c.e. would readily place that image in a political context.[21] The dragon stood for not only the great deceiver, Satan, but also a long line of national enemies that had advanced Satan's cause by thwarting the purposes of God's chosen people.

In the coming battle against the angels of God, Satan needs an ally

and creates one that is a parody and mirror opposite of Christ—the
Antichrist:

> And I saw a beast rising out of the sea, with ten horns and seven heads,
> with ten diadems upon its horns, and a blasphemous name upon its heads.
> And the beast that I saw was like a leopard, its feet were like a bear's, and
> its mouth was like a lion's mouth. And to it the dragon gave his power
> and his throne and great authority. One of its heads seemed to have a
> mortal wound, but its mortal wound was healed, and the whole earth
> followed the beast with wonder. Men worshipped the dragon, for he had
> given his authority to the beast, and they worshipped the beast, saying,
> "Who is like the beast, and who can fight against it?"(13:1–4)

This beast was, of course, a condensation of the salient features of
the four beasts in Daniel. The intended audience could hardly fail to
make immediate connections between the imagery surrounding this
beast and their feared worldly enemies: Rome, and the despised Roman
emperor and merciless persecutor of Christians, Nero. Much of the
urgency of this imagery is lost on contemporary Christians, but we must
remember that John's contemporaries took it as fact that Nero would
return from the dead to continue his persecution of Christians. Nero
symbolized the despotic character of the Roman Empire that continued to suppress and humiliate them. John's beast emerges from the sea
in a manner that makes clear just how antithetical Rome was to the
gospel of Christ. Just as Christ came to earth with the authority of God,
the beast or Antichrist comes with the authority of Satan. And just as
Christ rose from the dead, the beast recovers from a mortal wound
(which, incidentally, in the 1980s caused quite a stir in evangelical circles
when Ronald Wilson Reagan—each name having six letters—was shot
and yet survived).

In an obvious allusion to the three and a half years mentioned by
Daniel, John tells us that "the beast was given a mouth uttering haughty
and blasphemous words, and it was allowed to exercise authority for
forty-two months." As the beast ascends to power over humans, it becomes apparent that a struggle of cosmic proportions is taking place in
which each person must take sides. The faithful must resist the powers
of chaos by enduring the persecution they face in daily life. John helps
them make this choice by showing the consequences of unbelief: "If
any one worships the beast and its image . . . he also shall drink the wine
of God's wrath, poured unmixed into the cup of his anger, and he shall
be tormented with fire and brimstone in the presence of the holy angels
and in the presence of the Lamb."

What particularly troubles John is the continuing temptation for
Christians to soften the boundaries between themselves and others. His
ideal was to preserve an exclusive Christian community withdrawn from
the economic and political life of the empire. Members of the socially
prominent and wealthy families of the region, however, cooperated with

Rome and participated actively in its political and economic systems. Such participation was precisely what John needed to ward off. He thus tells of seeing "another beast which rose out of the earth" that helps promote the causes of the beast from the sea. The allusion is obvious. The beast from the land represents the provincial elite who do the bidding of the beast from the sea (Rome). This second beast, or the false prophet as he is sometimes referred to, assists Antichrist in creating a controlled economic system and forces each person "to be marked on the right hand or the forehead, so that no one can buy or sell unless he has the mark, that is, the name of the beast or the number of its name . . . six hundred and sixty-six." Roman coins, of course, bore the image and name of the current emperor, and thus John was warning that whoever used such coins and bore the mark of the beast would forfeit the possibility of salvation. His reference to having this mark on the right hand or forehead was obviously a parody of the Jewish practice of wearing phylacteries on the forehead and left arm. His cryptic reference to the number 666 was in all likelihood a punning device drawn from the practice of using both Greek and Hebrew letters as numerals. John apparently translated Nero Caesar into Greek, Neron Kaisar, and then transliterated the result into a Hebrew form whose numerical value was 666. His apocalyptic talents proved uncannily effective, as this number has for two thousand years been the prophetic obsession of an unending chain of soothsayers of the Second Coming.

The beast and his ally the false prophet relentlessly make war on the saints and blaspheme against God. Just as evil seems about to triumph, God directs his angels to act decisively to move the sweep of cosmic history toward its denouement. The beast is captured and, along with the false prophet, is thrown into a lake of fire. Then an angel seizes and binds the dragon, Satan, and throws him into a bottomless pit for a thousand years. During this millennium the 144,000 who have "been redeemed from the earth" rule with Christ over a rejuvenated earth. In this paradise will be "the souls of those who had been beheaded for their testimony to Jesus and for the word of God, and who had not worshipped the beast or its image and had not received its mark on their foreheads or their hands. They came to life and reigned with Christ a thousand years." John offers no explanation as to why this period will last precisely one thousand years and no more or less. Nor does he explain why Satan was merely bound for this time and then deliberately released at the end of the thousand years to once again make war on God's people. But final victory over Satan is assured. For after being set loose for one last desperate assault on all that is of God, Satan is once again captured and thrown into the lake of fire where he and the Antichrist "will be tormented day and night for ever and ever."

At this point God exercises final judgment on the human race. The book of life is opened, and all are judged by their earthly actions. The righteous receive their just reward and inherit "a new heaven and a new earth" in which they will experience eternal and unmitigated happiness. The cowardly, the faithless, and the spiritually polluted are thrown in the lake that burns with fire and brimstone. This final destruction of all those who are not of Christ is in keeping with an undercurrent of vindictiveness and morbidity that runs throughout the Apocalypse. The author is here inviting his readers to identify with the aggressor, God, and to take vicarious pleasure in the great suffering and tortures awaiting their human adversaries. John almost certainly intended his work to be read aloud before an assembly of Christians and to help them see themselves in this mythic context. His use of expressive and evocative language helped elicit from his audience the emotional charge they needed to withstand the temptations represented by the Antichrist (Rome's grand social and economic system) and his false prophet (the provincial elite). His apocalypse plays on the audience's fears and feelings of resentment and, by projecting them onto a cosmic screen on which victory is assured, produces the needed emotional catharsis. Adela Yarbro Collins notes that through its use of evocative symbols and artful plots,

> the Apocalypse made feelings which were probably latent, vague, complex, and ambiguous explicit, conscious, and simple. Complex relationships were simplified by the use of a dualistic framework. The Jews who reject and denounce Christians are followers of Satan. Those who do not have God's seal bear the mark of the beast and are doomed to destruction.[22]

The symbol of the Antichrist, the beast from the sea, gave John and his audience a mythic device with which to label and interpret their fears and frustrations. John's mythopoetic imagery helped explain and make bearable the tension between what was (i.e., the reality of their low socioeconomic status and powerlessness in the world defined by the social elite) and what should be (i.e., the acceptance of their beliefs and claim to righteousness by all others). By providing the emerging symbol of Antichrist with such an embellished identity, this otherwise obscure first-century author bequeathed an apocalyptic legacy that funds many Christians' interpretations of the world to this day.

The Antichrist in Early Christianity

As Christianity grew in stature and solidified in theology, so did the Antichrist legend. John's Book of Revelation emphasized the image of the Antichrist as Endtyrant. Never lost, however, were other dominant images of the Antichrist such as that of the False Prophet, the agent of Satan, or the monster of chaos. Thoughts about the Antichrist, like other theological topics, were shaped partially by biblical materials and partially by the shifting currents of popular culture. At times the tradition was pushed slowly forward by the scholarly efforts of monks and academicians who offered reasoned exegeses of sacred texts. In other instances political and social turmoil brought added urgency to the task of identifying an enemy who could be held responsible, and consequently thoughts about the Antichrist shifted more rapidly into new and conflict-laden territory. By the time Christianity reached the zenith of its influence on the thinking of learned persons in the Middle Ages, an entire theological scaffolding had been erected to support efforts to scout out threats—both real and imagined—to the believing community.

During the first three centuries of Christian thought, the identities of Satan and the Antichrist were frequently intertwined, with the early church fathers sometimes treating these two nefarious personae as identical.[23] Firmicus Maternus, for example, stated unequivocally that "the devil is Antichrist himself."[24] Other early Christian writers labored to differentiate between Satan and the Antichrist who, while possessed of Satan's demonic spirit, is yet a distinct personage who will appear on earth and attempt to deceive humanity just before the Second Coming. By the time of Jerome (c. 340–420) and Chrysostom (c. 345–427), the assumption that the Antichrist is the devil himself nearly died out of ecclesiastical tradition. In his commentary on Daniel, Jerome wrote, "Nor let us think that he [Antichrist] . . . is the devil or a demon, but one of men in whom Satan is wholly to dwell bodily." Chrysostom, offering an exegesis of Paul's reference to the "lawless one" in 2 Thessalonians, wrote, "But who is this one? Think you, Satan? By no means, but some man possessed of all his energy."[25] Following the lead of the Johannine epistles and the Book of Revelation, then, early Christians began to distinguish between Satan and the Antichrist. Whereas Satan represented the disembodied spirit of cosmic evil, Antichrist referred to the human person who is prophesied to appear in the last days with the purpose of advancing Satan's cause.

One of the leading patristic writers, Irenaeus (c. 160–230), helped preserve the apocalyptic element of early Christian faith in the church's emerging theology. He drew on Daniel and Revelation to argue that Satan was still endeavoring to thwart salvation by encouraging paganism, idolatry, sorcery, blasphemy, apostasy, and heresy. Identifying unbelievers of every kind as colleagues of Satan, Irenaeus was among the first to use apocalyptic thought to justify the persecution of all those existing outside the doctrinal boundaries of orthodoxy. Irenaeus taught that the armies of Satan would continue their vain warfare against the Christian community and, as the end time approached, would make one last concerted attack led by the Antichrist, an apostate, murderer, and robber who would have "all the Devil's power" behind him.[26] His contemporary, Tertullian (c. 160–230), expanded on 1 and 2 John to

argue that although every current heretic and rebel against Christ manifested the spirit of Antichrist, they were but forerunners of a single, horrifying Antichrist who had yet to appear. This distinction between the
yet-to-appear Antichrist and his present forerunners has persisted to
this day as a means for denouncing one's rivals for their Antichrist-like
nature while yet maintaining an eschatological outlook focused on the
enemy to be defeated by Christ in the final battle of history. Also note-
worthy is the fact that Tertullian, like many patristic writers, moved
away from identifying the Antichrist with Rome. He taught that the
Roman Empire was in fact the stabilizing force responsible for warding
off or restraining the imminent outbreak of Antichrist's chaos. This position proved to be important when, in the late fourth century, he emperor Constantine and his successor Theodosius converted to Christianity. Far from being Christianity's archenemy, Rome evolved into its chief
guarantor. Yet the Antichrist legend survived in popular thought, proving to be fluid and capable of adapting to changing sociopolitical conditions.

The greatest of Christianity's early theologians, Augustine (354–
430), lived to see both the decline of the Roman Empire and the failure
of the world to come to a screeching halt as predicted by apocalyptic
soothsayers. Augustine never abandoned Christianity's forward-looking
eschatological hopes, but he became an outspoken critic of apocalyptic
thinking. On this point he was profoundly influenced by a fellow North
African scholar, Tyconius (c. 330–390). Tyconius had written an influential study of Revelation that countered apocalyptic readings of its vivid
metaphors. Instead of looking for the Antichrist as a supernatural agent
who would appear outside the political and social borders of Christianity, he urged a "spiritualized" reading of Revelation in which the Antichrist was to be understood in terms of the struggle of good versus evil
within the church in every age. Augustine followed Tyconius's lead and
offered an ahistorical, more ecclesiastic, and antimillennial interpretation of Revelation. For Augustine, apocalyptic symbolism was to be
understood in terms of the continuing struggle between good and evil
in the heart of every Christian. In his classic *The City of God*, Augustine
developed a tradition of multiple Antichrists already living: All heretics,
all schismatics, every sinner was an Antichrist. Rather than looking to
some supernatural entity for the Antichrist, Augustine pointed directly
to all perjurers, cheaters, evildoers, adulterers, drunkards, slave dealers,
and usurers. As he wrote elsewhere, "For the Word of God is Christ:
whatsoever is contrary to the Word of God is in Antichrist."[27]

Augustine's interpretation of Revelation became the orthodox position of the institutional church and continues to this day to be the consensus position in both Catholicism and mainstream Protestantism. In
this way Augustine helped subordinate apocalyptic fervor to the ongoing life of the church community. He shifted attention away from in-

terpreting the human spiritual condition in the mythic terms of a battle
between two cosmic powers and instead prompted Christians to make
a frank appraisal of their own moral and spiritual resolve. Rather than
viewing the calamitous events of Revelation as portents of the end, they
should see how such events symbolically depict the recurrent travails
faced by every human. And rather than projecting absolute evil onto a
cosmic scapegoat, they must see the Antichrist in nonapocalyptic fashion as the very real tendency in everyone to sin. Apocalyptic thinking
about the end of the world and about the deceit of Antichrist continued to abound in Christianity, as the rest of this book will discuss in
some detail. But from Augustine onward, theological orthodoxy favored
a nonapocalyptic approach to Christians' future and their personal
struggles with evil.

Augustine's antiapocalyptic leanings notwithstanding, the historical
tradition of "naming the Antichrist" gained added momentum in the
seventh century with the emergence of a new and forceful rival to
Christianity—Islam. No group of unbelievers had ever exasperated, even
embarrassed, Christians as did the upstart Muslims. The followers of
Mohammed claimed to be the rightful heirs of the religion of Abraham,
Moses, and Jesus. Moreover, they accused Christians of having fallen
into idolatrous superstition when they misinterpreted the prophet Jesus
as a divine being equal to the transcendent Allah. Armed with no other
cognitive means for confronting persons inalterably different from themselves, church officials turned to apocalyptic categories. The Muslims,
it seems, were either the precursors of the Antichrist symbolized by the
beasts and plagues mentioned in Revelation or the very armies of
the Antichrist himself. Such rhetoric lent itself then, as it does today, to
the task of mobilizing military and political action against the infidel
Muslims. Pope Urban, for example, justified sending the Crusaders on
a bloody conquest of Palestine by announcing that "it is the will of God
that through the labours of the crusaders Christianity shall flourish again
at Jerusalem in these last times, so that when Antichrist begins his reign
there—as he shortly must—he will find enough Christians to fight!"[28]

Over the succeeding centuries the Antichrist legend was embellished
by many medieval writers. Among the more important of these medieval works was Adso's *Letter on the Origin and Life of the Antichrist*, written in about 950. Relying mostly on patristic teachings concerning the
Antichrist, Adso reveals the continuities in the Antichrist tradition that
seem to transcend the vicissitudes of time and social upheaval. Adso
sticks to the tradition that the Antichrist will be born a Jew (some biblical passages suggest a Roman heritage, thereby leaving room for theological disputes which continue to this day among premillennial biblical scholars). More specifically, Adso tells us, the Antichrist "will be born
from the Jews, namely from the tribe of Dan."[29] Adso also counters the
speculations that he will be born from a virgin and maintains instead

that he will be born from the union of a father and mother. "Neverthe-less," Adso maintains, "he will be conceived wholly in sin, generated in sin, born in sin. The devil will enter the womb of his mother at the very instant of his conception. He will be fostered by the power of the devil and protected in his mother's womb." The appearance of the Anti-christ will thus parody at every step the appearance of Christ. Just as the Holy Spirit entered Mary and surrounded her, so the devil will de-scend into the mother of the Antichrist and completely surround her with a totally inimical spirit of evil. Adso explains that he should be called the Antichrist because he will be contrary to Christ in all things.

> Christ came in humble fashion; he will come as a proud man. Christ came to raise up the humble, to justify sinners; he, on the other hand, will cast out the humble, magnify sinners, exalt the wicked and always teach the vices contrary to virtues. He will destroy the Law of the Gospel, call the worship of demons back into the world, seek his own glory, and call him-self almighty God. This Antichrist will have many ministers of his evil: many of them have already gone forth into the world such as Antiochus, Nero, and Domitian. In our own time we know there are many Antichrists. Any layman, cleric, or monk who lives in a way contrary to justice, who attacks the rule of his order of life, and blasphemes the good, he is an Antichrist, a minister of Satan.[30]

Having identified contemporary laypersons and fellow clergy who "at-tack the rule of their orders of life" as antichrists, Adso goes on to say that there is yet to come a single, dreaded Antichrist who will appear at the end of time and who will torture the people of God for three and a half years. He will then be killed through the power of Jesus on the Mount of Olives, opposite the spot where Christ ascended to heaven.

The scholarly construction of "the life of the Antichrist" reached its zenith among medieval clergy. In his *Antichrist in the Middle Ages*, Richard Emmerson shows that although the medieval Antichrist tradition was very complex and varied from author to author, it is nonetheless pos-sible to discern a standard and widely accepted medieval understand-ing of the Antichrist: who he is, when he will appear, what he will do, and what will become of him.[31] Interest in the Antichrist, of course, closely mirrors interest in apocalyptic thinking in general. Although there was a steady tradition of apocalyptic throughout the Middle Ages, it surely intensified in moments of social unrest and religious uncer-tainty. And as might be expected, efforts to identify the Antichrist or his predecessors in such periods of turmoil sometimes took the form of attacks on despised minorities or various political enemies.

The medieval tradition wavered somewhat between identifying contemporary heretics (especially Jews) as antichrists and expecting a single, specific individual who would come in the future immediately before the return of Christ. On the whole, the latter interpretation was the dominant one, and medieval clergy wrote at length about a man who would be born of a whore or some other evil woman, of Jewish parentage from the tribe of Dan. It was thought that from his birth onward, he would be possessed by the devil, who would instruct him in the powers of deception and wonder making. The various "lives of the Antichrist" state that he will enter Jerusalem, rebuild the temple, and convert the Jews, who will initially embrace him as their ally. He will gain both political and religious power, send out false prophets, destroy belief in Jesus as the Son of God, and institute a new law. This master of deceit will appear to perform miracles and will demand to be worshiped as God. When the biblical prophets Enoch and Elias appear to challenge his rule and convert Jews to the true Christ, he will kill them and persecute their followers. In his final parody of Christ, the Antichrist will attempt to rise to heaven from the Mount of Olives. At or about this moment Christ will return from the heavens, destroy the Antichrist "with the spirit of his mouth," and inaugurate the millennial period as described in Revelation.

Much of what was written about the nature and activity of Antichrist during the Middle Ages was prompted by the relatively disinterested motives of scholarly or academic inquiry into biblical texts. These traditions were thus reasonably free of polemical efforts to identify contemporary persons as being in league with this diabolical spirit. As Bernard McGinn concluded, the textual evidence indicates that the bulk of medieval apocalypticism was not primarily a manifestation of popular protest. It was, he wrote, "for the most part, an attempt by a group of educated religious literati to interpret the times, to support their patrons, to console their supporters, and to move men to pursue specified aims at once political and religious in nature."[32] Yet, ever since 1 John's first efforts to brand renegade Christians as antichrists, the symbol of the Antichrist has frequently been pushed into the service of ulterior social and political motives. The continued identification of Jews with the Antichrist illustrates this point, as does the Revelation of John's preoccupation with Rome and the social elite who participated in Rome's economic order.

In the twelfth century the Italian monk Joachim of Fiore pressed apocalyptic references to the Antichrist into the service of his own radical theological agendas. Joachim announced that the Antichrist was already alive and that at any moment, perhaps in the year 1260, the last chapter in world history would begin. Joachim went so far as to write that "just as many pious kings, priests, and prophets preceded the one Christ who was king, priest, and prophet, so many unholy kings, false prophets, and antichrists precede the one Antichrist who will pretend to be king, priest and prophet."[33] Joachim's apocalyptic manuscripts (both authentic and counterfeit) were soon the theological rage among medieval clerics, each providing intricate discussions of biblical prophecies and each complete with illustrations and timetables that graphically depicted the coming "Age of Grace" in which Antichrist would be defeated and righteousness would at last spread across the earth. Three consecutive popes approved of Joachim's reinvigoration of millennialist theology and supported his efforts. They were, perhaps, unaware of just how radically Joachim differed from Augustine's more conservative postmillennial teachings. And they were certainly unaware of just how easily Joachim's followers, especially those belonging to the so-called Spiritual Franciscans, would find specific kings and specific popes to be forerunners of this beast of iniquity. The net result of Joachim's efforts, then, was to place millennial speculations closer to the era's sociocultural tensions and therefore to encourage more fervent participation in the sport of apocalyptic name-calling.

By the fourteenth century the symbol of the Antichrist became increasingly politicized. "Naming the Antichrist" became a prominent part of several political and religious conflicts that surrounded the papacy in its fight with secular authorities and later with the leaders of the Protestant Reformation. As the Medieval era gave way to the era of Reformation, the concept of the Antichrist began to live up to its full potential as one of the most powerful symbolic weapons in the history of Western hate mongering.

The Antichrist in the Reformation Era

The use of apocalyptic rhetoric for political purposes was hardly new in the Reformation period. The Book of Daniel, 1 and 2 John, and Revelation all were political texts insofar as they interpreted current political foes in light of the cosmic battle between absolute good and absolute evil. Popes throughout the ages had frequently viewed their enemies in apocalyptic terms. The clearest such example was the ongoing feud between Emperor Frederick II and Popes Gregory IX and Innocent IV. When Frederick began to threaten the security of the Papal States and balked at embarking on his pledged crusade, Gregory excommunicated him and began accusing him of being the imperial Antichrist. Gregory's successor, Innocent IV, proved even more determined to cast Frederick's political ambitions in a diabolic light. Frederick responded in kind. One treatise written by a Dominican scholar in concert with Frederick boldly denounced Innocent as a pope in name alone. Likening Innocent to the beast rising from the sea, he wrote: "He has scandalized the whole world. Construing his words in the true sense, he is that great dragon who leads the world astray (Rev. 12), Antichrist, whose forerunner he says we are."[34] Another such treatise converted the name *Innocencius papa* to its numerical equivalents and found that "when the number is fully added up, the name of the marks of the beast, that is, of the Antichrist who is Pope Innocent, equals 666. . . . There is no doubt that he is the true Antichrist."[35]

The early voices of the Reformation also found the symbol of the Antichrist a powerful tool for characterizing the evils of the church. The English priest John Wycliff (d. 1384), for example, found himself at odds with the papacy when he condemned papal taxation as greed and declared the doctrine of transubstantiation to be unscriptural. As the dispute escalated, Wycliff sought to rally support to his cause by charging that the friars and bishops were agents of the Antichrist and the pope none other than the Antichrist himself. John Huss (1369–1415) walked a tightrope when he portrayed the papal office as the Antichrist while trying to avoid being burned at the stake. (This he unfortunately proved unable to do.) In response to charges of heresy, Huss sought to clarify that "I did not say [that the pope is Antichrist], but I did say that if the pope sells benefices, if he is proud, avaricious, or otherwise morally opposed to Christ, then he is the Antichrist."[36]

The velvet gloves came off for good when Martin Luther finally made a decisive break from the Roman Catholic Church. In his famed *Table Talk*, Luther referred to the pope as "the right Antichrist" and held that "the conviction that the Pope is Antichrist . . . is a life and death matter for the church."[37] Luther's view that the whole world was in tension between God and the devil prompted him to mythologize his enemies. To Martin Luther there were no matters of honest disagreement in religious or political matters. His opponents were partisans in the cosmic war between good and evil, and it was imperative that his followers see these disputes in terms equally as clear.

It was somewhat predictable that the social, economic, and political upheaval attendant to the Protestant Reformation would spawn a violent wave of apocalyptic rhetoric. As Christopher Hill, Paul Christianson, Katherine Firth, Bryan Ball, and others have shown, nowhere were apocalyptic symbols used for social and political purposes more vividly than in seventeenth-century England.[38] Reformation-era England witnessed not only upheavals of faith but also desperate political battlles between those defending the monarchy and those seeking radical political change. These conflicts between social class and political outlook were so great that those who participated could not envision compromise on any item. Once their opponents were understood to be agents of Satan, compromise was out of the question. Participants on all sides believed that victory must be total and unequivocal. For example, Protestantism's unquestioned tenet that the pope was the Antichrist had propaganda value for the Tudor government, especially in rallying unflagging support in the wars against Spain. If Catholic Spain were aligned with the Antichrist in Rome, then support of Drake and his navy against this diabolical enemy must be total and unyielding.

As the seventeenth century wore on, however, this zealous pursuit of enemies turned from foreign to civil affairs. Those grasping for greater political influence within England seized hold of the notion that the Church of England, with all its rituals and Roman-like customs, had never fully separated from the papal Antichrist. The attack on the theological integrity of the Church of England originated with a few radical Protestant sects but obviously carried political and social innuendos. Once the Church of England was identified with the despotic rule of the Antichrist, it was but a short step more to see that a monarchy that supported the church was likewise characterized by tyranny and deceit. Christopher Hill described how the dramatic happenings of the early 1640s transformed the battle against the Antichrist from one of national defense to one of civil protest. "The symbolism of Antichrist fanned the fire of rebellion, rousing utopian hopes, especially in the classes hitherto excluded from politics. Hill wryly observed that the sheer beauty of the symbolism of Antichrist was that it was fluid and ambiguous, allowing for groups with different political agendas to rally together against a common enemy and, if necessary, to redefine the enemy from time to time: "The symbolism of the Beast had its advantages. Its imprecision allowed differing interpretations to be put upon it, either by different people or by the same person in appealing to different groups. Antichrist stood for bad, papal, repressive institutions: exactly which institutions was anybody's choice."[39]

The political rebellion became bloody, and the aroused hopes eventually gave way to disillusionment. Compromise became expedient when it became clear to all that there was yet need for civil authority. Even the radical Protestants began to realize how pernicious the quest for the Antichrist could become and gradually abandoned their quest to identify him among their worldly adversaries. Most British Protestants returned to a more Augustinian or nonapocalyptic interpretation of humanity's chief adversary. The concept of the Antichrist was once again made into a spiritual symbol for the cloudy tendencies of the human heart. In his *Antichrist in Man, Christ's Enemy* (1656), the Quaker John Nayler spoke for the majority who were now leery of the polemical uses of Christian symbolism. Nayler turned apocalyptic thought inward and declared that "Antichrist is in everyman until he be revealed by the light of Christ within."[40] As Hill pointed out, if the Antichrist is in everyone, in the elect as well as in their adversaries, then he is no longer a political target. If Antichrist is in every man, he is indistinguishable from Satan or the general force of evil and, in a sense, ceases to exist as a separate person or enemy.

The fact that the quest for the Antichrist had turned out to be a blind alley led most of the British citizenry to cease identifying things of this world with Christ's kingdom and, as a corollary, to cease looking for anti-Christian enemies in this world too. But for others it proved only that the British system and the Church of England were corrupt beyond regeneration. These nonconformists, Puritans as they were often called, knew they must seek a new England in which to realize their millennial dreams. When they went into the wilderness of the New World on their errand for God, it was no surprise that they found the Antichrist already there waiting for them, scheming to thwart their errand at every possible opportunity.

TWO

Thwarting the Errand

The last conflict with anti-christ . . . in the utmost part of the world.

Cotton Mather, 1702

❧

The Reformation in England generated a series of ideological clashes that pitted citizen against citizen in heated political, economic, and religious struggles. The intensity of these disputes inclined many to invoke apocalyptic rhetoric concerning the struggle between absolute good and absolute evil. Among the most influential of the Protestant apocalyptists of this period was John Bale. His *Image of Both Churches* (1548), one of the first extended expositions of the Book of Revelation in English, interpreted the conflict between Protestants and Catholics as nothing short of the struggle between Christ and the Antichrist. Bale explained that the seven heads of the dragon mentioned in John's apocalypse symbolized seven historical appearances of the devil. The seventh head is filled with "all carnal wisdom . . . all devilish policies and crafts: this is the papacy here in Europe, which is the general Antichrist of the whole world."[1] The Reformation had turned the world into a battleground. True Christians must rally to the cause of God and combat the subtle plots of the papacy. Hard and fast commitments must be made. As Bale would have it, "Either we are citizens in the New Jerusalem with Jesus Christ, or else, in the superstitious Babylon with Antichrist the vicar of Satan."[2]

Bale's apocalyptic renderings of contemporary events proved contagious. John Foxe's *Actes and Monuments*, popularly known as "The Book of Martyrs," further embellished the English Reformation's role in inaugurating God's kingdom on earth. The first edition of Foxe's book in

1554 was a small octavo volume recounting the martyrdoms of those who came before the Protestant Reformation. By the time it reached its final form in 1583, it had expanded to a work of almost 2,500 pages which included a detailed account of the papal Antichrist's persecution of righteous English Protestants.[3] Foxe's "Book of Martyrs" was placed in every cathedral church by official decree and soon could be found alongside the family Bible in every Protestant home.

Part of the appeal of Foxe's book was that it set his contemporaries' religious struggles against the apocalyptic background of the war against the Antichrist. Foxe warned the Antichrist that his reign was about to come to an abrupt halt: "You see now, your doings, so wicked, cannot hide; your cruelty is come to light; your murders be evident; your pretty practices, your subtle sleights, your secret conspiracies, your filthy lives are seen, and stink before God and man."[4] Foxe explained that God had foreordained the entire sweep of human history to be a progressive march toward his establishment of a rule of righteousness. The final step in this historical journey was about to start, and English Protestants were in the vanguard. Beginning in 1300, God had summoned his servants to a renewed witness to him and against the persecutions of the Antichrist. The events of the sixteenth century proved that history was entering its final hour and that the battle against the Antichrist was ready to be launched in earnest. Faithful Christians were being called on to witness their faith through patriotism and opposition to Protestant England's enemies—Catholic Spain and Catholic France. This zeal to serve God by undertaking "battles" against Antichrist was to have a profound influence not only in Old England but in New England as well. As historian Peter Gay wrote,

> Anglicans and Puritans alike loved the Book of Martyrs, memorized it, told their children stories from it; the illiterate had it read to them and absorbed its message from its heart-rending woodcuts. . . . And less than half a century after Foxe's death, Englishmen took his book, and his philosophy of history, across the Atlantic into the American wilderness.[5]

Apocalyptic theology thus provided a well-developed philosophy of history that gave meaning and significance to English Protestants' efforts to oppose the ecclesiastical structure of Catholicism. What gave this view of history its urgency was the omnipresent but subtle deceptions of the Antichrist, who might take almost any form to undermine the cause of true Christianity. It is interesting to note in this context that those Protestants who most strongly emphasized justification by means of faith were also the most ardent in their belief in the plot of Antichrist against them. Having eschewed ecclesiastical or sacramental definitions of Christian "belonging," these Protestants equated piety with adherence to particular articles of faith. It was imperative, then, that they ward off the possibility that their members would be attracted to divergent theological beliefs. Continuous warnings about the wiles of the Antichrist helped arouse and maintain concern with crossing over theological boundaries. As Christopher Hill discovered, "the belief in Antichrist was strongest amongst those Protestants who most strongly emphasized justification by faith and were most hostile to the ecclesiastical establishment and its ceremonies."[6] This radical emphasis on salvation by means of faith rather than works was not characteristic of the faith of most British, who conformed to the highly liturgical and ritualistic Anglican Church. But among the nonconformists—the Puritans and related groups—this form of radical Protestant faith and its associated hyperalertness to the Antichrist continued in earnest.

Many English Protestants believed that the religious reformation in their land had not gone far enough, that the Anglican Church preserved too much of the ornate ritual and ecclesiastical structure of Catholicism. Nor did the Church of England put sufficient emphasis on the plain Bible-centered faith that according to a stricter Protestantism could alone guide them to salvation. A large group of these nonconforming English Protestants sought to purify the church even further. Known as Puritans, they separated from the established Anglican Church and clustered together in a number of fledgling denominations such as the Congregationalists, Presbyterians, and (although the relationship here is more complex) Baptists. It was among these separatist and nonconformist groups that the most interest was generated in leaving England for America. Part of the motivation was to erect a bulwark against Catholic Spain and Catholic France. Another part was to erect a bulwark against the unpurified form of Protestantism found in the Church of England itself. Following the lead of Bale and Foxe, these Puritan Protestants saw themselves occupying a unique role in God's providential actions in history. It was they who had been chosen to construct an earthly kingdom where pure faith and righteous government would exist side by side. Their mission to erect a holy commonwealth could hardly be separated from millennialist biblical faith. It stands to reason, then, that their "official" histories, such as William Bradford's *Of Plimouth Plantation*, were fraught with apocalyptic tension. As Bradford put it, they had left Europe because of the "wars of opposition [that] . . . Satan hath raised, maintained and continued against the Saints, from time to time, in one sort or another."[7] "By God's good providence," these defenders of the true faith had come to build a New Jerusalem in "those vast and unpeopled countries of America, which are fruitful and fit for habitation."[8]

Errand into the Wilderness

On May 11, 1670, Rev. Samuel Danforth delivered the annual "election sermon" intended to remind the local colonists of their solemn responsibilities. The sermon, "A Brief Recognition of New England's Errand into the Wilderness," gave salient expression to the Puritans' distinctive view of their role in God's foreordained plan for the world.[9] Danforth was speaking to the second generation of settlers in the New World. It was important that he, and every other minister in New England, regularly remind his parishioners of the godly "errand" their forebears had undertaken and warn them of the moral dangers that threatened them from every side. These annual election sermons, "jeremiads," as Sacvan Bercovitch calls them, became an early American institution designed to keep alive the early settlers' sense of special providence.[10] The purpose of these jeremiads was to take the community to task for any slackening of collective resolve and to highlight once again the cosmic significance of any progress they might make. By delivering these "state-of-the-covenant" addresses, the clergy hoped to keep alive the notion that God had a special purpose for gathering his saints in the American colonies. And finally, these jeremiads planted deep in the American psyche the conviction that both person and community life are to be measured by their faithfulness to the terms of God's errand.

To the Puritans' way of thinking, European Protestants had, for the most part, proved unequal to the task to which God had summoned them. For this reason God chose to send a certain small remnant forth to a new Zion where at last the world would witness a holy and uncorrupted commonwealth. Rev. Edward Johnson explained that when old England "began to decline in religion," Christ raised "an army out of our English nation, for freeing his people from their long servitude," and created "a new England to muster up the first of his forces in." New England was destined "to be the place where the Lord will create a new heaven and a new earth, new churches and a new commonwealth together."[11]

Colonial clergymen's tendency to mythologize their role in history gave apocalyptic significance to incipient American patriotism. Cotton Mather, for example, explained that the marching of God's saints into New England signaled nothing short of the "last conflict with anti-christ . . . in the utmost parts of the earth."[12] In his 1690 election sermon, delivered before the General Court of Massachusetts, Mather rhetorically asked the colony's forefathers to explain just why they had ventured into the wilderness:

> And the answer to it is not only too excellent but also too notorious to be dissembled. Let all mankind know that we came into the wilderness because we would worship God without that Episcopacy, that Common Prayer, and those unwarranted ceremonies with which the "land of our forefathers' sepulchers" had been defiled. We came hither because we would have our posterity settled under pure and full dispensation of the gospel, defended by rulers that should be ourselves.[13]

We should, perhaps, be cautious about taking at face value the professed religiosity of the early colonists. There is no certain way to gauge the depth and seriousness of statements like these made by the clergy at church or civic ceremonies. Nor can we help but wonder what the average layperson thought of such pretentious rhetoric. The first American colony, Jamestown, was largely a commercial venture, and most of those who joined the Massachusetts Bay Colony did so for economic rather than religious reasons. Yet the diaries of Plymouth's leader, Governor William Bradford, and the Massachusetts Bay Colony's governor, John Winthrop, reveal how seriously biblical faith was taken. It should be remembered, too, that lay interest in the clergy's sermons made their publication and sale a profitable commercial enterprise and created the nation's first literary tradition. Whatever the mixture of motives and reasons, the fledgling colonies did adopt Bradford's, Winthrop's, and Mather's mythic accounts of the colonization of the New England as their own official history. To this day, Americans retain the implicit faith that they are God's chosen nation. And also to this day, Americans show a tendency to demonize their enemies and view all that conspires to thwart their errand into the wilderness as somehow the subtle plot of the Antichrist.

Cotton Mather's father, Increase Mather, encouraged this mythologizing of the settling of New England, declaring that "there never was a generation that did so perfectly shake off the dust of Babylon . . . as the first generation of Christians that came to this land for the Gospel's sake."[14] Nor would Governors William Bradford or John Winthrop have found this an exaggeration, at least if Mather's descriptions were understood as referring to their noble intentions rather than the civil and religious waywardness that was embarrassingly manifested from time to time. The Puritans knew that a society dispatched on an errand must be organically bound together. There could be no divisions or conflicts of interest. From the outset, then, American Puritanism held a corporate conception of society in which all were bound together into what Bradford called one "civill body politick." The famous Mayflower Compact put such resolve into a political platform founded on obedience and submission to the word of God as interpreted by the New England clergy:

> In ye name of God, Amen. We whose names are underwritten . . . having undertaken, for ye glorie of God, and advancement of ye Christian faith . . . doe by these presents solemnly & mutualy in ye presence of God, and one of another, covenant and combine our selves togeather into a civill body politick, for our better ordering & preservation, & furtherance of ye ends aforesaid . . . unto which we promise all due submission and obedience.[15]

John Winthrop helped think through this same connection between sacred and secular order for the hearty souls who settled the Massachusetts Bay Colony. In order to plant his "choice grain" in the American wilderness, God had "sifted a whole nation" to set forth on his errand. They were not fleeing from persecution; they were instead executing a final flank attack on the forces of unrighteousness everywhere.[16] Their role, as John Winthrop frequently reminded them, was to exist "as a city upon a hill" where the "eyes of all people are upon us."[17] As part of God's program of instruction to the world, they were to provide the nations with a working model of a godly society and, by their example, lead the final assault on the Antichrist.

Winthrop counseled that the civil covenant they had made with one another required that "we must be knit together in this worke as one man, we must entertaine each other in brotherly affection."[18] The kind of social solidarity that Winthrop and other Puritan leaders envisioned was one in which there would be no rewards other than the reward of the errand itself. Social gradations, as historian Perry Miller pointed out, were to remain what God had originally appointed. There was to be no economic rivalry, and though there would be hard work for everybody, prosperity would be bestowed not as a consequence of labor but as a sign of God's approval of the errand itself.[19] For the first time in the history of humanity, there would be a society so dedicated to God's purposes that worldly success would lead not to sinful diversions but to the further glory of both God and the civil body politic.

John Winthrop kept a journal to record the momentous construction of the "city upon a hill." He was not, however, primarily concerned with recording personal reminiscences. Instead he was documenting the vast extent to which supernatural forces affected the colonists' individual and collective destinies. In 1635 he wrote that "it is useful to observe, as we go along, such special providences of God as were manifested for the good of these plantations."[20] The special providences that Winthrop observed were of the fates of those persons who subordinated their individuality to the purposes of the group and of those persons who blatantly acted out of self-interest. He took special note of how those who acted contrary to the corporate good soon drowned in a shipwreck, died in an explosion, or lost personal property. When a thief was found in the colony, he saw special evidence of divine providence, "showing the presence and power of God in his ordinances, and his blessing upon his people, when they endeavor to work before him with uprightness."[21]

God was not the only one with a vested interest in the activities of New England's saints. Winthrop reported that they were victimized by constant plots spawned by the devil to "disturb our peace, and to raise up instruments one after another." The devil conspired against them by sending adverse weather, Indian massacres, disease, and pestilences of every kind. Worse still, he struck right at the heart of the community by "sowing jealousies and differences between us and our friends at Connecticut."[22] The war with the Antichrist was not yet over. As

Increase Mather argued a few years later in 1682, their feared enemy was still dangerous, for "a dying Beast will bite cruelly . . . since he is going out of the world, we may expect he will give a cruel bite at the Church of God."[23]

And cruel bites they received. The Antichrist's own special demons, the Native Americans, resisted the colonists' evangelical advances and haunted their errand at every step. Diseases and natural disasters continued to plague the colonists, proof of the "special providences" of their immortal adversary. Worse still, the jealousies and differences that Winthrop reported grew at an accelerating rate. Most unsettling of all, apostasy had become rampant. The moral and spiritual fiber of the colonies was suffering from the continued immigration of rival sects and also on account of the devil's clever schemes to lead the second generation astray. There was obviously a need for vigilance against such supernatural assaults. Clearer boundaries must be established and maintained. Heretics must be identified. The Antichrist had to be named and banished from the "city on a hill."

Demons in the Shape of Native Americans

When William Bradford described how the Pilgrims eagerly anticipated arriving in the "vast and unpeopled countries of America," he could hardly have been unaware that the New World was already inhabited. By "unpeopled" he thus meant not yet populated by civilized Europeans. His narrative goes on to describe the spot destined to blossom into the New Jerusalem as "devoid of all civil inhabitants, where there are only savage and brutish men which range up and down, little otherwise than the wild beasts of the same."[24] Earlier explorers and Jesuit missionaries had already flooded Europe with accounts of "the nations of savages" that populated the Americas.[25] Foremost among these accounts were gruesome tales of Indian atrocities. No less shocking were descriptions of pagan religious ceremonies, since in their own way, these would prove the greater obstacle to sanctifying the New World.

Bradford's history of the Pilgrims' voyage conveys this trepidation and recalls how the decision to embark on their holy errand had been made in the face of what they fully expected to be the "continuall danger of the savage people; who are cruell, barbarous, and most treacherous."[26] The stories that had circulated around Europe were enough to make "the very bowles of men to grate within them, and make the weake to qauake, and tremble." This fear was fully understandable given the fact that the Pilgrims believed that the men who awaited them

> delight to tormente men in the most bloodie manner that may be; fleaing some alive with the shells of fishes, curring off the members, and joynts of others by peesemeale and broiling on the coles, eate the collops of their

flesh in their sight whilst they live, with other cruelties horrible to be related.[27]

The Puritans were at no loss to explain why these cruelties were already there to greet them on their arrival in the New World. In his lengthy history of the American colonies, *Magnalia Christi Americana*, Cotton Mather explained that Satan had beaten them to the New World and had already laid the traps with which he intended to snare his opponents. The Native Americans, Mather surmised, were Satan's first line of defense against the forces of righteousness:

> Though we know not when or how these Indians first became inhabitants of this mighty continent, yet we may guess that probably the devil decoyed these miserable savages hither in hopes that the gospel of the Lord Jesus Christ would never come here to destroy or disturbe his absolute empire over them.[28]

Jonathan Edwards later endorsed Mather's judgment about the Native Americans' subjugation to Satan's will, opining that "it is certain that the devil did here quietly enjoy his dominion over the poor Indians for many ages."[29]

It is important to remember that Mather, Edwards, and their contemporaries took for granted the Protestant axiom that the pope was the Antichrist. They were, therefore, reluctant to affix this term to those who currently occupied the wilderness that they coveted for themselves. Yet insofar as the term *antichrist* designates the forms and personages through whom Satan operates in this world, it is clear that the early settlers regarded the Native Americans in the symbolic universe as closely linked with the Antichrist tradition. From the Puritans' perspective, the Native American cultures established throughout the New World were the devil's "city on a hill." The Native Americans' lifestyles were symbolic opposites of their own Bible-centered piety. They had forsaken European civilization and were now cast adrift in a wilderness that appeared as an all-too-favorable environment for Satan's nefarious deeds. The lure of the devil was all about them as the imminent outbreak of sloth, avarice, jealousy, disobedience, heresy, and even witchcraft would soon testify. They knew that if they were to capture the devil's city and convert it to their own godly purposes, they would have to resist these calls of the wilderness. For example, Cotton Mather worried that it was the "terrible wilderness" itself that would prove fatal to the Puritans' errand. What he called the "dark regions of America" provided Satan with a perfect abode. Historian Richard Slotkin examined the Puritans' readiness for seeing the devil all about them in the inhabitants and landscape of the New World and contends:

> The wilderness was seen as a Calvinist universe in microcosm and also as an analogy of the human mind. Both were dark with hidden possibilities

for good and evil. Through the darkness the Indians flitted, like the secret Enemy of Christ or like the evil thoughts that plague the mind on the edge of consciousness. Like the devil, Indians struck where the defences of good were weakest and having done their deed, retreated to hiding.[30]

The belief that the Indians were, like the Antichrist, in league with Satan provided a noble justification for conquests into the American frontiers. The lofty goal of converting the pagan natives to Christianity featured prominently in all early discourse about the reasons for supporting settlements in the New World. King Charles asserted in 1628 that the conversion of the natives was "the principal Ende of this plantacion," and the original charter granted to Massachusetts charged the governor and company to "wynn and incite the Natives . . . [to] the onlie true God and Saviour of Mankinde."[31] Some, like John Eliot, took this charge in earnest and sought to strike a blow against Satan by converting his former associates to the true faith. On the whole, however, the time and energies expended by the Protestant settlers to convert the Native Americans proved largely wasted, and such efforts gradually waned over time. After all, unlike the Catholic French who equated conversions with nominal doctrinal understanding accompanied by outward participation in the sacraments, the Protestants identified conversion with the acceptance of complex theological ideas and a public narration of one's personal experience of grace. Cultural and linguistic barriers made it nearly impossible for Native Americans to comply with these stringent proofs of conversion, and Puritan energies were consequently redirected to more pressing circumstances. Even as early as the 1640s, a correspondent of John Winthrop's listed conversion of the natives a distant seventh on his list of reasons that God had brought his people to New England.

The Puritans' proclivity for demonizing their enemies served an even more important ideological function when it became necessary to murder the Native Americans wholesale. For a community that had conceived of itself as dedicated to the gospel of love, the widescale slaughter of Indians posed serious questions about the Puritans' character and moral resolve. Knowing that their adversaries were in league with Satan helped ease the consciences of God's chosen people. Within weeks of arriving on the shores of Plymouth, the Pilgrims had been forced of necessity to raid Indian storage bins for corn and native crafts. Violent skirmishes broke out from time to time, leading up to the Pequot War of 1637 in which the Puritans killed more than five hundred native men, women, and children in a single battle. By the outbreak of King Philip's War in the 1670s, there could be no more mistaking the fact that the interests of the Native Americans and the European settlers were inalterably opposed. The quest for survival robbed the colonists of many of their lofty moral principles and brought home the realization that, in a barren wilderness, might makes right.

In the face of such realities, the colonists gradually abandoned their original plans to Christianize the Indians and instead formulated a doctrine of holy war, which called for the obliteration of Satan's allies from the earth. Samuel Nowell, for example, explicitly interpreted the outbreak of King Philip's War as a preparation for Armageddon. He divined that "God in his providence keeps some Nations and people unsubdued, as he did with Israel of old . . . he kept some people unsubdued on purpose to teach Israel War."[32] The cosmic significance of the Native Americans, then, was to arouse the Puritans' combativeness on the eve of the final battle with Satan: "When God intended the Canaanites to be destroyed, he did forbid Israel to marry with them: they were to be thorns to them, and Israel was to root them out."[33] The Native Americans were no longer hapless souls who needed only the Gospel to find their way to civility. They had instead become demons who had to be defeated if progress were to be made in fulfilling God's errand.

In a period in which the ministers of New England were about to instigate the outbreak of the witchcraft hysteria that demonized the dissenters in their own villages, they first set about demonizing the Indians who threatened their community from without. The clergy were already aware that the Native Americans' religious ceremonies directly implicated them in "diabolicall worship." Observers recounted all the loud moaning and hideous movements involved in these ceremonies as proof that they were in league with the devil. Even Roger Williams, an able advocate of Native American rights, refused to endanger his soul by watching the devil's agents at work during these powwows.[34]

Further evidence of the Indians' intimate association with the dark regions of the spirit world came from Rev. John Emerson. Emerson wrote to Cotton Mather that sinister spirits were conspiring against the saints of New England. Good Christians, of course, were long accustomed to assaults from the spirit world. But now, according to Emerson, these spirits were tormenting them by taking the form of Indians and stalking them when they least expected. The proof that they were beset by repeated incursions from the spirit world was that Indians had recently been spotted in the very middle of their villages and would then disappear in almost the twinkling of an eye. Mather confirmed Emerson's suspicion concerning these demonic specters: "I entirely refer it unto thy judgment (without the least offer of my own) whether Satan did not Set Ambushments against the Good People of Gloecester, with Daemons, in the Shape of Armed Indians."[35] Demons, in the shape of Indians, were waging a "spiritual war" on those who would erect the holy city on a hill. As Mather described it,

> the Story of the Prodigious War, made by the Spirits of the Invisible World upon the People of New England, in the year, 1692 . . . [has] made me often think, that this inexplicable War might have some of its Original among the Indians, whose Chief Sagamores are well known unto some

of our Captives, to have been horrid Sorcerers, and hellish Conjurors such as conversed with daemons.[36]

Cotton Mather's study of the Indian wars reveals how the Puritans responded to the general decline in religious zeal by interpreting their struggles against an external foe in terms of apocalyptic mythology. With overt rebellion in the form of both heresy and witchcraft about to break out in the community itself, however, Mather and his colleagues were soon to have more sinister demons to name and combat.

Dissension in Utopia

The early settlers of New England thought of society as a unit bound together by the terms of their covenant with God. Society was not a simple aggregation of its individual members but an organism that functioned for a definite purpose, with all parts subordinate to the whole. Concern with the proper regulation of this social organism made the very concept of democracy a farce. Early colonial society was, as Perry Miller described it, conceived as "a dictatorship of the holy and regenerate."[37] The right to vote was restricted to church members, and full church membership, at least in the Bay Colony, required a narration of one's personal experience of regenerating grace. Religious holiness and civil righteousness were thus inseparable in the Puritan mind. The right of elected leaders to whip into line any who faltered at the task of serving "the errand" was unquestioned. Those who persisted in putting self-interest ahead of the welfare of the communal good had the liberty to leave New England, to be banished, or, if they returned, to be hanged in the Boston Commons.

Disputes over who did and who did not belong in the corps of the "holy and regenerate" raged from the start. At stake was determining who had a legitimate voice in shaping the nation's errand. Perhaps the most intense of these early boundary disputes was the debate over the "halfway covenant." The halfway covenant was a compromise according to which the children of church members, even if they did not undergo a distinct conversion and become full church members, could be considered "halfway" embraced by the covenanted community and have some privileges of church membership (e.g., receive baptism). This practice posed no great problem until grandchildren began to be born whose parents were only "halfway" members of the covenant community and someone had to decide whether or not the third generation was qualified to receive baptism. The controversy that arose was heated because, either way, one of the first generation's cherished ideals would have to be sacrificed. If baptism were denied to the children of unregenerate parents, then the holiness of the church would be preserved at the cost of numbers, and the "visible saints" would become a decreasing percentage of the population. If baptism were allowed, the churches would no longer possess a clear measure of holiness and would gradually become incapable of making clear moral or doctrinal pronouncements. Disputes over the halfway covenant exposed a fault line in the culture's religious foundation. Differences of opinion were difficult for either side to tolerate. Jonathan Edwards, for example, was ousted from his pulpit at Northampton precisely for his unwillingness to accommodate his parishioners' demands for more flexible standards of church membership. Modern readers are perhaps unlikely to take these historic disputes seriously. Yet they can, at the very least, appreciate the fact that early colonists believed they would be unable to protect their city on a hill from sabotage unless they could establish some kind of theological or moral boundaries to help them differentiate between "insiders" and "outsiders."

New England ministers relished the opportunity to remind the citizenry of the duties incumbent on those engaged in God's errand. One rhetorical technique for stemming the tide of declension was the "jeremiad" delivered in the form of sermons on fast or election days. These sermons identified deviance, or even potential deviance, and interpreted it in the mythic terms of God's never-ceasing battles against Satan. Beginning as early as John Winthrop's sermons aboard the *Arbella*, the New England clergy reminded those guilty of even the smallest neglect of duty that God stood vigilant, ready to chastise those who grew wayward. False dealings with God, betrayal of covenant promises, degeneracy among the young, or the shameless pursuit of either profits or pleasure were certain to bring swift revenge. Too, Satan was ever lurking about, ready to claim for himself any soul that opened the door to his influences. Evil was a force of great cunning and strength. Indeed, so treacherous was the pull of evil influence that according to Cotton Mather's "official history" of the colonies, God's providential order could at any moment be "overthrown and turned upside down [with] men speak[ing] evill of good, and good of evill, accounting darknesse light, and light darknesse."[38]

Cotton's father, Increase Mather, was among the first to take official stock of the "state of the covenant" in New England. As early as 1679 he helped convene an assembly of clergy and lay leaders to deliberate on the moral declension and religious apostasy irrupting all about them. Their report, published under the title *The Necessity of Reformation*, listed twelve general categories under which the iniquity of New England could be summarized.[39] First there was a great and visible decay of godliness. The members of the assembly had also witnessed several manifestations of insubordination to established authority. Furthermore, heretics were present in the shape of Quakers and Anabaptists. The long litany of vices seemed to be increasing: swearing, sleeping during sermons, lie telling, sex and alcohol abuse, lawsuits, the decay of family government, and unbridled greed in business dealings. All told, the citizens of New England had lost their civic spirit as defined by their moral leaders, and worst of all, they failed to display any inclination to reform.

It is clear, then, that deviance threatened the errand from the very beginning. But what is equally clear is that New England villages actually seemed to require and even elicit this deviance. As sociologist Kai Erikson noted, deviant behavior frequently helps a group by making the outer edges of group life more discernable.[40] Communities, we must remember, occupy cultural as well as geographical space. Because this "cultural space" sets the community apart as a distinct and special group, it is imperative that communities protect their moral and intellectual boundaries by providing clear-cut standards of conduct and belief. When a person's thought or behavior moves to the margin of these boundaries, it becomes deviant. The interesting sociological fact is that such deviant behavior actually protects boundaries by drawing attention to the dangers associated with any broach of the community's moral or religious borders. A community in the process of losing control over its members actually requires a certain amount of deviance so that it can rally a renewed defense of its boundaries. By naming someone to the deviant class, a community is able to accentuate the frightening consequences of noncomformity and dramatize how vulnerable a borderless society is to disruption by alien influences.

When a community "names" the deviant, names the Antichrist, it reminds its members who they are not and whom they must never allow themselves to become. It is thus understandable that within a generation or two of coming to the New World, the Puritans of New England would need to name deviants and, in so doing, draw attention to the dangers of boundary failure. Erikson's analysis of deviance in the early colonies suggests that it "is quite natural, then, that they would seek new frames of reference to help them remember who they were, and it is just as natural that they would begin to look with increasing apprehension at the activities of the Devil."[41] Confronted by the kinds of iniquities that Increase Mather and others observed, the New England Puritans learned to study with special care the shapes in which the devil appeared to them. Among the most interesting of those shapes were Roger Williams, Anne Hutchinson, and the alleged witches of Salem.

When Roger Williams arrived in Massachusetts, he was welcomed as "a godly minister."[42] Unfortunately, he did not find the New England churches nearly so godly. He rejected a call to serve the Boston Church because he "durst not officiate to an unseparated people." The New England Puritans had refused to separate officially from the Church of England for reasons of political expediency. Williams, however, demanded that New England churches formally deny any connection with the Romish practices of the Anglican Church. John Cotton and others knew that the Church of England still carried the "image of the Beast" of Revelation, but they shied away from any hasty break with the king's church. Williams soon found that the nonconforming were no more free in New England than they had been in England itself. Although his contention that the New England Puritans were uncomfortably close to the sphere of Antichrist was hard to dispute, ministers nonetheless joined together with other colonial authorities to fend off Williams's antiestablishment rhetoric. He further antagonized the colony's leadership by criticizing its practice of using the civil government to prosecute persons for failing to abide by religious precepts. Then, to make matters worse still, he denounced the colony's charter from the king as an unlawful expropriation of lands rightfully belonging to the Native Americans.

The problem with Williams's views was not that they were theologically unsound but that they failed to take into account the political and social realities of the age. What he soon discovered was that New England, eager to combat conspiracy, had erected dissension-squelching mechanisms no less effective than those it alleged existed in the Antichrist's Roman Catholic Church. New Englanders believed that they had avoided the source of the Antichrist's tyrannical power in Europe by keeping the churches separate from the state.[43] To Williams, however, the entanglement still existed, albeit in a new form. The state rushed in on its own to stamp out religious heresy by prosecuting persons for disrupting of the civil order, and so it did in his case. Williams's theological positions seemed to be pushing the church toward a more democratic system, which roused the fears of civil authorities as much as it did those of the clergy. Following a series of summonses before ministers and magistrates, the General Court found Williams guilty of disseminating "newe & dangerous opinions, against the authoritie of magistrates" and ordered him banished. The boundaries prevailed; the heretic was expelled.

The fight against antinomianism did not cease with the ostracism of Roger Williams. A new bout of boundary skirmishing broke out in the home of Anne Hutchinson, a woman in her middle forties who possessed a remarkable ability to debate the most obscure points of Puritan theology.[44] In 1634 Hutchinson emigrated from England to Massachusetts, where she soon won respect for her vigorous intellect and her kindly disposition. Her avid interest in religious issues led her to convene informal meetings of women at her house, during which she led discussions of the sermons of the previous Sunday. Hutchinson was quick to take exception to the local ministers' views and to engage in heated theological polemics. The points of theology that were in dispute were probably obscure even in her own day. Their importance, however, was never really theological but, rather, political. When Hutchinson began to argue that only two of the many ministers of the Bay Colony were "walking in a covenant of grace" and that all the others preached a "covenant of works," she exposed the weakest link in the community's delicate chain of command. The juxtaposition of "covenant of grace" and "covenant of works" revived the Protestant Reformation's rejection of Catholicism's belief in the efficacy of ecclesiastical and moral works. To Hutchinson and her growing group of supporters, this theological distinction bore directly on whether the clergy of New England were fit to govern the colony and whether they were justified in their tireless efforts to mold citizens' behavior ("works") to fit their moral standards.

After pondering for some time whether the Antichrist was embodied only in Muslims, Hutchinson finally concluded that the ministers of the Church of England and all who followed in their ways were antichrists because they did not preach the new covenant. What made Hutchinson's charges against the incumbent clergy's theological views so serious is that they went to the heart of New England polity. Indeed, the colonial preachers had subtly shifted their emphasis from salvation by grace alone to a person's compliance with the community's moral standards. The clergy argued, of course, that they had never returned to the discredited covenant of works; they were not arguing that outer conformity to social mores earned salvation but that such conformity was a convenient way to demonstrate salvation. On this basis they defended their practice of judging who had or had not experienced a true conversion and thereby screening candidates for church membership. They also maintained that even the surest saint must submit to church discipline and be governed by the will of the congregation, not because this would earn salvation, but because a person must be adequately prepared for the gift of grace when it came.

When Anne Hutchinson charged that godly behavior on this earth was no evidence of salvation, she drew attention to the fragile basis on which New England clergy sought to control the nation's errand. Sainthood in New England had become a political responsibility as well as a spiritual condition. For good or for bad, Hutchinson did not quite appreciate how the world had changed in ways that made the "covenant of grace" an insufficient basis for religion to serve as an agent of social control. Her opponents quite naturally saw her as an antinomian and accused her of advocating a religion that absolved its adherents from obedience to moral law. The case against her was more that of sedition than heresy. Although the arguments and legal exchanges were cloaked in the language of theology, they were actually about political and social insubordination.

In the beginning, Hutchinson had the support not only of about one hundred sympathetic citizens but also of Governor Vane, Rev. John Cotton, and her brother-in-law Rev. John Wheelwright. Unfortunately, Vane returned to England; Cotton was embarrassed into acquiescing to his pastoral colleagues; and Wheelwright did not have enough clout to keep himself from being banished from the colony. Once cut off from effective allies, Hutchinson was brought to trial "for traducing the ministers and their ministry." The troublesome point was that although the General Court knew what her punishment should be, it did not have a clue to what crime she had committed. The transcript of her civil trial preserves the confusion and frustration surrounding the colonial authorities as they tried to find a charge that would stick against their theologically adroit opponent. Even though Anne Hutchinson stood before the court a lone woman in poor health and without legal counsel, everyone who mattered could see that she was the devil incarnate, come to sabotage all that they held dear in life.

The opening sessions brought forward a host of theological technicalities concerning which Hutchinson was said to have fallen into doctrinal error. It was clear, however, that she was scripturally better versed and intellectually quicker than her accusers. Asked, for example, what right she—a woman—had to hold meetings in her house, she promptly replied that in Titus it is counseled that the elder women should instruct the young. But the trial was never about theology. And Hutchinson, given several opportunities to back down and act conciliatory, seemed hell-bent on undermining the authority of the idiots she saw before her, no matter what the personal cost. One after another, the assembled ministers offered testimony about the indignities they had suffered at the hands of the impudent Mrs. Hutchinson. Ex-governor Thomas Dudley sought to summarize the truth concerning her guilt:

> About three years ago we were all in peace. Mrs. Hutchinson from that time she came hath made a disturbance . . . [she has] vented divers of her strange opinions . . . she now hath a potent party in the country. Now if all these things have endangered us as from the foundation, and if she particular hath disparaged all our ministers in the land . . . why, this is not to be suffered![45]

With everyone agreed that Anne Hutchinson's "strange opinions" endangered the very foundations of Puritan society, it only remained to find legal grounds for banishing her from the holy commonwealth. Dudley again came to the rescue by uncovering the true source of this "potent party" of antinomianism. He reinforced the boundaries of orthodoxy by testifying that "I am fully persuaded that Mrs. Hutchinson is deluded by the devil." This had actually been suspected for some time. Just the year before Anne Hutchinson's close friend and supporter, Mary Dyer, had given birth to a stillborn and premature fetus, "so monstrous and misshapen" that Governor Winthrop was able to conclude unequivocally that the devil was working through these women. A few months later Anne Hutchinson herself gave birth to a deformed fetus that further implicated her in the nefarious actions of the archenemy of Christ and his church. As time would tell, a pattern was emerging that anyone whose talk or actions went against the grain of Puritan order risked being accused of collegiality with the devil.

Modern readers find it difficult to read the transcript of Anne Hutchinson's trial without viewing it as a cruel miscarriage of justice even by the standards of the time. This is, however, to fail to realize that it was a social drama whose outcome was certain from the outset. At the end of many hours of legal posturing with no hard evidence that Hutchinson had committed any crime, Governor Winthrop announced the court's verdict: "Mrs. Hutchinson, the sentence of the court you hear is that you are banished from out our jurisdiction as being a woman not fit for our society, and are to be imprisoned till the court shall send you away." Still baffled as to why her relentless logic had not carried the day, Hutchinson responded, "I desire to know wherefore I am banished." Winthrop, without hesitating, scolded, "Say no more, the court knows wherefore and is satisfied."

Of course, the court did know why Hutchinson had to be banished even if it did not have any formal laws or statutes to cite. As Erikson notes,

> The settlers were experiencing a shift in ideological focus, a change in community boundaries, but they had no vocabulary to explain to themselves or anyone else what the nature of these changes were. The purpose of the trial was to invent that language, to find a name for the nameless offense which Mrs. Hutchinson had committed.[46]

In brief, she was guilty of being deluded by the devil and voicing his subversive words. True, she cited the very theological doctrines on which the Puritan faith was initially constructed. She understood well Protestantism's emphasis on the decentralization of ecclesiastical authority and the primacy of each person's internal relationship to God. But Hutchinson was out of step with the new demands of commonwealth building and threatened to blur the moral and intellectual boundaries that restrained persons from straying outside their Puritan community. It was obvious to all the proper authorities that her crime was serving as an agent of the cosmic foe, Satan, and so banishment was the most lenient sentence she could possibly have hoped for.

Witchcraft and the Devil's Plot Against New England

The banishment of Roger Williams and Anne Hutchinson reveals how effective the New England clergy were in protecting their self-appointed errand into the wilderness. Their apocalyptic rendering of the colonies' historical importance led them to see cosmic significance in the give and take of everyday life. Rather than representing the real differences among competing groups of people, social and political struggles were seen instead as skirmishes between the people of God and their diabolical adversaries. Nowhere was this mythologizing of civil life more blatant than in the witchcraft episode of Salem in 1692. Much has been written about the Salem witchcraft trials; they have been interpreted as a symptom of sexual hostility, the consequence of generational conflicts, the result of food poisoning occasioned by fungus-tainted rye bread, and an outbreak of racial hostility stemming from the experiences of captivity by the Indians.[47] Perhaps the most compelling of these interpretations is Paul Boyer and Stephen Nissenbaum's careful analysis of the role of factional rivalries in the "naming of witches."[48] Those who still identified with the social and economic ideals stemming from the original "errand" found themselves surrounded by prospering neighbors whose social and economic ideals came from mercantile capitalism rather than religion. They vented their confusion and resentment in the principal means available to them: naming the enemy in the mythic terms of the cosmic battle between God and Satan.

In 1692 Salem Village had an adult population of 215 persons. Two generations of population growth and expanding economic opportunities were fast bringing them into new cultural territories unchartered in the Puritan worldview. Having inherited the "corporate" notion of society in which the private will was to be subordinated to the public good, they were ill prepared for the emergence of preindustrial capitalism and its pull toward an ethic of individual autonomy. The problems that confronted Salem Village were by no means unique in the late seventeenth century. All across New England, ministers and their congregations were having difficulties; farmers were resisting the economic system of mercantile capitalism; outlying areas were breaking away from their parent towns, and centers of social authority were shifting. But as Boyer and Nissenbaum point out, the tensions of late-seventeenth-century New England became especially intense in Salem Village. It was located just a few miles from the more prosperous and commercial Salem Town, and the proximity of Salem Town provoked endless political confrontations that revealed the village's increasing vulnerability. But Salem Town was much more than a political rival; it was also a symbol of the looming moral threat concerning the very nature of New England's errand. This symbolic rift came to a head in a series of disputes over who had the authority to call or dismiss the minister of Salem Village's church. In the midst of their debates over who would occupy the village's pulpit, the citizenry became acutely aware that they had divided into two opposing factions, which differed markedly in their economic prosperity and their willingness to accommodate the new economic order symbolized by nearby Salem Town.

The residents of Salem Village were divided by what finally boiled down to three main socioeconomic factors: church membership, wealth, and geographical proximity to the commercial enterprises in Salem Town. The ensuing witchcraft episode did not create these divisions, but

it did expose their symbolic significance. Boyer and Nissenbaum observe
that if we are

> to understand the intensity of these divisions, we must recognize the fact—
> self-evident to the men and women of Salem Village—that what was going
> on was not simply a personal quarrel, an economic dispute, or even a
> struggle for power, but a mortal conflict involving the very nature of the
> community itself. The fundamental issue was not who was to control the
> Village, but what its essential character was to be.[49]

The incident that ignited these volatile social tensions began with
the idle curiosity of some young girls who came together to play and to
speculate about boyfriends and the future. One of the girls devised a
small crystal ball from the white of an egg and in its murky fluid thought
she saw the outlines of a coffin. Nobody knew then, much less now,
what the girls actually experienced in their excitement and fright. They
never told. But the grown-ups began supplying their own interpretations of what was happening in their village, something they continued to do until more than 140 persons had been accused of witchcraft.
The parents were alarmed at their children's unruly behavior, which
they described as outbursts of "fits," "distempers," "odd postures," and
"foolish, ridiculous speeches." Under intense questioning from their parents, the children directed their attention at a young slave girl by the
name of Tituba who had apparently brought a great deal of occult lore
along with her from the Caribbean. A few weeks later, again under the
adults' directive questioning, the children accused two other local
women for tormenting them. These two, along with Tituba, were the
first to be arrested for suspicion of witchcraft.

Accusations and arrests multiplied in the following months. After
the initial arrest of a few social misfits and general malcontents, the
accusations began to target persons of increasingly higher social stature. A high percentage of those accused of witchcraft were persons of
real social respectability; those, that is, who were prospering from the
very social forces responsible for the reduced fortunes and prospects of
Salem Village's old guard. The young girls who supplied most of the
names at the beginning of the witchcraft epidemic had never even met
most of those whom they accused. But the girls had heard their names
mentioned around their homes and had picked up on their parents'
resentment of these strangers' education, wealth, and growing political influence. What information the girls could not provide on their own
was helpfully supplied by the adults who stepped in to make the accusations complete. Historical perspective allows us to see how members
of the older cultural order, unable to relieve their frustrations in any
normal political way, employed the only means at their disposal for
ridding themselves of unwelcome individuals: They accused them of
being agents of the devil. The village authorities went after the more

vulnerable of these social deviants not by making rational or empirical arguments but by keeping the dispute in the language of apocalyptic theology. The trials consequently revolved principally around private judgments of what ways of life constitute the way of God and what the way of Satan.

Published sermons and church records from Salem Village in the years surrounding the witchcraft trials leave little doubt about the role of religion in mythologizing the conflicts and tensions of social life. The minister, Samuel Parris, had already prepared the soil for such thinking by tracing the source of local grievances to actual, conscious collaboration between individual human beings and evil spirits. As Parris put it, there existed "a lamentable harmony between wicked men and devils in their opposition of God's kingdom and interests." In a sermon describing why King Saul had become "haunted with an evil and wicked spirit," Parris explained that Saul had gone for advice "to the Devil, to a witch."[50] Right after the young girls had first broken into their fits and convulsions and just two weeks before the first of the accused witches was arrested, Parris preached a sermon entitled "Christ Knows How Many Devils There Are." In this sermon he meticulously explained to the residents of Salem Village that Satanic influences were behind every vice and act that subverted Christ's moral order.

Parris originally stated that wicked people were in league or association with the devil. During the protracted witchcraft proceedings, however, Parris's sermons collapsed even this fragile distinction between the human and the supernatural by suggesting that the wicked persons in their midst actually were devils. He argued that although by the word *devil* "is ordinarily meant any wicked angel or spirit," it may also mean "vile and wicked persons—the worst of such, who for their villainy and impiety do most resemble devils and wicked spirits." Although it is technically true that a person could not become a devil in "nature," he or she might, like Judas, become a devil in "quality and disposition." More to the point, he added, "there are such devils in the Church."[51] This subtle theological shift justified the sense of outrage felt by his parishioners at the way in which their "errand" was being betrayed. In the guise of prospering merchants and their families, devils were afoot in Massachusetts. Parris's theological dissertations on the ways in which human persons might actually embody the devil in "quality and disposition" adequately formulated the citizenry's vindictive demand for revenge. Because the accused witches were actually devils rather than persons, if found guilty they must be dealt with accordingly. And sure enough, many of them were.

The governor of the colony, Sir William Phipps, requested the learned Cotton Mather to write a book that would explain and justify the witchcraft trials. Mather, for reasons that will be explained more fully later, was especially suited to the task. An archetype of the apocalyptic mentality, Mather understood that every event in the human world was shaped by the deeper cosmic forces set in motion by the battle between God and Satan as they struggled for control of the universe. His narrative of the witchcraft proceedings, *The Wonders of the Invisible World*, provides insight into the theological logic that made these trials an exercise in righteousness. "I have indeed," he wrote, "set myself to countermine the whole PLOT of the Devil, against New England, in every branch of it."[52]

For Mather, the witchcraft trials were to be understood against the larger background of the devil's plot to thwart the errand into the wilderness. He explained that "the New-Englanders are a people of God settled in these, which were once the Devil's territories."[53] They had formed a "true utopia" and were a chosen generation of men whose godliness and absence of vice were without parallel. As could be expected, their inroads against vice and iniquity irritated the devil and made him exceedingly disturbed. For precisely this reason, the "Devil is now making one Attempt more upon us; an Attempt more Difficult, more Surprising, more snarled with unintelligible Circumstances than any we have hitherto Encountered."[54] Mather continued by explaining that in the last days, the devil was growing more able, more adventuresome, more consternating. Now, just as New Englanders were poised to usher in a godly commonwealth, "an army of Devils is horribly broke in upon the place which is the Center . . . [even assuming] the shapes of innocent persons."[55] So malevolent was the devil's influence that he had succeeded in undermining proper authority and government and had even managed to raise "animosity and misunderstanding among us."

Amid such affliction and confusion, Mather counseled that the people turn to "the Glorious and Sacred Book of Revelation" to discover how the righteous might emerge victorious from this supernatural assault. Mather could see how this whole horrible assault by the devil on "the Center" was part of the end-times scenario of which Revelation had warned them. He was reassured that the Protestant Reformation had fully exposed the Antichrist and thus the hour of final victory was near.

> The Devil's Eldest Son seems to be towards the End of his last Half-time; and if it be so, the Devil's Whole-time, cannot but be very near its End. It is a very scandalous thing that any Protestant should be at a loss where to find the Anti-Christ. But we have a sufficient assurance that the Duration of Anti-Christ is [drawing to a close].[56]

Mather, whose Protestant faith identified the Antichrist with the papacy, could take consolation in the fact that true faith would soon triumph over this final assault of Satan and his eldest son. The witchcraft episode was one final test of moral resolve. Satan and the Antichrist were sure to be defeated if believers held steadfast to the inherited errand and resisted any temptation to follow competing impulses. Although both Cotton and his father Increase Mather were concerned that innocent persons might be mistakenly convicted of witchcraft, protection of the errand nonetheless required unyielding resistance against the devil's last attempt to undermine it. Naming the witches was thus essential to preserving the true faith. For although it was difficult for the clergy to rally opposition against abstract social transformations, they had long ago mastered the apocalyptic art of flaming the fires of passion against those whose nonconformity threatened to raise "animosity and misunderstanding among us."

Mather, Edwards, and the Colonial Apocalyptic

Puritan ministers rarely preached at length on the subject of biblical prophecy, as the practical task of generating a stable worldly order dictated against fanatic preoccupation with the collapse of worldly systems. Nor was the sober Puritan temperament comfortable with the obscurities and reckless predictions that accompanied the explicit emphasis on apocalyptic themes. But although colonial theologians were reluctant to allow the fantastic symbolism of Daniel or Revelation to distract their parishioners from the rigors of everyday Christian life, they nonetheless believed that these prophetic books provided important clues to the ultimate meaning of the American experience. John Cotton, Thomas Shepard, Ephraim Huit, William Aspinwall, and Thomas Parker all wrote serious treatises on biblical prophecies that circulated among the theologically curious in New England.[57] Michael Wigglesworth's widely read poems entitled "God's Controversy with New England" and "The Day of Doom, or a Poetical Expression of the Great and Last Judgment" exemplify New Englanders' interest in the details of Christ's imminent return.[58] New England intellectual life was steeped in the apocalyptic assumption that God was ceaselessly at work steering the course of human history toward a final kingdom. This final triumph of the saints over their persecutors was considered a future certainty. But in the meantime humans were expected to await the return of Christ by preparing themselves morally and spiritually while still attending to matters of this world. The clergy's job was to help their parishioners sustain their commitment to this moral and spiritual preparation. Toward this end the clergy frequently found it useful to use apocalyptic imagery as a homiletic or motivational tool. The laity found added incentive to tend to their worldly duties when alerted to the presence of invisible supernatural enemies who preyed on those with a weak or hesitating will.

No better examples of colonial apocalyptic thought exist than the writings of Cotton Mather and Jonathan Edwards. Both exemplify the

Puritan reluctance to emphasize apocalyptic ideas regularly in public settings. Yet both lived in fervent expectation of the grand destiny that awaited God's chosen people, and for this reason their understanding of the history of redemption united all their other theological interests. Mather and Edwards interpreted the meaning and significance of events transpiring in the world around them in terms of the prophetic categories in Daniel and Revelation. From the Salem witchcraft trials monitored so closely by Mather to the Great Awakening rejoiced in by Edwards, these Puritan divines were able to sift every worldly event through the sieve of the apocalyptic imagination. Although the Antichrist's evil and deceit were everywhere about them in the American landscape, each was convinced that the time of biblical prophecy was at hand and that the Antichrist was therefore in his final hour.

Cotton Mather's lifelong obsession with the devil was an inherited trait. Fearful of his own emotions, pleasures, and lusts, he interpreted his inner struggles to sustain piety in the apocalyptic categories of his father and grandfather.[59] Cotton's grandfather, Richard Mather, left England in 1635 because he and his neighbors lived in "fearful Desolation." He was certain that God favored England above all other nations and that he had inspired the Reformation there to lead England out of the Antichrist's dreadful clasp. But the citizens of England had not fully expunged the influences of papal religion form their shores and thus had not taken the Reformation far enough. Like virtually all Protestants, Richard identified Revelation's "beast from the sea" with the papacy and its ecclesiastical paraphernalia. Even though the Antichrist had seized hold of Christ's church and led millions of souls into apostasy, the day of reckoning was fast approaching. The Book of Revelation foretells the coming battle in which Christ would return and consume the Antichrist and his followers, leaving the faithful to reign on earth in a restored Edenic paradise. Richard's decision to leave England and join the Puritans in the wilderness was dictated by his belief that these gathered saints might contribute to the Antichrist's final demise. By staying true to their covenant with God, the godly citizens of New England would help usher in the prophesied utopian millennial age.

Cotton's father, Increase Mather, had continued the family's intellectual leadership in New England by graduating from Harvard and studying for the ministry at Trinity College in Ireland. His many sermons and published writings were, however, more acts of piety than of intellect. Increase's attempt at a scientific treatise on the movement of comets, for example, argued against reducing physical laws to so-called secondary causes and instead maintained that the movement of comets must finally be attributed to God's mysterious power.[60] This talent for detecting the causal influence of invisible powers served him in his quest to keep the second generation faithful to the founding settlers' holy errand. His *Discourse Concerning the Danger of Apostasy* chronicled the wiles of Satan in leading his contemporaries astray, and his *Essay for the Recording of Illustrious Providences* opened its readers' eyes to the miraculous examples of divine intervention in such otherwise mundane events as thunderstorms, close calls while at sea, and magnetic variations.[61]

When the Salem witchcraft trials accelerated into a frenzied miscarriage of justice, it was Increase who stepped forward to restore cultural order. His *Cases of Conscience* made a telling argument against the use of "spectral evidence" (testimonies of persons who had had visions of devils appearing in the forms of known citizens of the village and environs, thereby implicating them in his nefarious deeds). But as Increase Mather's biographer, Robert Middlekauff, comments,

> He did not do so out of scientific skepticism, or because he was a "liberal" in any sense, or because he doubted that witches were tormenting the people of Salem. Indeed, it was precisely because he entertained not a shred of scientific rationalism that he was able to argue that the methods of the court were unreliable.[62]

Whereas the less pious officers of the court had proceeded on the assumption that things in this world were what they appeared to be, Increase knew better. He contended instead that appearances must never be confused with true reality (i.e., the supernatural influences of Satan or God). Only a thorough, and ultimately apocalyptic, knowledge of Satan's ways could be used to sort out the truth from its alluring counterfeits. What gave Increase hope was the conviction he had inherited from his father that Satan's and the Antichrist's reigns were near their ends and that rational order would soon be restored to the universe. As he reached the end of his life, he devoted increasingly more attention to the revolutions, wars, famine, and pestilence that signified the imminent return of Christ and the final defeat of the Antichrist.

From childhood, Cotton Mather's mastery of languages and modes of theological disputation heralded his bright and promising career as a third-generation American clergyman. Cotton assumed the mantle of theological leadership from his father and grandfathers and eloquently championed the Puritan worldview well into the eighteenth century; a century, however, in which fewer seemed to care about an arcane theological vocabulary that was becoming hopelessly out of step with the colonial experience. Cotton Mather was a vain and irritable man who never quite understood the intellectual changes going on about him and who frequently gave way to fits of rage when any obstacle—external or internal—stood in the way of his passionate pursuit of personal and national godliness. Yet this tragic, even comical, Puritan sage was without question the leading theologian of his era and the proud expositor of America's role in ending the reign of the Antichrist.

Cotton inherited a conspiratorial view of the universe from his father and grandfather. Like Richard and Increase before him, Cotton took for granted that unseen and malevolent powers had the capacity to enter into people's innermost selves and prompt them to evil action. Cotton, in fact, went further in this regard than did his Puritan ancestors, who for the most part assumed that Satan could not exert power over a person so long as he or she resisted temptation. Cotton often implied that the devil's authority was uncurbed and that he could prompt even "innocent" persons into apostasy or morally revolting actions. He knew this from his own experience; his diary records recurring and often violent assaults from the devil.[63] He learned from an early age to expect buffetings from evil spirits, particularly after he had just performed some good act or in any way advanced in personal piety. His internal life thus represented a microcosm of the larger battles being waged between Satan and God. He girded his loins for this holy battle even in adolescence. Fasting by fourteen, Cotton delighted in the pleasures of asceticism and denial. "We must kill our lusts before they kill us," he repeated, knowing full well that people's inner corruption stripped them of their defenses against the devil. Although he married three times and fathered fifteen children, he despised and feared sexual gratification (as well as food and drink) throughout his life.

The demons that Cotton feared in his inner life also populated his public ministry. He, like his father, considered pulpit-inspired fear of God's wrath to be the principal bulwark against the moral declension rampant throughout the colonies. It was Cotton Mather's sacred vocation to rail against sinners and to decry every social or economic trend that might fan the flames of lust and pleasure. This may, in part, explain the fervency with which he believed that the end was imminent. Millennial rhetoric provided a convenient homiletic device with which to threaten unregenerate souls with the fate that would await them if Revelation's Book of Life failed to include their names. Mather's eschatology held together his entire theological system by providing its ultimate reference and dramatizing the ultimate grounds for embracing Christianty's gospel of salvation. Millennial faith gave Mather assurance that the sufferings of the elect would cease and the unregenerate would receive their just deserts. Christ would come and catch the world unsuspecting (i.e., except for those who listened to Mather predict first 1697, then 1716, and finally 1736 as the certain year prophesied in scripture for the Son of Man's return). He would come in clouds of smoke and fire, accompanied by legions of angels singing his praises. What Mather dwelled on most, however, was the glorious promise that Christ would destroy the Antichrist and his cohorts and then chain the devil for a thousand years before crushing him for good.

Perhaps no part of Revelation gave Mather more satisfaction than this vivid image of the physical smashing of all God's enemies. Throughout his life Mather feared and dreamed about death. Robert Middlekauf notes that "visions of his own death haunted him from an early age, and descriptions of the deaths of sinners—their corruption at last stopped, their polluted influence ended, their filthy voices silenced— gave him satisfaction all his life."[64] The urge to know in greater detail how all inner and outer demons would be destroyed once and for all prompted Mather to pore over the commentaries of every millennialist author on which he could lay his hands. He particularly absorbed himself in the writings of Joseph Mede and William Whitson, who fortified his confidence that the signs of the times fulfilled biblical prophecy and that the final destruction of the Antichrist was within sight.[65] The Salem witchcraft episode further convinced Mather that the cosmic powers had stepped up their border skirmishes in anticipation of the coming final battle. Cotton, like his father, believed that the Bible made it clear that there would be a widescale conversion of Jews to Christianity just before the Second Coming. (Paul wrote in Romans that "all Israel shall be saved.") With his father, Cotton Mather shouted hosannas every time he heard of a Jew who had been gathered into a Protestant church, and he prefaced one of his one works with an address calling out "Return, O backsliding Israel."[66] But despite the conversion of a Jew here and there and despite occasional earthquakes, wars, and eclipses, none of Mather's predictions came true. Indeed, the cohorts of the Antichrist— devils, witches, Quakers, Anabaptists, heretics, and Native Americans— that he so despised ended up outliving his efforts to rid them from the New World.

The apocalyptic speculations of Jonathan Edwards provide another look at the role of the Antichrist in colonial theology. One of the most brilliant and original minds that America has ever produced, Edwards followed in the footsteps of his grandfather, Solomon Stoddard, pastor of the church at Northampton, Massachusetts.[67] Graduating from Yale at the age of seventeen, Jonathan put his life and intellectual energies into running his church and producing masterly philosophical and theological treatises. Alarmed by the what he described as the "extraordinary dullness" of his congregation's religious life, he preached a series of five sermons in 1734 on the subject of salvation by faith alone. His words seem to have struck a responsive chord. A young woman of questionable morals was converted; other young people were excited by her example; and soon conversions began spreading like wildfire through the community. Edwards's newfound ability to stimulate his listener's "religious affections" made him one of the principal architects of America's revivalist heritage. His success at bringing sinners to repentance and conversion made him a focal point in the First Great Awakening, in which a wave of religious enthusiasm passed across the nation, producing a large number of converts to Protestant denominations in its wake. Other revivalists of the Great Awakening, such as George Whitefield and John Wesley were perhaps more charismatic preachers, but Edwards's *A Faithful Narrative of the Surprising Work of God* (1737), *Some Thoughts Concerning the Present Revival of Religion* (1742), and *A Treatise Concerning Religious Affections* (1746) have had profound influence on the subsequent history of revivalism and religious enthusiasm in America.

Apocalyptic elements are strikingly absent from most of Edwards's public ministry and early writings. One reason is that he was what today is called a *postmillennialist*, believing that human history will progressively usher in a godly kingdom before the return of Christ. Postmillennialism is tied to a certain optimism concerning the possibilities of human nature and consequently does not require ardent hope for a supernatural and instantaneous "solution" to the human situation. Yet in the quiet of his personal study where he spent hours every day, Jonathan Edwards engaged in a lifelong study of the Book of Revelation and the apocalyptic elements of the Old Testament.[68] Poring over the cryptic passages of these texts, Edwards concluded that we can be certain that the Antichrist had embodied himself in the Roman papacy. Edwards regarded Revelation 17:18 ("And the harlot that you saw is the great city which has dominion over the kings of the earth") as unequivocally disclosing the identity of this master of trickery and deception. This passage, he wrote, "is spoken the plainest of any one passage in the whole book. . . . 'Tis the only part of this prophecy but is spoken without allegory."[69]

Edwards believed that Christian faith carried with it an imperative to participate in the Antichrist's defeat. He maintained that just as the Old Testament prophecies concern Christ, the prophecies of the New Testament concern the Antichrist. Edwards pondered over these prophecies at length and at last worked out an elaborate history of the "work of redemption" that identified three distinct periods in God's plan for redeeming the world. In the first period, from the fall of Adam and Eve to the incarnation of Christ, Satan emerged as God's grand enemy who proved himself capable of conquering humanity. The second period, from Christ's incarnation to his Resurrection, struck a fatal blow against Satan, as Christ's death purchased humanity's salvation (notwithstanding the fact that the Jews, in "a most malignant manner," opposed the gospel) and paved the way for the final judgment that would transpire at Christ's Second Coming. The third period, from the Resurrection to the final judgment at the end of the world, has thus far been characterized by the two great works of Satan to forestall God's victory: the emergence of the Muslim kingdoms and the rise of the Antichrist.

The rise of the Antichrist, according to Edwards, was gradual. The Christian church corrupted itself in many ways as the popes claimed more and more power and robbed people of their ecclesiastical and civil liberties. Somewhere in this process the Antichrist seized control and emerged as the "master-piece of all the contrivances of the devil against the Kingdom of Christ."[70] The Antichrist and his minions turned the church into an agent of trickery and deception. Under Antichrist's direction the clergy held the Christian populace in ignorance, duping them with superstitions and false doctrines shrouded in the church's pretended miracles and pretentious displays of pomp. Most offensive of all, to Edwards, was the Antichrist's attempt to exalt "himself above all that is called God, or that is worshipped, so that he as God sitteth in the temple of God, shewing himself that he is God."[71] The Reformation struck a telling blow against the Antichrist and "the horrid practices of the Popish clergy." But even as the final destruction of Antichrist was at hand, the powers of darkness were rising one last time to exert themselves against the true gospel. Satan's influence was still strong, as Edwards knew all too well. The continued presence of heathenism, heresy, Islam, and unconverted Jews was evidence enough that the devil was still afoot. Edwards particularly noted Satan's cruel work in the recent promulgation of "corrupt opinions."[72] Among those groups who were hard at work sewing the seeds of infidelity were the Anabaptists who failed to make proper allowance for civil authority, sundry religious enthusiasts who falsely pretended to be inspired by the Holy Spirit, Arminians who attributed too much efficacy to human will, and—most heinous of all—Deists whose commitment to the era's scientific rationalism prompted them to deny revealed religion. The philosophy of Deism struck Edwards as perhaps the most dangerous of Satan's final assaults. Deism had emerged most forcefully out of Catholic France and was thus obviously tainted by the arrogant apostasy of the Antichrist. Its cult of reason and liberal democratic ideals was now rampant in the American colonies, causing "licentiousness in principles and opinions. . . . History gives no account of any age wherein there was so great an infidel apostasy of those who had been brought up under the light of the gospel."[73]

But all of this was of no final consequence. Scripture confirms that these desecrations and abominations are but the dying struggles of the old serpent. God's Spirit was about to be poured out over the world and to bring multitudes flocking to Christ. Edwards's chronological calculations assured him that the Antichrist would fall no later than 1866 (a figure he arrived at by adding the number 1,260, which represented the prophesied forty-two months of Antichrist's rule, to the number 606, which he claimed was the year in which universal episcopacy was proclaimed). The sixth vial mentioned in Revelation was about to be poured out. At any moment "the battle of the great day of God Almighty" would break out, a battle that he believed would conquer, but not terminate, the city of the world. Waged by human beings rather than angels, this battle would bring about a new political order based on the law of God. All of this would be accompanied by four spiritual (rather than physical) "comings of Christ," each of which would be

accompanied with a terrible destruction of the wicked, and the enemies
of the church: the first, with the destruction of the persecuting Jews, which
was amazingly terrible; the second, with dreadful judgments on the Hea-
then persecutors of the Church; the third, with the awful destruction of
Antichrist, the most cruel and bitter enemy that ever the church had; the
fourth, with divine wrath and vengeance on all the ungodly.[74]

At this point the righteous of the church who had been reviled and condemned by their persecutors would finally be vindicated. A glorious age
of peace and prosperity would dawn, marked by great holiness and temporal prosperity. Perhaps foreshadowing the colonies' revolutionary
stirrings, he added that "the absolute and despotic power of the kings
on earth shall be taken away, and liberty shall reign throughout the
earth."[75] Great light and knowledge would prevail, and religion would
be uppermost in the world. To complete the triumph, the pride and
cruelty of the wicked would be exposed, and they would be cast into
an everlasting fire.

Edwards saw the quickening of religion unleashed by the Great
Awakening as a certain sign that the history of redemption was fast
approaching its climactic goal. The Great Awakening had set a process
in motion that would culminate in the prophesied millennium. As we
shall see, however, many of Edwards's contemporaries saw the colonial war against papal France as a political means of overthrowing the
Antichrist. Edwards, too, was encouraged by the defeat of the Antichrist's French agents. But his revivalist impulse prevented him from
politicizing interpretations of the Antichrist or of the means by which
humans could help hasten the millennial dawn. To Edwards, political
events such as the French and Indian War were aids to the task of
bringing people to repentance, but they were not themselves the means
that would ensure Satan's final defeat. This great architect of American evangelism remained convinced that revivals, not wars, were the
most effective strategy for driving Satan and the Antichrist from American shores. The next generation of American clergy, however, saw the
threat of Antichrist in a far more politically charged context and were
consequently prompted to a more revolutionary formulation of apocalyptic mandates.

The Revolutionary Antichrist

In the late 1740s and the 1750s, eschatological expectations were high
in the colonies. The Great Awakening had aroused thoughts about
humanity's spiritual future. Meanwhile, the political unrest that led to
the French and Indian War prompted Bible-oriented colonists to speculate about the meaning of the turbulence that loomed ahead. Beginning
in this era and extending through the 1770s, American identifications
of the Antichrist became increasingly politicized.[76] The long-standing

identification of the pope with the Antichrist made Catholic France an easy target for the clergy's efforts to explain the cosmic significance of the colonies' enemies. No sooner had the colonists helped achieve victory over the French Antichrist than they discovered that the Anglican Church was itself steeped in the Antichrist's deceit, and by association, so was King George III.

There was, of course, nothing truly new in these politicized interpretations of the Antichrist; the notion that the church and the king of England were collectively the "beast from the sea" had been rampant in revolutionary England a century earlier. The colonists, however, were less likely to see the Antichrist cloaked in political garb than were the religious nonconformists still remaining in England. They viewed their local governments as approximating true theocratic rule, and challenges to this order by the likes of Anne Hutchinson had easily and lawfully been disposed of. Inspired by revivalist preachers such as Jonathan Edwards, most Americans believed that praying saints, not armed soldiers, would be the vanguard of a spiritualized kingdom. The new, politicized Antichrist emerged as part and parcel of a radical shift in the colonists' collective identity and collective aspirations. In a span of less than thirty years, the colonists created a national identity for themselves replete with a vivid sense of national mission. The colonists' quest for freedom from what they perceived as despotic rule acquired a noble-sounding form when clothed in the rhetoric of biblical witness against the reign of the Antichrist. Apocalyptic symbols gave the struggling colonists a sense of cosmic significance and also performed the vital function of mythologizing the political enemies who stood in the way of their divinely appointed destiny.

From 1754 to 1760, the British colonists in America found themselves in a protracted war against the French and their Indian allies. The clergy provided a clear sense of the significance of this struggle by interpreting it in the terms of biblical prophecy. Countless sermons delivered during this period interpreted the battle with Catholic France in expressly religious terms. As Nathaniel Appleton, a Calvinist minister in Cambridge, Massachusetts, explained, the French were "of the Church of Rome; which we Protestants maintain to be Antichrist." Appleton maintained that any war with France was an instrument of God's judgment and thus constituted "a Vial of his Wrath [poured] upon this Part of Antichrist."[77] In 1756 a minister by the name of Aaron Burr counseled the faithful to prepare for even worse times ahead, at the same time exhorting them to take heart in the knowledge that they were doing the bidding of God. For despite the blows that the Catholic beast had delivered to them, "the Destruction of Antichrist and the End of this Night of Popish Darkness is near at hand." God would smile on their faithful efforts and would send forth "a plentiful, outpouring of the Spirit of all Grace," and with the Antichrist at last defeated, Christ's millennial reign could begin.[78]

The French and Indian War prompted many clergy to abandon the language of religious love in favor of the rhetoric of religious hate. The clergy argued that just as in Old Testament times, God was commanding his people to take up arms in the defense of a holy cause. Robert Smith, a Presbyterian minister in Pennsylvania, preached that bloodshed was needed to purify the earth in preparation for the millennium. He explained that the colonial struggle was part of the larger turning of the wheels of divine providence and destined to bring even more "dreadful Vengeance to tumble Antichrist from his usurped Seat and give the Whore of Babylon her Double Cup."[79] Fighting the French, then, was the cause of God. Marching to battle hastened the destruction of the Antichrist, whose defeat would usher in a "Salvation, a Deliverance, by far superior to any—nay to all that New-England ever experienced."[80]

By the end of the French and Indian War, the American clergy began to blur any distinction between the Kingdom of God and the new nation the colonists yearned to create for themselves. Nathaniel Hatch convincingly argued that the clergy helped create a "collective identity" for colonial Americans by emphasizing that the first settlers had come not only for religious freedom but also for the sacred cause of political liberty.[81] For example, in his sermon honoring the victory over the French at Quebec, Samuel Cooper reflected on New England's history and maintained that the Puritan fathers had come to this wilderness because they were "smitten with a Love of Liberty, and possessed with an uncommon Reverence to the Dictates of Conscience."[82] In this way the clergy reshaped America's myth of origin in order to put greater emphasis on the meaning and purpose of the secular structures developing within and between the American colonies. In short, they were able to highlight the religious significance of the political values that bound the colonists together. This gradual coalescence of a national identity around the quest for civil liberty was hastened with the help of apocalyptic categories. As soldiers for Christ, the colonists shared a common enemy against whom they must collectively act. At the height of hostilities against the anti-Christian foe of French popery, James Cogswell delivered to the soldiers a sermon that outlined the American character as that of collective resistance to the Antichrist:

> I would entreat you to see to it that you engage in so noble a Cause for right Ends. Let your principal Motives be the Honor of God, and the Defence of your country. Fight for Liberty and against Slavery. Endeavour to stand the Guardians of the Religion and Liberties of America; to oppose Antichrist, and prevent the barbarous Butchering of your fellow Countrymen.[83]

Following the French and Indian War, the clergy continued to describe the Antichrist in terms of the obstacles that stood in the way of political liberty. The Antichrist had for centuries been thought to be implicated in the various "principalities and powers" that impeded the growth of true Christianity. Except in the revolutionary England of the 1600s, few theologians had concerned themselves much with the political and social faces of the Antichrist. It was enough for Protestants that they had the papal Antichrist to contend with. Throughout the 1760s and 1770s, however, American clergy warned of the growing "popery" in England, stressing the affinities of the Church of England with the Roman Antichrist. Ruth Bloch chronicled the second stage in this politicization of the American Antichrist, showing how the age-old view of the Antichrist as a tyrannical being soon made clear the resemblance of King George to Revelation's beast from the sea. The logic was clear and straightforward: If the Antichrist were the epitome of tyranny and if the British government were tyrannical to the core, then no colonist could escape the necessary conclusion that the British civil system that enslaved them was the worldly face of the dreaded Antichrist.[84]

Apocalyptic thinking surely did not cause the American Revolution. But at the level of popular culture, it did articulate the meaning and significance of the ideal order that the colonists were trying to bring about.[85] Thus, in 1766, the Sons of Liberty gathered in Boston to hear an address designed to stimulate continued resistance against the Stamp Act. The orator agitated his audience by reminding them that the Book of Revelation foretold the evil deeds that would be committed by the beasts from the sea and from the land. "I beseech you then," he continued, "to beware as good Christians and lovers of your country, lest by touching any paper with this impression, you receive the mark of the beast, and become infamous in your country throughout all generations."[86] This association of British tyranny with the work of the Antichrist emboldened colonists to act stridently on behalf of their fledgling nation. The *Maryland Journal*, for example, reported that upon hearing that the Continental Congress had finally declared America's independence, a group of soldiers celebrated by throwing down and decapitating "the IMAGE of the BEAST," a statue of George the Third.[87] In case any doubt remained, a pamphlet entitled "Concerning the Number of the Beast" appeared in 1777, confirming the identification of King George with the Antichrist. Its author carefully examined the Hebrew and Greek words for "Royal Supremacy in Great Britain" and was able to demonstrate to his own satisfaction that these words contained the hidden numerical value of 666, the sign of the Beast of Revelation.[88]

Colonial ministers drew on their apocalyptic vocabulary to find words that would sanction the patriots' cause and extol the sacrifices that lay ahead. Sermons during the war repeatedly stressed that America's political liberty was God's providential cause; British tyranny was the Antichrist's. Failure to act strenuously on behalf of God and liberty was therefore tantamount to a deliberate transgression against God. In the spring of 1776, for example, a chaplain in the American army was so enraged by the violence of the British army, "a piece of barbarity unknown to Turks and Mohammaden infidels," that he could only liken it to the "horrible wild beast" of Revelation. Duty to God in such circumstances called for more than turning the other cheek. "We must," he exhorted, "beat our plowshares into swords and our pruning-hooks into spears."[89] Americans were in this way helped to understand the struggle of freeborn men against political tyranny in the same way that they had learned to understand the cosmic battle of Christ's forces against Antichrist. Both were clear moral struggles against evil in which it was both possible and necessary to take an unambiguous stand.

The patriot clergy and lay essayists alike described the American forces as the soldiers of Christ. The revolutionary cause was depicted as a sacred quest against what was variously termed "all the powers of Hell," "the prince of darkness," "the serpent" "the dragon," or "the antichristian beast." The image of Britain as the Antichrist justified violent rebellion and also strengthened hopes in triumphant victory. Shortly after the battle of Lexington, the Massachusetts clergyman Elisha Fish reminded his fellow patriots that "although men or devils, earth or hell, Antichrist or the dragon rages, the people of God may still triumph in Christ, the Captain of their salvation."[90] Colonial patriots were able to see themselves as the vanguard of Christ, destined to be victorious. Their rebellion against tyranny would usher in a utopian era. The American democratic system would be as "a light to the nations," advancing the emancipation of all humanity by the contagion of its example.

The American republic emerged from the Revolutionary War as a nation with the "soul of a church."[91] That is, Americans emerged from their struggle for independence with an unquestioned belief that God had smiled favorably on their cause. The sense of collective identity that surfaced in the new republic had, at its very foundations, a certain assurance that the American way of life was nothing short of God's instrument for ushering in a kingdom of righteousness on earth. To be sure, a high percentage of America's "founding fathers" were champions of Enlightenment rationality and rejected the claims of all revealed religion—let alone the apocalyptic language of Daniel and Revelation. Such architects of the American identity as Thomas Jefferson, Thomas Paine, John Adams, and Benjamin Franklin looked askance at their compatriots' religious rhetoric. But both parties—religious and secular—agreed on one important thing: The creator had designed the universe with the intention that it would steadily give rise to a just and righteous order. The biblical and secularist sources of American identity thus concurred that historical progress was not only inevitable but also the very nature and purpose of existence.

Both visions of American destiny held that it was Americans' solemn duty to aid this progress and to resist all impediments to the gradual creation of a perfected order on earth. The colonial clergymen draped these assumptions in the mythic cloth of apocalyptic faith. In this way they invested the emerging American political order with ultimate meaning and significance. Their politicized renderings of apocalyptic discourse showed the first Americans that it was their sacred duty to resist the Antichrist, that is, to resist every impediment that, like King George, prevented the spread of godly society. Although not all Americans have believed in the mythic dimensions of the American national identity, these conceptions continue to this day to enable Americans to demonize their enemies and to know without the slightest inkling of doubt that in God they trust.

The rhetoric of the revolutionary Antichrist redirected American apocalyptic thought in ways that enabled religious Americans to work in and through the same political structures as their secular neighbors. Instead of waiting for progress to be initiated and achieved by a supernatural agent (i.e., Christ, upon his return), the colonial clergymen focused on humanity's responsibility for rearranging the political and social structures that would permit the fostering of Christian culture. In the theological terms of the twentieth century, they eschewed a premillennial interpretation of apocalyptic faith (i.e., Christ must come first before any real spiritual renovation of the earth can begin) in favor of a postmillennial interpretation (i.e., Christ will be fully present only once they have reshaped their world into a morally and religiously pure order). When the war ended, the American clergy were euphoric in anticipating the next stage in their preparation for the imminent millennium. All that remained was for the churches to extend pure Christian faith to the whole American populace and then throughout the world. If accompanied by a systematic concern for moral reform, evangelical efforts would of themselves usher in the Golden Age. The prospects for this utopian age had not seemed so auspicious since the founding of New England. As the chaplain to the Continental Congress, George Duffield, boldly proclaimed, "Vice and immorality shall yet here become banished . . . and the wilderness blossom as the rose."[92]

The millennium awaited the building of a Christian Commonwealth in the new republic. The only task that remained was to identify the lingering pockets of Antichrist's resistance.

Three

Impediments to Christian Commonwealth

We are entering, fellow-citizens, upon a period foretold by prophets of old—looked for and longed for by lovers of their country in past generations—a period of the overthrow of despotism, and the downfall of Anti-Christ.

Ladies' Christian Commission, 1865

ଛ

Between 1780 and 1880, American Protestants busied themselves with the task of building a Christian commonwealth. The tyrannical British Antichrist had been defeated in the Revolution, and millennial optimism ran high. Americans were confident in their election as God's chosen people. They had emerged from the Revolution as a new Israel, providentially guided to lead the world to political liberty and moral perfection. Their destiny was to be an example to all the world that democratic government and gospel faith could work in tandem to produce a righteous commonwealth.

A few clergy believed from the outset that democratic government alone was insufficient to save humans from their own sinful tendencies. In a sermon delivered in Boston in 1776, Samuel West tried to qualify the heady utopian faith that fueled the Revolution by cautioning that "nothing can prevent our success, but only our sins."[1] West's pronouncement proved prophetic. Irreligion and moral sloth were deeply rooted in the human condition. Democracy, equality, and the granting of political liberties could only exacerbate, not remedy, these remaining impediments to the creation of a Christian commonwealth.[2] Another clergyman, Nicholas Street, spoke for those whose Christian values were threatened by the licentiousness ushered in by Americans' newly found freedom. Street compared Americans with the children of Israel who, freed from Egyptian bondage, fell into vices of their own making and as a consequence wandered aimlessly in the desert rather than entering the promised Canaan:

> We in this land are, as it were, led out of Egypt by the hand of Moses. And now we are in the wilderness, i.e. in a state of trouble and difficulty. . . . And thus we in this land are murmuring and complaining of our difficulties and ill successes at times, thinking our leaders to blame, and the like, not considering at the same time that we are practicing those vices that have a natural tendency to destroy us.[3]

Street knew all too well that proliferating moral and religious vices "forebode ill concerning us as a people." If public virtue failed and the people grew vicious and profane, God would have no choice but to multiply the nation's distresses and bring his people to repentance and reformation. Street gave an example of the kind of vices that threatened the Christianization of America: Soldiers were ignoring the Sabbath, and many of them had been known to engage in profanity and swearing. As the nineteenth century dawned, Protestant clergy added to Street's list and identified many additional obstacles delaying Americans' entrance into the Promised Land: atheism, Deism, Masonry, intemperance, slavery, immigrants, non-Protestants such as Catholics and Jews, Mormons, the sinful nature of city living, and the Civil War.

All of these impediments were at one time or another interpreted as cunning devices of the devil to recapture the city on a hill. Yet the period between 1780 and 1880 was for the most part one in which Antichrist rhetoric receded from American mythic discourse. True, the Antichrist reared his pernicious head to inspire Deism and later to urge on the opposing side in the Civil War (either the North or the South, depending on the angle of one's apocalyptic vision). Many millennial sects such as the Mormons, Millerites, Shakers, and sundry communal groups kept discussion of the end times from disappearing from the national consciousness altogether. But even these groups were more concerned with overcoming their members' moral declension than deciphering diabolical plots aimed against them by the Beast.

The impediments to Christian commonwealth were vexing to Protestant churches, but none of these impediments was rooted in a social base sufficiently powerful to threaten their hold on their members' loyalties. Hence members of Protestant reform movements during the nineteenth century were frequently zealous in their efforts to uproot sources of apostasy and moral turpitude, but they were neither sociologically nor psychologically seduced by them. Accordingly, there was no need for Protestants to interpret their "enemies" in such apocalyptic categories as the author of Revelation resorted to when trying to make sense of his community's beleaguered place in the world. As a consequence, the Antichrist was largely absent during the confident expansion of American Protestantism in the nineteenth century. It seemed that the Antichrist was saving his energies for the battle that would begin in earnest in the late 1880s as the century's main intellectual and cultural currents swelled into what became known as modernism.

The Antichrist in the Age of Enlightenment

By the 1780s it had become clear that the establishment of the American nation was in itself insufficient to launch the millennium. Millennial hopes instead fixed on the gospel-inspired extension of knowledge, science, and morality. Under the clergy's very noses, however, Americans were coming under the influence of a new understanding of what constituted knowledge, science, or morality. The Age of Enlightenment blossomed in Europe at almost the exact moment that the colonies began their quest for independence. The writings of British philosophers like John Locke and David Hume had stripped the pursuit of knowledge from pious submission to religious authority. Reason and empiricism were fast becoming the final arbiters of what could be deemed truth. In his *Essay Concerning Human Understanding* (1690), Locke asserted that all knowledge derives from sense experience. His empiricist position directly challenged long-established theological convictions that knowledge is either innate or revealed. In actuality Locke thought of himself a defender of faith, as is evidenced by his later work *The Reasonableness of Christianity* (1695). He did not, for example, doubt the inspiration of the Bible or the divinity of Jesus, as did many of his contemporaries. But despite Locke's personal piety, his philosophical writings emboldened those who embraced science, not scripture, as the sole path to valid knowledge about their world. Locke championed the view that humanity's rational powers, if rightly disciplined and employed, could extend their knowledge of the world and provide the means of solving the problems confronting them in their collective pursuit of happiness. For this reason he personified the humanistic confidence of the age and left for later generations a psychological theory of human cognition that made religious faith appear both superstitious and a hindrance to true human progress.

This was the Age of Reason. The educated public throughout the Western world was aglow with confidence in humanity's ability to know the world through the use of reason alone, unaided by the dogmas of religion. Newton's scientific discoveries portrayed the universe as a lawful, machinelike entity that behaves in a rational, even mathematical manner. The workings of the universe correspond to human logic. From this discovery, Enlightenment thinkers concluded that reason was the key to nature's secrets and would ultimately provide complete knowledge of the universe. French *philosophes* like Voltaire and Diderot inspired fellow eighteenth-century intellectuals to reexamine religion in light of the era's confidence in reason. For some, the result was outright incredulity and ridicule. Others, however, opted for a rationalized form of religious belief and embraced the period's Deistic religious philosophy.

Deism had roots in both the Enlightenment and what was known as the "latitudinarian" sentiment among many eighteenth-century Englishmen who sought to overcome the divisions among Christians by identifying a certain core of reasonable claims on which all Christians could agree. Lord Herbert of Cherbury helped articulate the central tenets of the Deist position when he listed what he thought to be the five basic truths common to the foremost religions of the world. Briefly stated, they were the beliefs that God exists, that he is to be worshiped, that the practice of virtue is the true worship of God, that humans should repent their vices, and that there is an afterlife in which there will be rewards and punishments. There was, however, nothing distinctively Christian about Deism. It mentioned nothing about any special work of Christ, the existence of miracles, or the reliability of scripture. It also lacked mystery, ritual, or any emotional appeal. But it did make possible a "rational faith" that for many in the Age of Reason was the only viable alternative to having no religious faith at all. Though skeptical of revealed religion and claims concerning miracles or the supernatural, Deism nonetheless affirmed the existence of God as First Cause of the universe. It also affirmed the importance of moral conduct as a means of living in concert with the lawful design that God imparted to nature. Many thoughtful persons of the age thus embraced Deism as the only religion compatible with reason and science.

Thomas Paine, Benjamin Franklin, and Thomas Jefferson were among those who helped introduce to American intellectual life Enlightenment humanism and the Deistic religious philosophy that typically accompanied it. Deist sentiment was not new in America, but it had been previously confined to the aristocratic elite. The outbreak of the French Revolution, however, set loose an impassioned popular antipathy toward institutional authority, and Deism grew into a widespread movement. The Deistic tracts of Thomas Paine, Ethan Allen, Elihu Palmer, and others attacked the churches as the great enemy of progress. Compared with humanism's bold belief in the inevitability of progress, biblical faith seemed meek and backward. Church membership dropped to 5 or 10 percent of the American population. Indifference to religion prevailed, and the clergy had to warn the nation of the error of its ways and to "name" the heretical author of this rationalist cancer in their midst.

The first step in the clerical apocalyptic smear campaign against Deism was to link it with the dangerous excesses of the French Revolution. The French Revolution had at first appeared to Americans as a continuation of their own triumphant quest for liberty and democracy. Its egalitarian values and rationalist philosophy were delivering death-blows to the papal Antichrist, who had for too long enjoyed unrestricted privilege in the French social and political orders. But as the bloodshed continued and chaos reigned, the revolution's egalitarian politics struck fear in those who felt themselves appointed to the task of preserving America's own fragile political order. Many began to suspect that the French Revolution was a clever scheme of the Antichrist, who had become ever more vicious and desperate in his final days. The Antichrist, it seems, had found it a strategic moment to abandon the form of the pope and instead embody himself in the skeptical and Deistic philosophies that were driving humans to the brink of self-destruction. In the words of Nathan Strong, the Antichrist had chosen British and French intellectuals to usher in "the last stage of anti-christian apostasy."[4] In 1793 Rev. Joseph Lathrop had been enthusiastic about the imminent fall of the Beast at the hands of the French revolutionaries. Just five years later, however, he became aware of Satan's adroit maneuvering and began to warn his fellow Americans that the devil was now parading in the disguise of rationalistic philosophy. First clothed in ancient paganism and then in popery, Satan had, according to Lathrop, reappeared with the French Revolution dressed in "deism, materialism, atheism, and every species of infidelity."[5]

In the eyes of American clergy, there was a direct link between the anarchy set loose by French revolutionary thought and the moral dangers of the Deistic religious beliefs popular with their own countrymen. On the morning of May 9, 1798, Rev. Jedidiah Morse delivered a sermon that exposed this link so forcefully that shock waves were felt across the nation for years to come. Morse claimed to have in his possession documents that proved that the French Revolution had been plotted by a secret association of anarchists known as the Bavarian Illuminati. This diabolical group had now gained control of the Masonic lodges throughout England and America and, from this power base, were now plotting to overthrow the American government. He warned that even as he spoke, secret agents were sowing the seeds of revolution throughout New England.[6]

Morse's Bavarian Illuminati scare obviously hit an exposed nerve in American Protestantism. Even though Morse never produced any evidence to substantiate his claims, for the next several months sermons and popular tracts sounded alarm at the conspiracies being hatched by the Bavarian Illuminati and kindred groups of infidels. Timothy Dwight, president of Yale College, used his July 4 sermon that year to warn that spies, saboteurs, and—worst of all—infidels were lurking all about them.

Dwight explained that the French *philosophes* and the Order of the Illuminati were the unclean spirits coming out of the mouth of the papal Beast, as prophesied in the Book of Revelation.[7] An anonymous tract written in 1798 saw in the French-inspired infidelity a danger of such magnitude that it dwarfed the apostasy created over the years by the papacy. The Beast's "little horn" was not the pope, as Protestants had traditionally concluded, but must instead signify the French Revolution.[8]

Protestant ministers were slowly awakening to the potential gulf between America's religious heritage and its newly made commitments to the political ideals of liberty and democracy. Harvard divinity professor David Tappan described the dangers of "pursuing the splendid phantom of an undefined, romantic liberty and equality, which would at once clash with social order, moral justice, and the present frame and condition of man."[9] Democratic values fostered a cultural ethos in which people tended to ignore the strictures of religion and follow their own predilections instead. Faced with declining church attendance and ubiquitous moral declension, many clergy agreed with Abraham Cummings, who repudiated "the false doctrines of liberty and equality, which have contaminated millions of mankind."[10] Indeed, to most Americans in this age, it was inconceivable that there would be any final divorce of religion from the matters of civil government. Without the guiding light of gospel faith, the nation would lose its moral compass and would no longer be carried forward with the sweep of divine providence. As William Symmes put it in 1785, "a nation favored with gospel privileges cannot slight and neglect their religious advantages, without endangering their civil liberties."[11] Surrounded on all sides by Deism and infidel philosophy, Timothy Dwight in 1798 echoed this seeming truism by reminding his readers that "Rational Freedom cannot be preserved without the aid of Christianity."[12] Any citizen who promoted infidelity, then, was a false patriot "who contradicts and counteracts his own pretensions of love to his country."[13]

Although few religious Americans were willing to go as far as Tappan and attack democratic values, most were becoming aware that a free society provided a new battleground in the ongoing war between the Antichrist and the forces of God. In his *Sacred Cause of Liberty*, Nathan Hatch describes how American clergy realized that the Christian republic they yearned to create could be more effectively destroyed through heresy than through any external political or military threat.[14] The Antichrist could more quickly create disorder throughout a free society from within by spreading infidelity than by seeking to overthrow it militarily from without. By the 1790s, ministers had come to the opinion that the symbol of Antichrist could no longer be restricted to the papacy but should instead be applied to the moral and intellectual cancers in their own midst. Analyzing the weakness of the pope in 1799, David Osgood concluded that the marks of the beast and of the dragon, so visible and manifest upon it in ancient times, were nearly obliterated. The mother of harlots had either become a reformed prostitute, or having passed the days of vigour and passion, was a mere withered form in the last stage of decrepitude, retaining only the shadow and skeleton of former times.[15]

Protestantism's long linkage of the papacy and the Antichrist was at last weakening as the Beast began taking on new shapes closer to home. For this reason the symbol of the Antichrist should, in Timothy Dwight's words, be "far more justly applied to the collective body of modern Infidels."[16]

In his *A Dissertation on the Prophecies Relative to Antichrist and the Last Times* (1811), New Hampshire clergyman Ethan Smith continued to weaken the automatic connection of the Antichrist with the Roman Catholic church. The Roman hierarchy, he maintained, is but the "false prophet" or second beast of Revelation who does the bidding of the actual Antichrist whom he equated with the "atheistical powers" of the day. Smith specifically cited Voltaire, Rousseau, Hobbes, and Hume as among those who had infected Americans' thinking with the Antichrist's infidel philosophy. The atheistic and anarchical ideas so currently fashionable were "uniting the rivulets of Infidelity into a powerful current. . . . directing this mighty deluge against the principle of the Christian religion, and of all virtuous civil government; this was to be the development of the infidel Power under consideration; this is the Antichrist of the last times."[17]

It was not until 1880, when "modernism" had fully taken hold of American intellectual life, that these new conceptions of the Antichrist caught the attention of most defenders of the faith. In the meantime, however, a number of lesser impediments inspired by Satan and his agent, the Antichrist, preoccupied those seeking to bring about the Kingdom of God on earth.

The Millennium Through Moral Persuasion

In the first decade of the 1800s, Protestants began to develop new strategies for promoting religion in a nation in which religion was officially separated from the public realm. For the most part, the churches retreated to the "private" sphere of evangelical ministry and concentrated on doing what they knew best: revivalistic preaching and the winning over of individual souls. Scattered revivals throughout Virginia, the Carolinas, and rural New England began to generate a new wave of religious excitement. Then in 1802, a revival at Yale College conducted by Timothy Dwight elicited conversions from one-third of the student body. Dwight's sermons in the college chapel focused on the infidelity that accompanied the "freethinking" views associated with the era's intellectual life. He forcefully argued that infidelity to God inevitably led to political anarchy and countered that the best foundation for democracy was evangelical, gospel faith. Dwight's revivals were consequently designed to bring audiences to "true" patriotism as much as they were to encourage biblical witness. Among the many students who followed his logic and became convinced of the connection between evangelical faith and democratic liberty were Lyman Beecher and Nathaniel Taylor, men destined to carry Dwight's message forward by conducting similar revivals across the country.

The American population during these years was moving westward, first to western New York and then Kentucky, Tennessee, Ohio, Michigan, and Illinois. Under the leadership of Beecher, Taylor, and others, revival meetings followed. Itinerant revivalist preachers crossed the frontiers, conducting emotional revivals designed to win new converts committed to constructing a Christian society. Winthrop Hudson drew attention to the fact that the western revivalists were dealing with a moving, floating, migrating population.[18] Accordingly, they had to push for a much quicker decision than their eastern counterparts did, and so a new breed of American revivalism was born, as the "camp meeting" preachers turned on all the heat they could and appealed to the emotions more than to the intellect. The "Second Great Awakening" flourished across the American West for nearly two decades as these revival meetings produced large numbers of converts eager to make the world holy in anticipation of Christ's return to judge the living and the dead.

Distinctive to the era's religious thinking was its increasingly Arminian tone. That is, revivalist preachers modified the traditional Calvinist doctrine concerning people's inability to achieve salvation through efforts of their own. The strict Calvinistic position maintained that salvation was totally outside human hands and that true conversions were initiated only by the actions of an inscrutable and somewhat capricious God. The Second Great Awakening veered from traditional Calvinism and popularized the view that humans could choose or willfully decide to bring about their own spiritual regeneration. This new faith in persons' ability to take control over their own eternal destiny was better adapted to the confident, young American nation. The new theological climate also supported an optimistic program of social action, encouraging the belief that regenerated persons, acting in concert, could gradually construct a social order pleasing to Christ.

The Arminian tone of the Second Great Awakening convinced many that it was not enough for the churches to be concerned with winning individual conversions. They also needed to remake society. It was the churches' responsibility to direct "saved" Christians into both morally pure lifestyles and forms of volunteer service that would progressively regenerate the whole of American society. The first of these goals—encouraging saved persons to pursue piety and moral perfectionism—was hardly new to Christian ministry. The second, however, was unusual

in the history of Christianity and reflected the churches' innovative adaptation to the American separation of church and state. Although the
churches could not directly dictate civil law or polity, they could encourage individual church members to organize and use free, democratic organizations to advance their moral interests. Revivalist preachers
maintained that sin was the condition of selfishness and that if one's
conversion were genuine, it would shift "the controlling preference of
the mind" from a "preference for self-interest" to a "preference for disinterested benevolence."[19] Literally thousands of converted individuals
decided to become soldiers for Christ by joining one or another "reform
society" dedicated to eliminating one of the remaining impediments to
the Christianization of America. The president of Williams College, Mark
Hopkins, voiced the era's optimism when he predicted that the time would
soon come when "wars, and intemperance, and licentiousness, and fraud,
and slavery, and all oppression" would be brought to an end "through
the transforming influence of Christianity."[20]

A new national religious consensus was building, in which Christians understood their duty to be the creation of a millennial society.
Working in a democratic society without religious enfranchisement,
Christians set themselves to the task of promoting revivals, establishing churches, and participating in the newly emerging "reform societies"
designed to eliminate any remaining imperfections in American society. This new and uniquely American form of religious and moral action, known as *voluntaryism*, was seen as the ultimate vehicle through
which God's providential work would be accomplished. Americans were
certain that their nation was destined to lead the way in the moral and
political emancipation of the world. It was thus imperative that they
harness their collective moral will by forming voluntary societies designed to rid the world of moral evils. Among the first to be formed were
missionary societies designed to bring the gospel to the Native Americans, pioneers on the western frontier, and foreign lands. Bible and tract
societies, Sunday school societies, and education societies followed in
their wake. Soon a host of organizations emerged dedicated to humani-
tarian reform and the eradication of the seemingly countless moral ills
still lingering throughout the land. Societies promoting temperance,
antislavery, and antimasonry soon flourished across the republic. The
millennium would be ushered in on American soil by sheer persistence
and moral persuasion. Writing in midcentury, Horace Bushnell extolled
the ability of free men and women to change the social order through
cooperative, voluntary agencies:

> The wilderness shall bud and blossom as the rose before us; and we shall
> not cease, till a Christian nation throws up its temple of worship on every
> hill and plain; till knowledge, virtue and religion, blending their dignity
> and their healthful power, have filled our great country with a manly and

happy race of people, and the bands of a complete Christian commonwealth are seen to span the continent.[21]

The era's confident vision of the future reflected a postmillennial
piety. It rested not on hope in the Second Coming and miraculous transformations but on gradual changes effected through the exertion of
moral resolve. Timothy Dwight epitomized the era's confidence that the
millennium was something to be expected in the "medium-term" future.
He noted that "almost all judicious commentators have agreed that the
millennium, in the full and perfect sense, will begin at a period, not far
from the year 2,000." The new order would not come about in the twinkling of an eye but would be realized gradually and through human
instrumentalities. It was to be accomplished "not by miracles, but by
means."[22]

The millennial faith that America could become an ideal society
through well-intentioned moral crusades helped create a sense of common national purpose. This purpose, at least until the outbreak of the
Civil War, was possible largely because Protestantism still possessed the
social resources needed to forge consensus around its moral vision. Historian Robert Wiebe observed that throughout most of the nineteenth
century, Americans took for granted

> every man's ability to know that God had ordained modesty in women,
> rectitude in men, thrift, sobriety, and hard work in both. People of very
> different backgrounds accommodated themselves to this Protestant code
> which had become so thoroughly identified with respectability. . . . In an
> island community people had little reason to believe that these daily pre-
> cepts were not universally valid, and few doubted that the nation's ills
> were caused by men who dared to deny them.[23]

Those who did dare to deny them risked being the target of a reform
society expressly designed to persuade them otherwise.

Protestants enjoyed a sufficiently broad social base that dissenting
ideas or lifestyles never really threatened to undermine what Peter
Berger calls "the plausibility structure" that guides members of a society toward those ideas that should be considered knowledge (or moral
truth) and away from ideas that are obviously untrue. Because nearly
every respected member of American society subscribed to "the Protestant code," the century's moral crusades were conducted with a certain self-assurance, and the embattled rhetoric of apocalypticism rarely
reared its head. The Antichrist was thus largely absent. Of course, when
Catholics and Jews began to arrive on American shores in startling numbers, new plots from the Beast would be detected. Similarly, when it
became apparent that differences in interpreting the moral character
of slavery would split the nation, apocalyptic rhetoric surfaced long
enough to sharpen each side's ideological commitments. But as the cases

of antimasonry and temperance show, "naming the Antichrist" was rarely necessary in the nineteenth century's moral crusades. There was little cause for the churches to demonize their enemies until the last two decades of the century, when those who "dared to deny" the Protestant code appeared poised to usurp their socioeconomic power base and thus undermine the very structures that until then had permitted their belief systems to enjoy unchallenged "plausibility."

Antimasonry was one of the most intriguing weapons in voluntaryism's arsenal for converting the world and initiating the millennium. Freemasonry was an association of men who used the symbol of the building trade to represent their commitment to teach basic moral truths and promote the brotherhood of mankind. With European roots going back to the mid-1600s, Freemasonry came to the United States about 1730.[24] The Masons were a secret organization, and their initiation ceremonies and oaths were to be kept in confidence. The organization's principal goal was (and is still today) to help its members seek the "light" through instructional sessions that explore principles of morality and religion. Seeking to be free from sectarian disputes, the Masons kept their teachings free from distinctively Christian doctrines and encouraged wide-ranging philosophical discussions on issues of morality and religion. As a consequence, they attracted the period's freethinkers, who had had more than a little exposure to Deism and Enlightenment rationality. Benjamin Franklin, for example, joined one of the early Masonic lodges in 1731 and was later elected the provincial grand master of Masons in Pennsylvania. The Masonic membership included something of a "who's who" of the Revolutionary era: Paul Revere, John Paul Jones, Alexander Hamilton, Patrick Henry, and George Washington. Nine signers of the Declaration of Independence and thirteen signers of the Constitution of the United States were Freemasons. Masonry thus drew from the ranks of the nation's intellectual and social elite. This fact alone drew it to the attention of those clergy concerned that the Deistic and rationalistic views of the nation's leaders were responsible for decreasing church attendance and evidences of vice.

The introduction of Masonry into American society paralleled the rise of Deism and religious freethinking. Masonry drew its membership from the literate and wealthier elements of society who were also those most likely to be drawn to antireligious attitudes. For this reason they were an easy target for churchgoing citizens seeking someone to blame for the era's religious waywardness. As early as 1737 the *New York Gazette* reported the existence of Masonic lodges and, since they conducted their rituals in secrecy, suggested that they were engaging in immoral practices. Because the Masons met behind closed doors, took oaths of loyalty, and operated with a general tone of mystery, they were open to suspicion, and many people believed that they were engaged in the work of the devil. Before the Revolution, however, no one was able to mount a successful campaign against them.

Buoyed by the public's awareness of the Masonic affiliations of such national heroes as George Washington and Benjamin Franklin, the Masons attained the peak of their popularity immediately following the war. In the 1790s and early 1800s the number of Masonic lodges increased at a faster rate than did the churches. As Randolph Roth's research demonstrates, the Masonic lodges functioned similarly, but perhaps even more effectively than churches in terms of creating social networks among citizens of the new republic.[25] Lodge affiliations fostered mercantile and manufacturing agreements and thus helped create a public image of the Masons as a group of prospering aristocrats. None of this sat very well with their more plebeian neighbors, who saw their own economic prospects dwindling in the nation's new economic order. This was particularly true of the clergy and their core constituencies, who saw the Puritan commitment to somber morality and provinciality being replaced by a general temper of comparative light-heartedness and open-mindedness. The clergy responded with a salvo of jeremiads castigating citizens of the new republic for their waywardness and infidelity. Vernon Stauffer comments in his history of the growth of antimasonry among Protestant clergy that

> they were men of the past, callously unresponsive to the spirit of the new age. They were an embittered minority, exerting themselves to keep a struggling and confident majority a little longer under their thumb. They were mischievous meddlers in the affairs of others, using religion as a cloak to hide their social and political self-seeking.[26]

It is in this social context that we can understand Rev. Jedidiah Morse's obsession with the threat that Freemasonry posed for Americans when he mounted the pulpit on May 9, 1798. He had just discovered a book written by an Englishmen, John Robison, that directly linked the Masonic lodges with a secret society that had been in existence in Germany for more than thirty years, The Illuminated. Rev. Morse, father of Samuel Morse who invented the telegraph, was seeking to transmit an electrifying message of his own:

> I hold it a duty, my brethren, which I owe to God to the cause of religion, to my country and to your, at this time, to declare to you, thus honestly and faithfully, these truths. My only aim is to awaken in you and myself a due attention, at this alarming period, to our dearest interests. As a faithful watchman I would give you warning of your present danger.[27]

Morse proceeded to explain that the Bavarian Illuminati were organized with the express aim "to root out and abolish Christianity, and overthrow all civil government."[28] They had successfully infiltrated French society and masterminded the atheistic French Revolution. Their conspiracy was now spreading to America, where they were already using various secret means to subvert the national order by condoning sexual promiscuity, condemning the principles of patriotism, seeking to eliminate all private property, and plotting to get control of all cultural agencies such as the schools, literary societies, and newspapers. Morse curiously omitted Robison's major allegation, the charge that the Illuminati had taken control of the Masonic lodges and were now using this chain of secret societies to overthrow the American government. In his footnotes to the printed sermon, however, Morse repeated Robison's charge that Freemasonry was now a principal instrument through which the Illuminati were hatching their plots against the American way of life.

It was not long before ministers and newspaper editors took up Morse's cry of warning and antimasonry began to rage across the nation. For the next forty years antimasonry ranked among the principal causes listed by Protestants caught up in the Second Great Awakening's revivalistic and moralistic ethos. Antimasonry also became organized as a political party and during the 1830s was actually the largest party in some parts of the country. The Antimasonry Party, along with the Jacksonian Party and Workingman's Party, attracted the support of people who found themselves at a disadvantage in the postwar scramble for wealth and power. Antimasonry was thus a means of lashing out against aristocracy and privilege in the name of democracy and equality. The reactionary character of the movement was, however, principally moral rather than political in nature. It expressed the conspiratorial fears of those who felt their Christian values to be endangered. Above all, they believed that Masonry loomed across the cultural horizon as "an engine of Satan . . . dark, unfruitful, selfish, demoralizing, blasphemous, murderous, anti-republican and anti-Christian."[29] Masonry was, as Yale's president Timothy Dwight protested, the very means by which the Antichrist or Beast of Revelation sought to take back his lost territory:

> The sins of these enemies of Christ, and Christians, are of numbers and degree which mock account and description. All that the malice and atheism of the Dragon, the cruelty and rapacity of the Beast, and the fraud and deceit of the false Prophet, can generate or accomplish, swell the list. No personal or national interest of man has been uninvaded; no impious sentiment, or action, against God has been spared.[30]

Dwight's insinuation that Masonry was connected with the Antichrist was strident even in the context of the antimasonry hysteria. Most Protestants were confident of their ultimate triumph over the moral imperfections still lingering throughout the country. Few felt threatened or upstaged by competing intellectual or cultural systems. Theirs was a postmillennial faith that optimistically sought to transform American culture through sheer moral persuasion. But as Dwight's reference to the Antichrist's presence reveals, the moral crusaders were far more likely to characterize their enemies in apocalyptic rhetoric when they found themselves confronting impediments anchored in a sociological power base equal to or greater than their own.

A second of the nineteenth century's moral crusades, temperance, similarly links the Second Great Awakening's reform movements with sociological power struggles; in this case they involved a growing class hatred, ethnic prejudices, and a general fear of America's increasing cultural diversity. Early-nineteenth-century reformers found themselves awash in an alcoholic republic. Per capita alcohol consumption in the early 1800s was double what it is today.[31] A major reason for this was the absence of any reliable source of alternative beverages. Safe, clean drinking water was scarce in both rural and urban areas. Fruit juices were available only on a seasonal basis. Rum, whiskey, beer, and wine provided the only consistently safe source of liquid refreshment, and taverns provided one of the few sources of entertainment and social interaction in a society largely lacking in recreational opportunities. With the taverns, of course, came card playing, gambling, and general carousing.

Ever alert to the connection between loose living and errant thinking, Cotton Mather was among the first to detect heresy in intemperance. "The flood of drinking," he declared, had begun to "drown Christianity" and arouse the "anger of the Lord."[32] The Second Great Awakening alerted large numbers of regenerate Christians to the moral dangers of intemperance and led to the formation of reform societies determined to do something about this blight on the American cultural landscape. Temperance historian W. J. Rorabaugh notes that "in many localities revivals were held, church rosters bulged, and then six months or a year later temperance societies were organized."[33] Thousands of local and regional temperance societies appeared, and by 1826, the first national organization, the American Society for the Promotion of Temperance, was launched. Other national organizations soon followed, including the Anti-Saloon League, the Catholic Total Abstinence Movement, and the National Temperance and Prohibition Council. The rationale for the temperance crusade was provided by Lyman Beecher in his *Six Sermons on the Nature, Occasions, Signs, Evils, and Remedy of Intemperance*. Intemperance, he argued, is "not consistent with a credible profession of Christianity. . . . Men who are mighty to consume strong drink, are unfit members of that kingdom which consisteth not in 'meat and drink,' but in 'righteousness and peace.'"[34] For the most part, temperance advocates portrayed addiction to drink as a failing of human will rather than a devious plot of the devil. Temperance propaganda focused less on the religious evils of intoxication than on its economic and social consequences. It argued that alcohol causes persons to squander their wages, plunges them into bankruptcy, and pauperizes their families; moreover, intemperance lowers a person's efficiency and reliability as a worker and thus hindered the economic prosperity of the entire nation. By increasing the amount of crime, poverty, and disease, drinking imposed an extra burden on society by adding to the cost of maintaining jails, poorhouses, and public charity.

What began as a call for temperance in drinking gradually escalated into a demand for total abstinence. The push for prohibition mounted late in the nineteenth century and eventually culminated in the enactment of the Eighteenth Amendment. Drunkenness, once thought of primarily as a failing of the human will, was increasingly viewed as the consummate work of Satan, who seized on this diabolical means of thwarting the enactment of God's kingdom on earth. As one prohibition party maintained in the 1890s, "We have pledged ourselves to labor for the development of a better manhood and womanhood among us, but how can we hope to succeed if we allow Satan's stronghold to flourish?"[35] The reasons for this intensification of religious rhetoric are not hard to find. Immigration had brought wave after wave of non–Anglo-Saxon Protestants to American shores. Irish, Catholic, Polish, and Italian Catholics had flooded into American cities. Most arrived in the land of opportunity poor and badly educated. The heavy drinking and associated vices common among these immigrant groups became an identifiable symbol of how unlikely it was that they would ever fully be assimilated into the moralistic ethos of evangelical Protestantism.

Norman Clark's statistical analysis of the voting patterns that led to Prohibition indicates how clearly the whole temperance movement was a symptom of complex rural–urban conflicts that have shaped many social and political tensions in American life. Yet as Clark demonstrates, it was not an urban or rural location that fostered temperance convictions, but membership in a social class whose rural values (belief in Anglo-Saxon racial purity, Protestant religious commitment, a high value placed on thrift, cleanliness, and individual responsibility) were at odds with what they perceived to be urban values (racial amalgamation, religious pluralism, sloth, hedonism, graft, and crime).[36] But in all of this, the "religious core" of American culture still perceived themselves to be the dominant and most prestigious element of society. It was thus more natural for them to use progressive political reform legislation rather than to resort to apocalyptic rhetoric. The social contexts of other nineteenth-century moral crusades, notably abolition, were entirely different, however. Here the Antichrist would be much more active.

Slavery, the Antichrist, and the Civil War

The reformist impulse reached its peak by the middle of the nineteenth century. Evangelical piety and democratic institutions seemed perfectly suited to each other. Together, they would offer the world a contagious example of a complete Christian commonwealth. Voluntaryism had succeeded in promoting the formation of schools, hospitals, prisons, and charitable programs for the poor. Other reform movements strengthened popular support for temperance, a healthful diet, and even women's suffrage. But one moral blight still loomed over the nation's conscience. Slavery had proven impervious to Northern Protestantism's techniques of moral persuasion. The debate over slavery was far more than a dispute over labor systems. It was, to Northerners and Southerners alike, a climactic test of the nation's moral resolve. For example, the General Assembly of the Presbyterian Church adopted a manifesto as early as 1818 that declared the institution of slavery as "utterly inconsistent with the law of God." Yet the Southern Presbyterian Church later affirmed that "we hesitate not to affirm that it is the peculiar mission of the Southern Church to conserve the institution of slavery, and to make it a blessing both to master and slave."[37] When deeply rooted economic and social differences give rise to religious–moral posturing of this sort, dialogue becomes impossible. Both sides began to see the Antichrist lurking behind the enemy's lines; compromise was by this time out of the question. The Presbyterian, Methodist, and Baptist denominations splintered, and a few years later, so did the nation.

The religious condemnations that fueled the nation's civil strife had been incubating for a long time. Protests and denunciations of black servitude in the colonial tobacco industry went back to the mid-1600s. Revivalist piety in the early nineteenth century fanned these smoldering abolitionist sentiments and sparked the formation of abolition societies in much the same way it had stimulated temperance or antimasonry movements. Abolition, in fact, had a demographic appeal almost identical to antimasonry's.[38] Abolitionists, like antimasons, challenged the moral character and right to leadership of all who habitually lived in sin. Both were expressions of a commitment to egalitarianism and social benevolence (even though most abolitionists also believed that slaves belonged to an inferior race and were consequently in need of the leadership of whites). Yet, even more than antimasonry, abolition had a clear political agenda. Abolitionists were self-styled champions of the Western ideals of equality, freedom, and liberty; these ideals, they knew, were the vehicles through which God's providence would lead America toward its cosmic destiny. Slavery threatened these ideals and, in so doing, called into question America's worthiness to sustain God's providential errand. The intensity with which slavery's persistent presence struck at Americans' moral conscience is registered in the conclusion to Harriet Beecher Stowe's best-selling *Uncle Tom's Cabin*. Stowe's novel depicts the nation's capacity for moral resolve as having been paralyzed by the institution of slavery. Her story ends with the warning that the "wrath of Almighty God" would soon descend on Americans if they did

not immediately mend their erring ways. The wrath she predicted was
not long in coming.

Yankee Protestants led the way in picturing the nation as divided
between two distinct civilizations.[39] Freedom and slavery were two
opposing principles that could not both be incorporated into the American nation. Two ways of life and two different moral commitments were
juxtaposed. Christ was polarized against the Antichrist; the time for a
cataclysmic showdown was at hand. A number of popular tracts helped
place the imminent confrontation in overtly apocalyptic terms. A British clergyman, Michael Baxter, toured the United States preaching a
message from his subsequent book, *The Coming Battle and the Appalling
National Convulsion Foreshadowed in Prophecy Immediately to Occur During
the Period 1861–1867*.[40] L. S. Weed, a Methodist minister from Brooklyn, wrote that the twelfth chapter of Revelation contained an explicit
prediction of the Civil War and its inevitable outcome. Weed was convinced that the scriptural account of the final battle between Archangel Michael's host of angels and the Dragon and Beast proved beyond
doubt that the Confederacy would go down to certain defeat. Weed's
exegesis of Revelation was intended to show that the inevitable suffering that lay ahead would ultimately be redemptive. War would bring a
purging and bestow a "vindication for all coming time" on the nation's
moral character. Weed was confident that the approaching apocalypse
would prepare America to stride boldly forward on its errand to bring
democracy and gospel faith to every nation on earth. For this reason,
the war would be the "first great conflict to precede the millennium."[41]

The apocalyptic expectations held by Northerners at the dawn of
the Civil War were vividly portrayed by Hollis Read in a book published
in 1861, *The Coming Crisis of the World: or, the Great Battle and the Golden
Age*. Bible prophecies, Read explained, were certain that "Satan's empire is to be broken up." He believed that the intricate chronology of
Revelation could be unraveled to show that "God shall . . . in some remarkable manner avenge the cause of his elect" within the next five or
six years.[42] What made Read's and other apocalyptic pronouncements
so convincing is that they coincided with an established theory that the
millennium would begin in about 1866. According to a host of Bible
interpreters, the Antichrist had risen to power in about A.D. 606 which,
when added to the 1,260 years of his prophesied reign (3.5 "prophetic
years," with each year equaling 360 human years), adds up to 1866.[43]

Most Americans probably looked askance at the prophetic excesses
of individuals like Read and Weed. Almost all, however, had been raised
in a theological milieu that interpreted America as God's chosen nation.
A nation of Bible readers could hardly escape viewing the outbreak of
the Civil War as a moral conflict set against a larger cosmic backdrop.
The North, the soldiers of Christ, was standing witness against the South,
the vanguard of the Beast. A collection of essays published by the Ladies'

Christian Commission in 1865 put the whole matter as clearly as did any tract of that era. Entitled "Christ in the Army," the pamphlet pondered the deeper meaning of American military force and the decisive role the Lord intended it to play in the advent of his kingdom:

> The Lord is mustering the nations to the last great struggle between freedom and slavery, truth and error, and wish it as we may, He does not design that we bury the power He has forced upon us. . . . We are entering, fellow citizens, upon a period foretold by prophets of old—looked for by lovers of their country in past generations—which kings and prophets waited to see, and have not seen—a period of the overthrow of despotism, and *the downfall of Antichrist*; and it is evidently the design of Almighty God that the United States of America should be found prepared for taking their part, whatever it may be, in that great struggle.[44]

When a mortar shell burst over Fort Sumter, South Carolina, in the early morning of April 12, 1861, the full tragedy of the "American apocalypse" exploded on the nation's psyche. This war, destined to claim the lives of more than 600,000 citizens of the republic, proved a nearly insurmountable threat to the destiny of a united people. Both Northern and Southern clergy defended their causes by explaining that they alone carried forward the authentically American mission.[45] Each side invoked the sanction of the nation's God, and each understood its military to be the vehicle through which divine providence would ultimately triumph. James Silver's study of Confederate morale and church propaganda shows how effectively Southern clergymen—like their Northern counterparts—were responsible for creating an apocalyptic state of mind in which compromise became impossible.[46] Preachers exhorted their parishioners to endure any and all hardships in their battle against the devil, "perhaps the strongest ally of the Yankees."[47] Thomas Smyth wrote in the April 1863 *Southern Presbyterian Review* of "God's manifest presence and providence with the Confederacy." God had entrusted the Southern people with "an organized system of slave labor, for the benefit of the world, and a blessing to themselves while imparting civil, social, and religious blessings to their slaves."[48] Yankees, in contrast, were notoriously indifferent to the welfare of slaves, as could be expected from a Northern culture that bred intemperance, avarice, licentiousness, profanity, desecration of the Sabbath, theft, murder, and lewdness. The Confederacy, according to Southern preachers, was "the cause of God himself," and just as it was for David in his divinely appointed struggle against Goliath, "to fight is now . . . a religious duty."[49]

Fight they did. Having identified their enemies as agents of Satan, both sides could see themselves draped in the mantle of divine blessing. Engaged in a cosmic war of good and evil, they were participants in the American apocalypse. Their enemy was the Antichrist, and the angelic trumpets had called for the battle hymn that would mark his certain demise. So deeply had the apocalyptic mentality seeped into the nation's collective mind that Julia Ward Howe was moved to write a poem that serves as a rallying cry for strident crusaders to this day. Her "Battle Hymn of the Republic," first published in 1862, demonstrated just how easy it was for the participants in this national struggle to see their cause in a cosmic light:

> Mine eyes have seen the glory of the coming of the Lord:
> He is trampling out the vintage where the grapes of wrath
>   are stored;
> He hath loosed the fateful lightning of his terrible swift
>   sword:
>
>   His truth is marching on.
>
> . . . Let the Hero, born of woman, crush the serpent with
>   his heel,
>
> . . . He has sounded forth the trumpet that shall never call
>   retreat:
> He is sifting out the hearts of men before His judgment-seat:
>
> Oh, be swift, my soul, to answer him! be jubilant, my feet!
>   Our God is marching on."[50]

Ernest Tuveson, noting that Howe's original version of the poem read, "He is trampling out the wine press," discerns apocalyptic significance in this imagery of harvest and the completed cultivation of the soil. Tuveson concludes that "the grapes are 'ripe' because the day of Antichrist is closing. Clearly [for Howe] the Civil War is a major part of the 'reaping' of the accumulated evils of the long reign of the Beast."[51] The poem ends by reclaiming God's and America's ultimate mission on earth—the Redemption. The downfall of the Antichrist accomplished, divine grace will transform human nature and "transfigure you and me." God's chosen nation will thus emerge from the conflict purged and empowered to continue marching on.

Immigration and Early Nativism

The instinct toward territorialism is found throughout the animal kingdom. Individuals or small clan groups demarcate a certain spatial area as their own and fend off all who encroach on their territory. They also seek to ward off outsiders by means of various boundary-posturing behaviors that demarcate the borders of their "turf" and make clear that intruders are unwelcome. Laying down a scent of urine, growling, and loud chirping are examples of the aggressive techniques with which clan groups demarcate and defend group boundaries.[52] Among humans, such

boundary-posturing behavior tends to express itself in what is referred
to as *tribalism*. According to the eminent biologist Garrett Hardin,

> Any group of people that perceives itself as a distinct group, and which is
> so perceived by the outside world, may be called a tribe. The group might
> be a race, as ordinarily defined, but it need not be; it can just as well be a
> religious sect, a political group, or an occupational group. The essential
> characteristic of a tribe is that it should follow a double standard of mo-
> rality—one kind of behavior for in-groups relations, another for out-
> group.[53]

The act of "naming the Antichrist" frequently functions in the same
way as tribalistic boundary posturing does. From the author of 1 and 2
John to contemporary "Bible prophecy" writers, the detection of the
Antichrist has fostered group cohesion and provided an enemy against
whom even the harshest actions can be taken in the name of righteousness. Apocalyptic categories clearly distinguish between the forces of
good and those of evil and hence provide a powerful justification for
tribalistic behaviors. Such has been the case over the course of American history as Jews, Catholics, and sundry "foreign" influences began
encroaching on white, Anglo-Saxon, Protesatnt (WASP) turf. By identifying unwanted newcomers as cohorts of the Antichrist, self-identified
"native" Americans have been able to justify even the most aggressive
of territorial behaviors as acts of religious piety.

What is striking about the nineteenth century is how seldom the
nation's white, Anglo-Saxon Protestants actually felt their territory to
be endangered. The hegemony they enjoyed over the nation's "official"
religious–moral outlook made rival ideas and groups appear as an occasional nuisance but rarely as a threatening predator. Throughout the
1800s, however, Jews and Catholics continued to immigrate to the
United States in astonishing numbers. The 1820s witnessed 143,000 immigrants to the still-fledgling nation. The 1830s saw 600,000 more enter
the so-called melting pot, and from there the tide of immigration swept
across the nation's shores in even stronger force: in the 1840s, 1.8 million; in the 1850s, 2.6 million, in the 1860s, 2.3 million, in the 1870s,
2.8 million, in the 1880s, 5.2 million, and in the 1890s, 3.7 million. This
influx of new peoples, most of whom did not share the Puritan heritage of the founding colonists, was destined to invoke tribalistic behaviors from the self-proclaimed "native" Americans. Protestants had long
taken as fact the equation of Catholics with the Antichrist. And since
the Middle Ages, there was also a tradition that the Antichrist would
be born a Jew. It is not surprising, then, that nativistic reactions against
Jewish and Catholic immigrants would often take the form of apocalyptic name-calling. As we shall see, the twentieth century has seen
more than its share of vitriolic descriptions of the Jewish or Catholic

identity of the Antichrist. Although the social threat posed by immigrants did not become serious until late in the century, the 1800s nonetheless witnessed the emergence of "tribalistic" patterns that factored prominently in the long-term history of the American Antichrist.

Minority status was certainly not new to the few Jews who ventured from Europe to New England.[54] Compared with the entrenched anti-Semitism and ghetto conditions of Europe, life in the American colonies was relatively hospitable to Jews. The tolerant spirit fostered by the Enlightenment and the fluidity of colonial social structures combined to keep religious and ethnic prejudices at a tolerable level. The approximately two thousand Jews living in the colonies in 1776 might even have had cause to hope that their civil and religious liberties would at long last be secure in the new American republic. There was, for example, the Fourth of July parade in Philadelphia in 1788 at which Protestants took great care to prepare a separate table with special foods that the Jewish citizens could eat without violating their dietary laws. The esteemed physician Benjamin Rush remembered that great care also

> was taken to connect Ministers of the most dissimilar religious principles together, thereby to show the influence of a free government in promoting christian charity. The Rabbi of the Jews, locked in the arms of two ministers of the gospel, was a most delightful sight. There could not have been a more happy emblem contrived, which opens all its power and offices alike, not only to every sect of christians, but to worthy men of *every* religion.[55]

However uplifting this story of religious liberty in the American colonies may be, it is unfortunately a misleading symbol of Jewish life in America. Every available index of life in eighteenth- and nineteenth-century America substantiates the more pessimistic interpretation that anti-Semitism suffused the spirit, if not the letter, of the American legal and cultural systems. It was true, of course, that Article 6, Section 3 of the United States Constitution officially barred any religious conditions for holding federal office. But twelve of the original thirteen colonies entered the national era with statutes that expressly restricted Jews from holding state offices. The majority of Americans took it for granted that the civil and religious orders were not entirely separable, since the moral condition of the former was thought to rest wholly on the widespread diffusion of the latter. Protestantism was, without any need for further demonstration, assumed to be the truest expression of gospel faith. Although most agreed that Jews and other non-Protestants were to be tolerated, it by no means followed that they should be allowed to govern.

Rev. David Caldwell typified the genteel anti-Semitism of the era when he urged his fellow citizens of North Carolina to adopt a provision in the state constitution whereby

> no person, who shall deny the being of God or the truth of the Protestant religion, or the divine authority of the Old or New Testaments, or who

shall hold religious principles incompatible with the freedom and safety of the State, shall be capable of holding any office or place of trust or profit in the civil department within this State.[56]

Citizens of neighboring South Carolina similarly adopted a constitution that made "the Christian Protestant religion . . . the established religion of this state." Georgia's constitution required that state representatives be "of the Protestant religion," and Delaware's constitution required that all state officers swear a Trinitarian oath. New Jersey, meanwhile, stipulated that "all persons professing a belief in any Protestant sect . . . shall be capable of being elected into any office." Many American citizens even considered the federal constitution to be a betrayal of the nation's deepest values. Rev. Henry Muhlenberg of Pennsylvania lamented that "it now seems as if a Christian people were [to be] ruled by Jews, Turks, Spinozists, Deists, [and] perverted naturalists."[57] Rev. D. X. Junkin similarly maintained that the United States Constitution "is negatively atheistical. For no God is appealed to at all. In framing many of our public formularies, greater care seems to have been taken to adapt them to the prejudices of the INFIDEL JEW, than to the consciences of the Christian millions."[58]

Legal restrictions aimed at keeping Jews outside the boundaries of mainstream American life tell only part of the nativistic resentments they faced. Nearly every friendship between a Christian and a Jew was tinged with condescension and patronization. The pressure to convert to the "true faith" was felt from all sides. When the American Society for Evangelizing the Jew was formed in 1816, it quickly produced more than two hundred local auxiliaries. Even as the number of Jews in the United States gradually grew (to a total of 250,000 by 1880), their numbers were still too small to prevent the persistence of denigrating stereotypes. Jewish peddlers and shop keepers were routinely portrayed as greedy and deceitful. Jews were faulted for not remaining quietly in the background of American life and were consequently thought to be clamorously self-assertive.[59] Although too small in numbers to be suspected of posing a serious subversive threat, Jews were nonetheless largely unwelcome in the self-proclaimed "land of the free."

Somewhat ironically, Protestants disparaged Roman Catholics even more than Jews. Anti-Catholic prejudice had been smoldering among Protestants for more than two centuries before the colonists' declaration of independence, and few were prepared to grant concessions to the papist minority. It is estimated that there were no more than 32,000 Catholics in America by 1776, constituting only 1 percent of the total population.[60] Even with such small numbers opposing them, however, Protestants were of no mind to relax their vigil against the papal Antichrist. Seven of the original thirteen state legislatures moved quickly to enact laws restricting the rights of Catholics to hold office. Vermont's constitution, for example, required that all officeholders take an oath in which they "professed the Protestant Religion," and South Carolina expressly established Protestantism as the state religion. Too many generations had exerted too much effort to establish a nation free from papal corruption to now turn around and allow the Beast to enter right through the front door of American democracy.

Anti-Catholicism remained more of a religious sentiment than an active political agenda for the first few decades of the American republic. By the 1820s, however, the immigration of Irish Catholics to the United States escalated dramatically. Unbearable economic conditions in their native land drove nearly 4.5 million Irish to emigrate to America over the next hundred years. Famine brought about by disastrous weather and backward farming techniques, heavy taxation, and inhumane wage scales forced these desperate souls to leave their homeland behind and seek better lives in the land of opportunity. Unfortunately, nativistic reaction met them almost immediately upon their arrival. Most of these non-Protestant "foreigners" were poor, badly educated, and culturally naive by Yankee standards. Their unexpected and uninvited presence in America was costing many native citizens their jobs and raising taxes for everyone. Government funds were increasingly needed to address the problems created by such massive infusions of poor, illiterate immigrants. It is estimated, for example, that by 1835 well over half the paupers in American cities were foreign-born Catholics. Many native Americans began to suspect that foreign countries were deliberately getting rid of their "refuse" by shipping them overseas. Resentment understandably began to build. Rev. Lyman Beecher gave a unique twist to these nativist fears in his reactionary *Plea for the West* (1834), in which he claimed that the pope, in concert with several reactionary kings of Europe, was orchestrating a massive influx of Catholic immigrants into the Mississippi Valley region. This conspiracy was intended to overrun Protestants and force Americans to return to "feudal institutions."[61]

Compounding this early nativist reaction was the zealous evangelicalism spawned by the Second Great Awakening. By the 1820s and 1830s, thousands of Americans had been drawn into the revivalist-inspired frenzy for bringing the whole national population to the "true" gospel faith. Evangelical fervor naturally intensified awareness of Catholic–Protestant differences. From the Protestant perspective, Catholics severely deviated from Bible teachings. Permitting them to gain a foothold in American society would create a clear and present danger to the nation's self-appointed destiny. Thirty five religious newspapers were operating in the late 1820s, and each one of them railed against the dangers of Romanism. Editorials offered lengthy accounts of the idolatry, blasphemy, and moral weakness permeating the Catholic faith. More alarming still was the constant threat that all Catholics owed their ultimate allegiance to a foreign dictator, the pope, and could never be counted on as loyal, patriotic citizens. In 1829 a revivalist preacher whipped a group of Bostonians into such a frenzy that they launched a three-day assault on the homes of Irish Catholics. A few years later, in Charlestown, a group of five hundred Protestants marched on the Irish section and burned down a number of houses.[62] And in August 1834, many of these same persons participated in burning down the Ursuline convent in Charlestown.

The 1830s saw the nativistic rhetoric assume a new and commercially potent form—the anti-Catholic "exposé." Volumes such as *Priestcraft Unmasked* and *Priestcraft Exposed* were among the first of many books to offer unsubstantiated rumors of Catholic scandals while earning their authors a healthy profit. Rebecca Theresa Reed, an "escaped" nun, regaled eager listeners with her tales of the dreadful happenings within the walls of her former convent. Her disclosures were published in 1835 in a book entitled *Six Months in a Convent*, which sold more than 200,000 copies within a month. *Six Months in a Convent* actually had few lurid revelations to offer: Reed showed life in a convent to be boring but hardly immoral or lascivious. The public's appetite for learning of sexual and other improprieties within Catholicism was whetted, however, and in 1836 Maria Monk produced her infamous *Awful Disclosures of the Hotel Dieu Nunnery of Montreal*. Monk recounted how she had been raised a Protestant before entering the Hotel Dieu convent in Montreal to be educated. Eventually embracing Catholicism, she took her vows and was given instruction by the mother superior to "obey the priests in all things." All too soon she discovered to her "utter astonishment and horror, [this entailed engaging] in the practice of criminal intercourse with them."[63] Such illicit fornication frequently produced babies that, Monk confessed, were immediately baptized and then strangled. Monk claimed that nuns were routinely executed for refusing to obey the lustful will of the priests and she herself discovered the large hole in the basement down which the bodies of murdered nuns and babies had been thrown.

Needless to say, the first edition of *Awful Disclosures* was an immediate commercial success. The Protestant press proclaimed the work to be a frank and credible exposition of the tawdry corruptions rampant throughout the Catholic church. Sales continued at record pace, and the book eventually finished among the best-sellers of the nineteenth century. The fact that an impartial inspection of the Hotel Dieu convent by two Protestant clergymen proved all the accusations groundless and that ample evidence existed to indicate that Maria Monk was herself of questionable character (she later died in prison after being arrested for robbing her customer in a brothel) did nothing to dampen public enthusiasm for this shameless nativistic propaganda.

By the 1850s the immigration of Catholics to the United States had escalated to the point that Catholics appeared to constitute a serious social, political, and economic threat to Protestantism. Stronger measures seemed to be called for. In 1849 Charles B. Allen of New York founded a secret patriotic society, the Order of the Star-Spangled Banner. A few years later the order was set up on a national basis, with local, district, state, and national councils. Only American-born Protestant males without Catholic parents or wives could become members. When advanced to higher levels they were required to swear that they would not appoint foreigners or Roman Catholics to public office. The order was organized along the lines of a secret lodge, and its members frequently responded to questions about their organization with the pat reply, "I don't know," thus giving rise to the nickname, the Know-Nothings. Although the Know-Nothing movement professed opposition to all immigrant groups, it is clear that its members were principally motivated by their intense hatred of Catholics. Historian Ray Billington surmises that

> every Know-Nothing firmly believed that Papists should be barred from
> every office in the national, state and local governments and, if possible,
> driven back to the priest-ridden lands from whence they had come. The
> Know-Nothing party was really a No-Popery party, despite all the gloss
> and fancy phrases in its pronouncements.[64]

Throughout the 1850s the Know-Nothings proved to be a powerful political party, directly influencing a number of close elections at the state and national levels. The movement failed to sustain itself, however, as the nation moved closer to the Civil War. Hatred of Catholics had to be placed on the back burner when the struggle over slavery escalated into armed conflict.

By the 1880s, however, anti-Catholicism resurfaced across the land. With the Civil War settled, the country's WASP citizenry once again sought to assert their prominence in all things American. Anti-Catholic organizations were organized at various local, state, and regional levels. In 1887 the American Protective Association was formed and gradually grew into the largest of the century's anti-Catholic organizations. With a membership that may have reached 2.25 million, the A.P.A. is a classic instance of nativistic fear mongering.[65] The A.P.A. played on long-standing fears that Catholics were incapable of being loyal Americans because they swore allegiance to the pope. One means for exacerbating these fears was forged "pastoral letters." These forgeries were ostensibly secret communications from Catholic bishops instructing church members to engage in such seditious activities as murdering all Protestants and helping overthrow the "heretical" government of the United States. Initiates to the A.P.A. took a series of oaths of loyalty to both the organization and the nativist ideology that they believed could alone preserve the nation's moral character. Swearing not to permit a

Roman Catholic to become a member of the order or to countenance the election of a Catholic for any public office, the members vowed:

> I hereby denounce Roman Catholicism. I hereby denounce the Pope, sitting at Rome or elsewhere. I denounce his priests and emissaries, and the diabolical work of the Roman Catholic church, and hereby pledge myself to the cause of Protestantism to the end that there may be no interference with the discharge of the duties of citizenship, and I solemnly bind myself to protect at all times, and with the means in my power, the good name of the order and its members, so help me God. Amen.[66]

The American Protective Association, like the many nativist organizations that followed it, thrived on suspicion. Plots against God-fearing white Protestants were thought to be everywhere, thus requiring a redoubling of efforts to guard the nation's symbolic boundaries. In his study of Americans' enduring "fear of conspiracy," David Brion Davis points out that calling attention to subversion promotes in-group cohesiveness. The fear of conspiracy also helps clarify in-group values and gives a person's ego a heightened sense of imputed righteousness.[67] All of these are beneficial to tribal identity; unless, of course, one happens to be among the out-group and thus someone toward whom civil behavior is not expected.

By the late nineteenth and early twentieth century, religious rhetoric featured importantly in efforts to distinguish between the forces of good and the disintegrating influences of Babylon. Josiah Strong, in his widely circulated *Our Country: Its Possible Future and Its Present Crisis* (1885), reminded his fellow citizens that America was uniquely vulnerable to the devil's strategies precisely because of their accustomed tolerance and democratic principles. Yet it was time for alarm and a rethinking of the prudent application of these principles. Strong enumerated "seven perils" threatening the nation. First among them was immigration. He noted that "during the last four years we have suffered a peaceful invasion by an army, more than twice as vast as the estimated number of Goths and Vandals that swept over Southern Europe and overwhelmed Rome."[68] This army, Strong contended, was in one way or another responsible for each of the other six assaults on American life: Romanism, Mormonism, intemperance, socialism, wealth, and "the city." It was clear that Strong and others like him knew that a new, and more militant, strategy was called for. Such reactionary sentiment helped form the social basis for the emergence of fundamentalism in the first two decades of the twentieth century. It also formed the ideological roots of a resurgence of Americans' nativist fears of subversion from within and the consequent rediscovery of the Antichrist. Aiding both of these later developments was the gradual evolution of a premillennialist, apocalyptic strand of religious thought.

Countervailing Voices: Premillennnial and Apocalyptic Stirrings

Nineteenth-century American Protestantism was largely a "religion of civilization." That is, most churches subscribed to the belief that evangelical faith and concerted moral persuasion alone were capable of transforming the United States into a civilization pleasing to God. The era's postmillennial outlook made no distinction between divine providence and the material progress of the American nation. Yet against this background of confidence and optimism, a few countervailing voices could be heard. Many of those raised in the milieu of moral reform societies became disaffected by the world about them. Either the guilt induced by personal shortcomings or a growing suspicion of all worldly structures caused many to conclude that imperfect humans would never give rise to a perfect order. It seemed increasingly clear to such persons that the millennium could be initiated only by the Second Coming of Christ. Insisting on this premillennial return of Christ, these Protestants found themselves encouraging one another to separate from the secular world and to focus instead on their own personal holiness in the knowledge that Christ's final judgment would soon be upon them.

The first significant wave of premillennial interest arose in England during the 1820s. Dozens of apocalyptic books were published during the decade, and most made their way across the Atlantic. A series of Bible prophecy conferences at the estate of Henry Drummond, a socially prominent millenarian and member of Parliament, issued a six-point statement that captured the essence of the early premillennial cause:

1. World history is divided into a series of epochs or "dispensations." Our own dispensation will end cataclysmically in judgment and destruction of the church in the same manner in which the Jewish dispensation ended.
2. The Jews will be restored to Palestine during the time of judgment.
3. The judgment to come will fall principally upon Christendom.
4. When the judgment is past, the millennium will begin.
5. The second advent of Christ will occur *before* the millennium.
6. The 1,260 years of Daniel and Revelation 13 ought to be measured from the reign of Justinian to the French Revolution. The vials of wrath (Revelation 16) are now being poured out and the second advent is imminent.[69]

From the premillennial perspective, history was spiraling downward toward its tragic denouement, not advancing toward moral perfection, as the principal denominations were preaching. The church and nation together had been judged and found wanting, and both would soon end in cataclysmic destruction. This more pessimistic, premillennial outlook was at first slow in attracting American adherents. But a combination of factors made this apocalyptic piety more attractive as the century wore on.

Among the first Americans to seize on the premillennial gospel were several small, communally oriented religious groups. For example, the Shakers, Rappites, and Mormons all were enthusiasts of the Second Coming. Mother Ann Lee brought her United Society of Believers in Christ's Second Coming, more commonly known as the Shakers, to America in 1774. The Shakers were an intense biblically oriented sect who believed themselves to be the advance guard of the coming millennial order. Ann Lee's numerous trances and visions enabled her to convince her followers that Christ's Second Coming would be in the form of a woman. Most thought Ann Lee to be that female embodiment of Christ. The Shakers exuded an enthusiastic spirituality that attracted a sizable following, reaching as many as six thousand members by the 1840s. They particularly effective in recruiting former Baptists who sought a more intense commitment to ongoing prophecy and pietistic perfectionism than their former churches could offer. Distinctive of the group was Mother Ann Lee's insistence that since Adam and Eve, sexuality had been the root of all human sin. Because the Kingdom was literally at hand and procreation thus unnecessary, the Shakers used celibacy as a central part of their efforts to separate from the sinful world and elevate themselves from the animal to the spiritual plane. The Shakers' celibacy and pristine communal lifestyle no doubt prompted most contemporaries to be more amused than outraged by the group and its beliefs. Yet the Shakers succeeded in persuading mid-nineteenth-century Americans to reflect more seriously on Bible prophecy and the possibility that Christ's Second Coming would be a far more dramatic event than was generally considered.

The followers of George Rapp were also ardent Bible students and fervent believers in the imminent Second Coming. The "Rappites" grew out of German pietism and, like the Shakers, believed that they must separate from the secular world in order to found a communal society based on strict personal discipline. Organizing first in Harmony, Pennsylvania (1807), and then in New Harmony, Indiana (1815), the Rappites strove to construct a pietistic society that would be pleasing to Christ upon his return. From the same strain of German pietism came the Bethel commune in Missouri, the Aurora commune in Oregon, and the Amana colonies in Iowa. All espoused some degree of millennial faith and helped keep concern with Bible prophecy from receding too far from American religious awareness.

The Mormons, or the Church of Jesus Christ of Latter-Day Saints, made the expectation of Christ's imminent return the core doctrine of their dynamic faith. Living in Palmyra, New York, in the 1820s, Joseph Smith was visited by God and Jesus while walking alone in the woods.

Jesus told him that he was being called on to serve as a prophet in the latter days, to separate himself from all existing and apostate denominations, and to bear testimony to the full gospel that would shortly be revealed to him. Some months later the angel Moroni led Smith to a set of buried golden plates that contained the lost record of Jesus' ministry in North America—the Book of Mormon. The Mormons immediately found themselves to be religious outsiders. They claimed, after all, to be the recipients of a new revelation thought to complement and even supersede the New Testament. As if that alone were not sufficient to antagonize churchgoers and religious skeptics alike, the Mormons' practice of polygamy set them even further away from the cultural mainstream. First in New York, then Ohio, and subsequently in Missouri and Illinois, they met up with intolerance and fierce opposition.

Much like the community to whom 1 and 2 John were addressed, the Mormons were acutely aware that many professed Christians denied the gospel faith as they themselves understood it. The Antichrist they faced was thus not a horned beast rising from the sea but those persons who failed to accept the full revelation of Christ to the world. Citing 1 and 2 John, the *Encyclopedia of Mormonism* explains that "Antichrists are those who deny the divinity of Jesus Christ or essential parts of his gospel and actively oppose the followers of Christ or seek to destroy their faith."[70] The Book of Mormon itself uses the term *antichrist*. Although it explicitly refers to only one person as the Antichrist, the Book of Mormon profiles the subtle and sophisticated aspects of persons who deny "essential parts" of the gospel. Sherem (c. 540 B.C.E.), for example, rejected the prophetic teachings of the Nephite prophets, claiming that "there is no Christ, neither has been, nor ever will be." Sherem was stricken by God and moved to confess that he had been deceived by the devil in denying the Christ.

It was Korihor (c. 74 B.C.E), however, whom the Book of Mormon explicitly labels "Anti-Christ" because he taught that there was no need for a Christ and that none would come.[71] Korihor is portrayed as an extremist, rejecting all the teachings of the church as foolish tradition designed to subject people to corrupt and lazy priests. Korihor, like Sherem, confessed that he had been deceived by Satan. His sorry life underscores the danger of Satan's deceiving otherwise decent persons with doctrines that seem plausible to the carnal mind but result in putting them out of harmony with God's true teachings. In the broadest sense, then, anyone who counterfeits the true plan of Christ's gospel and is either openly or secretly in opposition to Christ is an Antichrist. Predictably enough, the Church of Jesus Christ of Latter-Day Saints came into contact with many of these, both those outside their gathering of saints and those inside their own ranks who were deceived by Satan into adopting apostate views.

Undoubtedly the most significant premillennial voice of the nineteenth century belonged to William Miller.[72] Miller (1782–1849) was a farmer from upstate New York who claimed to have been a staunch Deist in his early adulthood. While attending a local revival meeting, he underwent a conversion and undertook a disciplined course of Bible reading, using a King James version that in the margins contained Archbishop Ussher's chronology of dates and events.[73] For reasons that are unclear, Miller became obsessed with the Books of Daniel and Revelation and devoted countless hours trying to determine just when Christ would return to pass judgment on the earth. At last, Miller began to see that these texts contained a complex timetable forecasting the precise hour of the Second Coming. Miller adopted the standard evangelical custom of equating each biblical day with a human year. Based on this assumption, he was able to discern that the "seventy weeks" referred to in Daniel translates into 490 human years. Ussher's chronology indicated that Daniel made this prediction in 457 B.C. Miller simply added 490 years and arrived at A.D. 33. This was, of course, the precise year of Christ's death and resurrection. Miller then applied this same method to Daniel's reference to "two thousand and three hundred days and then the sanctuary shall be restored to its rightful state." Lo and behold, the Bible was clearly stating that the world as we know it would end in 1843! This was only 25 years from the time of his mathematical discovery.

Miller referred to himself as a "worm," a "poor feeble creature" who was too feeble, wicked, and weak to be a spokesman for God. Uncomfortable speaking before others, he nonetheless accepted an invitation to speak before a Baptist revival in 1831 on the subject of his study into Bible prophecy. His lecture was received enthusiastically, and suddenly this shy farmer was transformed into a commanding expositor of premillennial theology. The next year he published a pamphlet aptly entitled *Evidences from Scripture and History of the Second Coming of Christ About the Year A.D. 1843*. A year later he was granted a license to preach as a Baptist minister, and his apocalyptic message began to attract the attention of ministers and laity alike.

In 1839, while attending a Christian conference in New Hampshire, Miller met a Boston minister by the name of Joshua Himes. An active reformist in the abolition and temperance movements, Himes was enthralled by Miller's calculations and his ability to see how contemporary events were rapidly fulfilling the biblical prophecies connected with the end times. Himes joined Miller and brought to the movement a certain marketing savvy that catapulted the adventist cause into the center of national attention. Himes bought a circus tent that could seat four thousand people, reportedly the largest tent in North America. Soon Himes launched the first Adventist newspaper, the *Signs of the Times*, and then a number of periodicals, with titles such as *Advent Witness*, *Voice of Warning*, and *Midnight Cry*. Himes also orchestrated the printing of

Adventist charts, pamphlets, and hymnbooks as well as setting up conferences throughout New England at which those with active apocalyptic imaginations could meet and share perspectives on the "signs of the times."

It is estimated that fifty thousand Americans became committed Millerites. Thousands of others were fascinated with the adventist message yet hesitated to commit themselves fully to the cause. Several factors lent themselves to the creation of a climate favorable to premillennial faith. The Second Great Awakening had gradually died out by the late 1830s. Many were left yearning for an additional "dose" of spiritual enthusiasm and were ready to embrace a new and more daring theological system. Indeed, many of Miller's first invitations to speak on Bible prophecy came from ministers eager to find ways to light new fires of enthusiasm in congregations whose spirituality had become sedate since the revivals of earlier years. The financial panic of 1837 also pricked the bubble of religious and nationalistic optimism. Farmers and businessmen alike felt the hardships of depression between 1837 and 1844, making it difficult for various reform movements to raise money for their causes or to attract enthusiastic new recruits. It was only natural that some who had been reared in the buoyant optimism of "voluntaryism" finally began to despair of lesser reform efforts and sought a more immediate and total resolution of the world's imperfections. The stage was thus set for many to find in Millerism an answer to their prayers for a better life. Millerism was, in the words of David Ludlum, "the summation of all the reforms of the age."[74] That is, an immediate judgment day was the shortest possible route to millennial perfection, the boldest panacea of the era. In the twinkling of an eye, the tables would be turned, with the last becoming first (accompanied by the sweet vindication of being able to watch the first become last).[75]

The Millerites were not without their critics. Opponents rejected the Millerites' claims of biblical authority. Ruth Alden Doan showed that it was not so much that other Protestants denied the legitimacy of the biblical texts themselves but, rather, that the Millerites reached different conclusions when interpreting them.[76] The Millerites saw God as a transcendent ruler who stood in judgment over Americans' values and found them wanting. The majority of evangelical Christians could hardly believe their ears; although imperfections admittedly remained, most Protestants staunchly believed that their gospel-inspired nation was fast approaching the fulfillment of God's providential plan for creation. The cultural dominance long held by mainstream evangelical Protestants had made it possible for them to gloss over many theological distinctions. The Millerites now appeared on the scene, setting up a biblical standard of belief at a time when evangelical Protestants as a group found it comfortable not to take hard and fast theological positions. Lacking any systematic rejoinder to the Millerites' claims, most critics resorted to an *ad hominem* strategy, labeling them lunatics or deluded fanatics. Because premillenial beliefs were so far outside the dominant "plausibility structure" of American life and thought, such labels tended to stick. In fact, many persons were admitted to insane asylums on the grounds of "Millerite-induced insanity."[77]

Millerites were forced to respond to the incredulity and derision they encountered from others. In July 1843, the most prominent Millerite in Ohio, Charles Fitch, offered a compelling explanation for the hostility they were facing. Fitch declared that "whoever is opposed to the PERSONAL REIGN of Jesus Christ over this world on David's throne, is ANTICHRIST."[78] Those Christians who scoffed at the Millerite message and clung to the biblically unsound notion of postmillennialism were agents of the devil. In time, they would get their just deserts. Disbelievers, the Antichrist, are "all those to whom Christ will say, at his appearing, 'Those mine enemies who would not that I should reign over them, bring hither and slay them before me.'"[79] As for just who these Antichrists might be, Fitch confidently identified "the entire Roman Catholic Church." He was no less forthright in indicting the majority of Protestants, charging that "inasmuch as all these multiplied sects are opposed to the plain Bible truth of Christ's personal reign on earth, THEY are ANTICHRIST."[80] Fitch concluded that Antichrist "is everything that rises in opposition to the personal reign of Christ on David's throne, and to the revealed time for his appearing: and here we do find the professed Christian world, Catholic and Protestant, on the side of Antichrist."[81]

The Millerites had originally intended to work within the existing churches as they proclaimed their message of Christ's return. They wished only to arouse the church and warn the world of the imminent end. But when it became clear that their brand of Bible interpretation brought them to theological positions at variance with the nation's dominant religious outlook, they increasingly found themselves relegated to the cultural fringe. Most Millerites concluded that this was just as well. They needed to be separate in order to maintain their unblemished holiness before the Lord. David T. Arthur points out that the theology of the Antichrist provided a justification for maintaining these newly erected borders: "By applying the terms 'Antichrist' and 'Babylon' to all of nominal Christendom they were able to conclude that separation was a duty; indeed, it was a command from God. The churches were damned and lost. Salvation lay only in separation."[82]

Unfortunately for William Miller, 1843 came and passed without the Second Coming. New calculations were made that reset the date to October 1844. But there still was no cataclysmic destruction of the unbelieving Antichrists. The "Great Disappointment" of 1844 dealt a serious blow to the adventist, or premillennial, cause. Some, like Miller himself, did not readily concede error but instead maintained that they had been misled by Bible scholars and historians whose dates had just been proved faulty.[83]

The most innovative response, however, was by Ellen Gould White (1827–1915), whose numerous visions afforded her the certain knowledge that October 1844 had indeed been a signal moment in the end-times scenario. The "cleansing of the sanctuary" on this date had not, however, referred to Christ's Second Coming to earth but, rather, to his ascendancy to the most holy place in a heavenly sanctuary where he would begin his final preparations for his return. In short, she lengthened the eschatological timetable while keeping Miller's general framework intact. It was revealed to her that Christ would not return until more Christians lived up to his moral demands, including the keeping of the true, scriptural Sabbath of Saturday. Ellen Gould White became the prophetess around which the Seventh-Day Adventist denomination was organized.

The Seventh-Day Adventists have subsequently grown to over 500,000 members in the United States and continue to be one of the fastest-growing religious groups in the country. Ellen Gould White's writings make clear for all those in the adventist tradition that the

> Antichrist, meaning all who exalt themselves against the will and work of God, will at the appointed time feel the wrath of Him who gave Himself that they might not perish but have eternal life. All who persevere in obedience, all who will not sell their souls for money or for the favor of men, God will register in the book of life.[84]

The notion of Antichrist thus serves Adventists both as a symbol of theological waywardness and as a symbol of God's final judgment on unbelievers.

To be sure, the premillennial beliefs espoused by the Millerites and others were far from typical of nineteenth-century American religious thought. Timothy Miller's study of evangelical Protestantism in the 1800s demonstrates that "the most significant millenarian doctrines of the mid-nineteenth century were not those of William Miller, but those grown out of evangelical Protestantism's crusade to Christianize the land."[85] The excesses and obvious embarrassments in which Miller's premillennial prophecies frequently entangled him actually did more to deter than to attract others to the cause of Bible prophecy. But premillennialism was a cause whose time would come. Sociological and intellectual trends in the latter part of the nineteenth century forced conservative evangelicals to take hard and fast ideological stands that had been unnecessary a generation earlier. Fundamentalism soon grew out of the nineteenth century's premillennial stirrings and emerged determined to confront mainline Protestantism with a vengeance. The theological battle lines would be drawn more clearly, and the fight was destined to become intense. Such profound ideological campaigns can perhaps be waged without a God. But as Eric Hoffer has argued, they cannot be zealously fought without a devil.[86] Thus the American Antichrist was destined to be rediscovered as the emerging fundamentalist leaders tried to find the source and moral character of the apostasy that surrounded them.

Four

The Battle Against Modernism

It is the Christian apostasy which produces the Antichrist.

Samuel J. Andrews, 1898

❧

Liberal Protestantism reached the zenith of its cultural influence between 1880 and 1925. The mainline denominations, buoyed by the continued advances of the natural and social sciences, prepared to enter a progressivist era in which reason and faith would join together. Liberal confidence in humanity's rational powers left little room for premillennial religion. The majority of American Protestants consequently ignored the Bible's apocalyptic elements and instead saw God's providential spirit at work in the cultural progress they saw all about them. But for every action there is an equal and opposite reaction. In this case it was the emergence of a new and potent force in American religious life—fundamentalism. What distinguishes fundamentalism from mainline Protestant denominations is its opposition to the twentieth century's principal intellectual trends. Rather than accommodating the progressivist elements of the wider culture, fundamentalism opposes them. Over and against the scientific temperament of the twentieth century, fundamentalists champion the inerrancy of biblical texts. This insistence on the literal truth of scripture sets fundamentalists apart from the wider culture and gives them a distinctive identity. Nowhere is this commitment to biblical inerrancy more evident than in fundamentalists' enthusiasm for precisely those texts that other denominations discreetly ignore—the apocalyptic books of Daniel and Revelation. Using interpretive methods that resemble those of William Miller, fundamentalists insist that these apocalyptic texts reveal the significance of the events now transpiring all around them. The "signs of the times" are everywhere corroborating biblical prophecy that we are thus nearing the end-times scenario so vividly depicted in Revelation. Judgment is at hand. It was therefore imperative that conservative Christians separate themselves from the apostasies rampant in secular culture and instead remain loyal to the fundamentals of biblical faith.

Turn-of-the-century Protestant conservatives also rediscovered the Antichrist as a potent symbol of the cosmic evil that engulfed them. To this day, the sermons and writings that define fundamentalist attitudes toward the world are concerned with detecting the Antichrist's presence in the modern world. In fact, without the concept of the Antichrist, there would be no twentieth-century fundamentalist movement. That is, fundamentalism was from the outset a religious movement that sought to identify and oppose all that threatened to subvert old-fashioned gospel faith. Commitment to the fundamentalist cause has meant commitment to oppose almost every intellectual trend distinctive to the modern era. These trends are, from the ultraconservative point of view, nothing less than the Antichrist's means of infiltrating American culture. "Modernism" has therefore given the fundamentalist movement something tangible to fight. Because modernism has continued to make inroads into American religious and cultural life, it has also given fundamentalists good reason to yearn for the destruction of the world about them.

The Rise of Modernism

Much of what is considered "modern American culture" originated in the last two decades of the nineteenth century.[1] The natural and social sciences, biblical scholarship, and increased awareness of non-Western civilizations all took hold among the educated public well before the dawn of the twentieth century. Together they created a new intellectual climate that strengthened the tendencies toward rationalism, secularism, and humanism that had been present in American thought since the Age of Enlightenment. Biblical scholarship, for example, undermined the authority of the Bible. Seminary and university professors used the methods of literary criticism to study the origins and subsequent changes in biblical texts. Their sophisticated analyses established beyond scholarly dispute that the Bible was the work of numerous authors who collected, edited, and arranged their source materials according to their own, historically conditioned conceptions of religious truth. Modern scholarship therefore made it impossible to view the Bible as a "delivered once and for all" revelation from God. It was instead viewed as a collection of ancient mythic writings whose original purpose was to witness to its authors' personal faith, not to convey factual information. It is, after all, difficult to defend the doctrine of biblical inspiration when confronted with irrefutable evidence that the supposed "books of Moses" were written by several different writers at different times in history. Educated persons were similarly dissuaded from simple biblical literalism when they learned that the so-called prophecies in Isaiah and Daniel were written after the events they supposedly "predicted."

These unsettling intellectual discoveries were compounded by the study of comparative world religions and other academic inquiries into non-Western civilizations. Increased travel and the study of other cultures tended to challenge belief in the uniqueness of the Judeo-Christian heritage. Western scholars were discovering that what was recorded as the "absolute" moral or religious truth was principally a matter of cultural conditioning. All told, a new and more relativistic understanding of moral and religious truth was entering American intellectual thought.

By the late 1870s Darwin's theory of evolution had been accepted by nearly every important American scientist. This new scientific discovery filtered into the educated public's awareness in a surprisingly brief period of time; the theory of evolution meshed perfectly with Americans' progressivist and forward-looking character. It seemed almost ideally suited to an optimistic people eager to learn that progress and development were intrinsic to the very laws of nature. The challenge that evolutionary biology presented to biblical religion, however, was both obvious and dramatic. Educated persons were forced to acknowledge that the Book of Genesis (and, by implication, any other biblical text) did not contain factual information. What was at stake, furthermore, was not just information about the origins of life on this planet but also the methods of reasoning that science and biblical religion represented. This discrepancy among competing "truth claims" caused many to feel a tension between their heads and hearts. Most eventually acknowledged that the scientific method was a more reliable approach to factual knowledge yet continued to acknowledge the Bible's value as a source of moral instruction and spiritual edification. This forced option between the competing intellectual claims of science and the Bible prompted many Protestant seminary students of the era to think their way out of the ministry and instead to become pioneers in the fledgling fields of psychology and sociology.[2] Some of the period's most important thinkers, including G. Stanley Hall and George Herbert Mead, went into the social sciences hoping to reconfirm the basic tenets of their Protestant faith (e.g., the importance of a reasoned or moral outlook on life, the inevitability of progress, and the possibility of humans' opening up their lives to a higher spiritual power), but to do so on new and more tenable intellectual grounds.

Religious thinkers of the era were challenged to make religious belief more compatible with the modern world; and they found themselves undertaking what historian William McLoughlin described as "an enormous rescue operation to sustain the culture. They had to redefine and relocate God, provide means of access to Him, and sacralize a new world view."[3] Ironically, it was precisely the era's evolutionary and psychological sciences that furnished the tools for this theological rescue operation. The liberal or progressive Protestant theology of the late nineteenth century turned evolutionary science into a captivating metaphor for God's presence and activity in the world. The progressive evolution of life was seen as a perfect testimony to the immanence of God's providential spirit. This stress on divine immanence made it possible to affirm God's presence in the natural universe and to suggest that God was available to each person through the hidden recesses of his or her own unconscious mind.[4] In such paradigmatic works as John Fiske's *Through Nature to God* (1899), Lyman Abbott's *The Theology of an Evolutionist* (1897), and John Bascom's *Evolution and Religion* (1897), evolution became the new paradigm for Christian cosmology. Fiske, despite his avowed intention to preserve a personal deity, repeatedly described God in such pantheistic terms as "the Power which is disclosed in every throb of the mighty rhythmic life of the universe." Fiske and other theistic evolutionists believed that humans are inwardly linked with God's providential spirit. He declared that "the lesson of evolution is that . . . [the soul] has been rising to the recognition of its essential kinship with the ever-living God."[5]

Lyman Abbott, too, deemed it time to jettison traditional theological language. Modern religious thought, he argued, must understand God as the necessary postulate of the evolutionary movement of life. God was no longer to be understood as a separate entity residing in a celestial kingdom, but as "the Infinite and Eternal Energy from which all things proceed" and which is present within "all the multifarious forces of nature."[6] Abbott spoke for many scientifically inclined members of his generation when he reasoned that the "foundation of spiritual faith is neither in the church nor in the Bible, but in the spiritual consciousness of man."[7] Abbott was not alone in confidently proclaiming "the spiritual consciousness of man" to be the foundation for a modern spiritual faith. The writings of William James and various "mind-cure" writers also popularized the view that we all are, at least potentially, in tune with the Infinite. The increasingly pantheistic metaphors in which educated Americans defined God implied that the only thing that separates them from God was their own self-imposed mental habits. Notions of sin and humanity's unbridgeable distance from God were giving way to a psychologized piety that made no distinction between the divine and human realms.

Intellectuals of the era were confident that the world was on the brink of a new age in which science and religion might merge into a single theoretical system. Churchmen like Horace Bushnell and Henry Ward Beecher typified the impact of modernism on the liberal or progressive wing of Protestant religious thought. They embraced the evolutionary and psychological metaphors of their day and turned them into an optimistic vision of how humans might at last learn to live in complete harmony with God's immanent spiritual presence. Both Beecher and Bushnell believed that natural laws and forces are merely the material expressions of God's providential activity. Because they believed that every human being possessed the psychological capacity to become inwardly receptive to "a flowing-in" of God's spirit, they could look optimistically to such sciences as psychology for progressivist insights into their religious nature. Such accommodations to scientific thought would make religious faith viable to many whose intellectual commitments would otherwise render the Judeo-Christian tradition untenable. But to a growing number of premillennial Protestants, this liberal or modernist style of religious thinking constituted the greatest achievement of the Antichrist in disseminating apostasy throughout the Christian world.

Modernism was not simply an intellectual transformation. To understand why so many came to resent modernism's incursion on traditional American life, we also need to consider its social and cultural dimensions. Immigration, urbanization, and industrialization combined to launch American life along a new and vaguely defined path. The thirty years following the Civil War saw almost every urban center in the Northeast triple in size. Boston, New York, and Philadelphia grew from large towns to massive metropolitan complexes in the span of just one generation. To add to the confusion, most of the forty million immigrants who arrived on the nation's shores in the last half of the century headed straight for the cities. Even as early as 1860, fully 37 percent of all city dwellers had languages, customs, and religious affiliations different from those of their Yankee "hosts." Suspicious of one another, immigrant groups tended to retreat into self-imposed isolation. The United States was no longer a melting pot but now a grab bag of divergent peoples.

Slums, crime, and political conflict cluttered the American cityscapes. Social blight served as a constant reminder of how far the nation had drifted from the Puritan ideal of a corporate commonwealth in which kindred spirits worked toward common goals. The loss of social homogeneity proved to have a profound impact on the country's self-interpretation. Those Americans belonging to the pace-setting cultural mainstream were, for the first time, required to come to terms with "the other." White, Anglo-Saxon Protestants and their way of life were being displaced from the center of the national experience, and many began to point fingers at those they held responsible. A Methodist minister in

New York singled out a few of the culprits by compiling a long list of what he designated "forces opposed to the extension of Protestantism." He warned that urban crowding, saloons, Romanism, Judaism, and a "foreign element which refuses assimilation" were slowly chipping away at the nation's moral and spiritual leadership.[8] This list is, in retrospect, a kind of sociological epitaph of the WASP hegemony over American cultural life. The increasingly pluralistic character of American society threatened to make "legislative, social, and religious problems difficult of solution."[9] In other words, Protestantism was losing the social base it needed to impose its religious and moral vision on the rest of the nation.

The problems of industrialization went hand in hand with migration to the cities. The factory soon replaced the farm as the symbol of the nation's productivity, leaving wage earners utterly mystified. An agrarian economy provides individuals with a relatively simple vision of economic opportunity: Success is a function of the expenditure of time and energy. An industrial order, however, does not permit such straightforward calculations. Who understood stock markets, trusts, cartels, monopolies, or recessions—much less how to overcome them? Or for that matter, how was the entrepreneurial elite able to amass such fortunes while the average worker struggled just to make ends meet? Most Americans were equally uncertain whether organized labor or early political efforts to curb unrestricted capitalism were to be embraced or eschewed. In short, Americans lacked rules for reducing their new complex world into understandable concepts.

Before the 1870s, small-town life had been the country's norm. American communal life had been relatively cohesive, forged as it was around a consensus about the values of its predominantly Protestant, Anglo-Saxon populace. Human relationships were shaped within consensually validated norms and patterns. The interdependence of small-town life helped elicit conformity to these norms and patterns. Voluntary cooperation, spontaneity, and gregariousness were both virtues and practical necessities. In contrast, urban living generated its own special values which were destined to come into conflict with those of America's small-town heritage. Contractual agreement, systematic performance, and well-partitioned social roles undermined the moral orientation and social sense of those not reared in urban ways. Historian Robert Wiebe summarized the impact of these changes:

> The health of the nineteenth-century community depended upon two closely related conditions: its ability to manage the lives of its members, and the belief among its members that the community had such powers. Already by the 1870s the autonomy of the community was badly eroded. . . . America in the late nineteenth century was a society without a core. It lacked those national centers of authority and information which might have given order to such swift changes.[10]

Cultural spokesmen, particularly those of the nation's churches, struggled to articulate a new "core" for American society. Many in the mainline denominations were drawn to the "social gospel" movement that sought to apply the Christian ethic of love to the social problems facing urban, industrial America. Washington Gladden and Shailer Mathews were among the early leaders in the effort to develop a Christian ministry that initiated projects of social improvement in the nation's cities. The best-known architect of the social gospel movement was Walter Rauschenbusch (1861–1918). Referring to himself as a "Christian socialist," Rauschenbusch vacillated between optimism and realism as he sought to develop a theological critique of the structural impediments to a more equal distribution of wealth in the United States. The social gospel movement he inspired helped carry the progressivist spirit of the nineteenth-century reform societies into the twentieth century and its new array of social problems. Renewed efforts to bring gospel faith to bear on the need for housing, food, shelter, and medical care characterized many of the mainline churches as they sought to accommodate the new social environment.

Other Protestants, however, were not nearly so sanguine about the prospects of reforming the kingdom of evil in which they found themselves. Better, they thought, to concentrate on rescuing souls from this world than to waste time and energy on the hopeless task of regenerating a fallen world. Premillennial faith assured these persons that the only hope for this world rested in the Second Coming and that it was their solemn duty to separate themselves from the sinful world so that they might be pure before Christ upon his arrival. It was among those who opted for this response to modernism that fundamentalism germinated and thrived.

Call to Battle Royal

Modernism posed a serious threat to religious orthodoxy. The danger came not so much from the secularist expressions of modernism as from the extensions of modernism into the church itself. W. T. Gaston understood the apocalyptic significance of modernism's incursion into Christianity and described the challenge in militant terms: "The religious battle of the last days is clearly drawn before this generation. It is between natural and supernatural religion."[11] The naturalist tendencies of liberal theology were leading Christians into apostasy. "The modernist pulpit," declared one contributor to the *Pentecostal Evangel*, "is preparing the audience, the constituency, for the Antichrist."[12] Modernism was thus prompting American Protestants to sever the ready identification of the Antichrist with the papacy. It was fast becoming clear that the Antichrist was afoot here and now, using the fertile ground of modernist thinking to sow his seeds of apostasy and deceit.

As early as 1879 a prophetic conference was held in New York City to gauge the signs of the times and provide premillennial interpretations of American decay. Rev. Harry Parsons, pastor of Buffalo's Lafayette Street Presbyterian Church, came prepared to speak on "The Present Age and Development of Antichrist." As he looked out at the world about him, he became even more convinced that it was no place for God-fearing persons. Careful attention to Bible prophecies convinced him that the purpose of this age was "the gathering out of the nations those persons who shall afterward reign [with Christ] on earth."[13] The people of God must be gathered together, separated from the corrupting influences of those destined to face the wrath of God at judgment. It was important, then, that all faithful Christians know how to detect the presence and activity of Antichrist lest they unwittingly be led astray.

Parsons was certain that the Antichrist would prove to be more than a mere principle or set of vaguely defined social forces. He interpreted Revelation and Daniel as describing a distinct person who would rise to political power and provide Christ with a personal adversary. But it was also important to understand that the Antichrist was not only a being to be encountered in the future; he was also already active. Parsons explained that the Antichrist had already deployed the "recruiting forces" with which he intended to ensnare all those who strayed from steadfast loyalty to Christ: rationalism, skepticism, atheism, pantheism, and socialism. The most effective way to counter Antichrist's recruiting forces was not the social gospel's strategy of trying to ameliorate social, economic, and political problems. Instead, the Antichrist was to be warded off through evangelism and the winning of individual souls. As Parsons argued, "The Word of God declares that the purpose of preaching the Gospel of the Kingdom in the world is to save the people out of it called the Church and not to make the world better."[14] Put differently, Parsons already knew that neither he nor other premillennialists belonged in the new American culture. It was therefore preferable to separate themselves from this culture rather risk being co-opted by it.

What Parsons regarded in 1879 as Antichrist's recruiting forces had, twenty years later, grown into a full-fledged assault force. Rev. Samuel Andrews warned Christians in 1898 that "the battle of ideas" was coming to "its final, and bloody, stage." His *Christianity and Anti-Christianity in Their Final Conflict* was a discourse on the nature of Antichrist, enabling all to see how the heresy of modernism had deceived the masses and brought the world to the brink of its final ruin.[15]

Andrews had resigned as a Congregational minister to serve as a clergyman for the newly formed Catholic Apostolic Church. This new sect had been formed to return Christianity to its biblical roots and thereby prepare the faithful for the imminent Second Coming of Christ. But to Andrews's chagrin, few took biblical prophecy concerning the end-times very seriously. Most of the population appeared to be either modernist Christians who believed in the world's continual upward progress (and "can find no place for any development of evil and an Antichrist") or secular modernists who believed that Christianity would soon pass away altogether as the world evolved into a more scientific era. Andrews believed that the prophetic passages of Daniel and Revelation showed both parties to be sadly mistaken. The prophecy concerning the emergence of a deceptive "beast" in the final days was already coming to pass. As Andrews's reading of 1 John convinced him that "it is the Christian apostasy which produces the Antichrist."[16] The ideas promulgated by modernist Christians and rationalist skeptics were the very means by which the Antichrist would deceive the church and assume political power. Andrews, who expected a personal Antichrist to rise to political prominence in the near future, had no difficulty naming the tendencies that were currently preparing his way: modern pantheistic philosophy, the New Christianity, the deification of humanity, modern biblical criticism, modern science, modern literature, the periodical press, and Christian socialism.

Andrews's list of the tendencies preparing the way for the Antichrist was in many ways astute. He had, after all, identified what were to be the major strands of twentieth-century intellectual thought. He was, moreover, probably correct in his belief that these intellectual tendencies would displace the church and scripture from the center of that thought. Yet in retrospect, Andrews's arguments seem less striking for their logical force than for the psychological functions they served. By the 1890s the center of intellectual authority in America had shifted from the church to the university. University researchers were making startling discoveries in almost every conceivable field, and their scientific methods of inquiry consequently seemed to be making older, prescientific ways of thinking anachronistic. Andrews and others were thus confronted with a growing rift between their biblically grounded beliefs and the increasing prestige and scope of modern intellectual life. This incompatibility between religion and modernism was publicly embarrassing, and it put a strain on personal faith as well. The intellectual temptations posed by modernism would have to be explained and disposed of.

Psychologist Leon Festinger used the term *cognitive dissonance* to refer to such incongruity between two competing beliefs or sources of information.[17] He showed that because the experience of dissonance is psychologically uncomfortable, people try to reduce or remove the tension arising among discrepant beliefs. Important to our purposes is that Festinger's research indicates that the level of psychological dissonance persons experience increases dramatically when their initial beliefs were acquired solely through attachment to social groups rather than being grounded in some kind of "testable physical reality" that provides independent support. Festinger further demonstrated that both the number and "attractiveness" of those persons disagreeing with previously held beliefs affect the degree of dissonance they will experience. The greater the dissonance is, the more psychologically driven they will be to find ways of restoring congruity or logical clarity in their beliefs. According to Festinger there are at least three strategies by which people might try to reduce cognitive dissonance: (1) changing their own beliefs, (2) trying to persuade others who disagree with them to change their beliefs, or (3) reinterpreting the disagreement so as to deny the validity of opposing beliefs or knowledge.

Andrews's attempt to link modern intellectual life with the Antichrist was precisely such a strategy for reducing the dissonance that modernism had thrust on so many turn-of-the-century Protestants. Andrews, of course, was unwilling to change his own beliefs, and he realized the futility of trying to get many "modernists" to acknowledge the error of their ways. Instead, his act of naming the Antichrist was intended to undermine the integrity and motivations of all who pitted modernism against the fundamentals of biblical faith. By associating modernism with the Antichrist, Andrews was able to help his readers respond psychologically to both the public ridicule and the private doubts that modernism had engendered. Although a *d hominem* arguments may be fallacious in terms of formal logic, they are decisive in the apocalyptic point of view. Because modernism represents the cunning deception of the Antichrist as foretold in biblical prophecy, the religiously faithful need not be surprised that many find it intellectually valid. The Antichrist is, after all, the master of deceit and counterfeit. All but the most vigilant will be taken in by his cunning. By "naming the Antichrist," Andrews reinterpreted the conflict between modernism and biblical faith in such a way as to leave no doubt where God-fearing Christians' loyalties must lie. His constituency no longer had to trouble themselves with reasoned refutations of modernism's intellectual claims. Instead, all modern science and philosophy could be dismissed outright as an act of religious loyalty.

Andrews's long list of "tendencies preparing the way for Antichrist" demonstrates a special sensitivity to the kinds of difficulties that modernism posed to ultraconservative Protestants, for example, his railings against the pantheistic philosophy that guided so many of his contemporaries' efforts to make religious sense out of evolution. Never in his attack on pantheism did he attempt philosophical arguments about the logically problematic aspects of these speculative efforts to find God in the natural universe. For Andrews it was sufficient to point to the moral and religious consequences to which pantheistic ideas would inevitably lead. He took it for granted that every kind of evolution-based philosophy was destined to end in the glorification of humanity. Current public interest in the writings of Hegel, Emerson, Tennyson, Spencer, Schopenhauer, and Fiske was leading to the exaltation of humanity's innate potential at the expense of conventional Christian doctrine. Such a deification of humanity

> paves the way for the Antichrist because he will demand the homage of
> the world on the basis of being a representative of our "common divine
> humanity." . . . We see how broad and deep a foundation is thus laid in
> the philosophical teaching of the essential unity of the Divine and human
> natures, for the deification of the Antichrist.[18]

For that matter, Andrews believed that the whole of modern science "fosters habits of thought embarrassing to religious conviction." Not only does science deny the biblical account of creation, but the entire world-view with which it is associated undermines belief in the Second Coming of Christ and the imminent appearance of the Antichrist. For this reason, "men of this class are pre-eminently fitted to become, first the votaries, and then the slaves, of the lawless one."[19]

It was even easier for Andrews to find the workings of Antichrist in modern biblical criticism. He knew that his readers were familiar with scholars' attacks on the allegedly obsolete moral and scientific ideas contained in the Bible. Practitioners of the "higher criticism" of the Bible were encouraging people to move away from a literal interpretation of scripture. They advocated instead a more symbolic approach to read-ing the Bible that would separate its valuable moral insights from the crudely supernaturalist thinking of a prescientific age. Andrews felt no obligation to examine the academic soundness of biblical scholars' con-clusions. It was instead sufficient that he draw attention to the apoca-lyptic significance of any attempt to veer away from biblical literalism. He was certain that "this overthrow of the faith of men in the Bible is a great step forward in preparing the way for the Antichrist."[20] Once his readers knew that biblical scholarship was the work of the Antichrist, it would not be necessary to inquire any further into its academic mer-its. The categories of apocalyptic thinking could now take over and bring the reader to an acceptable resolution of the intellectual conflict.

More interesting still is Andrews's mode of repudiating both the periodical press and Christian socialism. What connects these two top-ics in Andrews's mind was that both forced him to realize that a sizable portion of the nation's intelligentsia no longer viewed the world through biblical categories. Given the fact that so many of his compatriots had fallen into apostasy, neither he nor fellow premillennial Christians could any longer sanction such traditional American values as democracy, equality, or even freedom of expression. Modern literature and the pe-riodical press were prime vehicles for the era's secularistic and human-istic leanings. Andrews had to confess that these depended on consumer sales and consequently "must reflect [the public's] beliefs and opinions." But, he pointed out, this is precisely what premillennialism wants us to understand: The general public is under the rule of the Antichrist, and only the loyal remnant walk in the way of the Lord. In an apostate era such as ours, democracy serves to create a sphere of lawlessness conducive to the Antichrist. The Antichrist will come as a "direct or indirect expression of the popular will," and for this reason democracy itself "serves to prepare the way of the Antichrist by making the popular will supreme."[21] In this regard, Andrews voiced the distrust of the general public, free speech, and democratic principles that characterized premillennialism for at least the next hundred years. The fledgling fundamentalist movement in which he participated had a certain "over againstness" from its very start; it defined itself in opposition to a world that was rapidly passing it by. The Antichrist proved a potent symbol for making cognitive sense of that opposition and even transforming it into a test of religious loyalty.

The "over and againstness" of Andrews's piety made him eager to separate from, not transform, the world about him. He understood contemporary calls for Christian socialism as yet another campaign directed by the Antichrist. To Andrews, socialism was little more than the economic side of democracy. It meant further enfranchising those members of the general public who showed little sympathy for preserving the interests of those who watched eagerly for the Second Coming. He observed that

> it is obvious, without special remark, that the socialist ideal of a kingdom of perfected humanity through a new social order will greatly help Antichrist in the establishment of his rule over the nation. The eyes of all are turned forward, their minds are full of vague but ardent expectation . . . [in this way] socialism will serve as a powerful lever by which Antichrist may overthrow the existing political governments, and the field be cleared for the final conflict.[22]

Biblical conservatives no longer needed to ask what was wrong with the world. They knew full well that the answer was modernism. Nor did they question why the church's work was so consistently frustrated. The reason was fast becoming obvious: The Antichrist was already among them, arranging the world according to his own apostate design. William B. Riley, an evangelist and minister to students at the University of Minnesota, wrote a volume entitled *The Menace of Modernism* (1917) that made it clear that more concerted action was necessary to combat the inroads being made by the Antichrist. Riley's campus ministry made him especially aware of how the modern educational system was surreptitiously bringing the nation's youth to the brink of apostasy. Thinking especially of university professors, Riley warned that 1 and 2 John expressly instruct that "all who participate in [modernism] are, alike, members of Antichrist."[23] In John's day as in the present, the "greatest enemy of any Church of Jesus Christ is the man who remains in her, assumes to be one of her teachers, calmly wears her good name, and yet denies the deity of Him who brought her into being . . . modernism is such an enemy."[24]

   The time was fast approaching to engage this enemy in open combat. Evangelist John Roach Straton, for example, accepted a challenge to debate the "fundamentals" of Christianity with Unitarian minister Charles Potter. The series of debates, staged before independent judges, joined fundamentalism and liberalism a year and a half earlier than did the memorable Scopes trial in Dayton, Tennessee.[25] Potter was deemed the winner of the first debate, Straton the second. When they met for the third debate, partisans of both sides understood the seriousness of the ideological clash in which they were engaged. They debated back and forth on such issues as the existence of miracles, the virgin birth, and the infallibility of the Bible. When the judges announced Potter the victor, Straton and his supporters were certain that their loss could not be explained according to any fair principles of moral decency or sound judgment. They responded to the dissonance that this negative verdict engendered in a manner that foreshadowed much of the twentieth century's use of apocalyptic symbolism. As Potter was leaving the site of the debate, he was besieged by a crowd of irate women who hurled epithets, calling him "Antichrist," "Satan," and "Devil."[26] Fortunately for Potter, the members of his church had gauged the intensity of their opposition's zealousness and had hired two private detectives to guard him without his knowledge. With their help he was able to escape one of the many skirmishes in what Andrews had called the final and bloody stage of "the battle of ideas."

   By the second decade of the century, a considerable number of Americans were aware that they had been intellectually and socially displaced from the nation's symbolic center. Nor was the dissonance and displacement they faced likely to be temporary. A campaign needed to be waged to regain the territory lost to the Antichrist. It was time for antimodernist Christians to fill in the ranks and develop a more effective strategy for retaliation. Curtis Lee Laws, editor of a Baptist paper, *The Watchman Examiner*, coined the word *fundamentalists* and used it to denote all those who were ready "to do battle royal" for the fundamentals of the faith.[27] A broad-based religious impulse was emerging in American culture, one destined to carry forward the assault on Antichrist.

The Dawn of Fundamentalism

The Western apocalyptic tradition was rich in the symbolic imagery necessary to do battle against modernism. It is undoubtedly for this reason that the premillennial beliefs gaining popularity in the late nineteenth century became the driving force of what became known as *Protestant fundamentalism*.[28] *Fundamentalism* is an elusive word. It refers not to any one denomination but to a particular theological outlook that has champions in many conservative religious organizations. In the broadest sense, fundamentalism refers to concern with evangelism and biblical values such as has been found historically in conservative Protestant religion. Yet in a narrower sense, fundamentalism must be considered as a subset of conservative, Bible-oriented faith. What distinguishes fundamentalism from other expressions of conservative religion is its self-conscious opposition to the influences that modernism has had within both the church and the wider scope of American culture. Fundamentalists, in short, eagerly adopt the posture of religious and cultural "outsiders."

The "over-and-againstness" that gives fundamentalism its distinctive theological cast is reflected in its emphasis on three interconnected themes or commitments: biblical inerrancy, separatism, and premillennialism. This insistence on biblical inerrancy signals opposition to religious liberalism and also directs attention to the significance of apocalyptic texts such as Daniel and Revelation for describing the contrasting fates that await faithful Christians and their modernist adversaries. Wary of secular culture and of the fashionable churches as well, fundamentalists insist on separating themselves from any conscious participation in the wayward tendencies that characterize "worshipers of the Beast." Certain that the hour of final judgment is upon them, twentieth-century fundamentalists have developed a distinctive piety centered largely on their shared hatred of the Antichrist who, in his final days, has grown desperate in his quest to overthrow the forces of God. In order to defeat this cosmic enemy, fundamentalists have found it necessary to separate themselves from all the ecclesiastical, political, and cultural structures in which they have detected his conspiratorial presence. Their premillennial faith has compelled them to become, like the communities to which both 1 John and Revelation were addressed, a people apart.

These theological tenets of evangelism, biblical inerrancy, separatism, and premillennialism came together in the relatively short period between the mid-1880s and 1920. In the span of just one generation, a new ideological synthesis was created that would help millions of Bible-believing Americans to take stock of the new world emerging around them. Critical to the process that brought these strands together were the rise of a theological notion called *dispensationalism*, a series of Bible conferences and urban revivals that gave premillennialism a surer footing on American religious soil, and the appearance of several new premillennial publications, including *The Scofield Reference Bible*. Each of these factors helped breathe new life into the figure of the Antichrist.

Perhaps the most important theological innovation in the construction of American fundamentalism was the newly coined doctrine of dispensation.[29] The concept of dispensationalism refers to the separation of the history of salvation into distinct periods or dispensations.

Apocalyptic writers throughout the centuries divided the history of God's dealings with humanity into distinct periods or epochs. The modern version of such dispensationalist understandings of history developed among a British sect known as the Plymouth Brethren. One of the Brethren's most popular teachers, John Nelson Darby (1800–1882), visited the United States seven times between 1862 and 1877 and on each occasion won more converts to this version of premillennial faith.

One of Darby's most ardent American followers, C. I. Scofield, defined the term *dispensation* as "a period of time during which man is tested in respect of obedience to some specific revelation of the will of God."[30] Although history is not progressive in the sense of improving the human condition, it does change as God progressively alters his methods of dealing with humanity. Step by step, God leads humanity to the terms of final judgment. As Scofield explained, the various periods or dispensations

> are marked off in Scripture by some change in God's method of dealing with mankind, in respect to two questions: of sin and of man's responsibility. Each of the dispensations may be regarded as a new test of the natural man and each ends in judgment—making his utter failure in every dispensation.[31]

According to dispensationalism, we now live in the next-to-last epoch of human history. This epoch, usually referred to as the "Church Age," is situated between the fifth dispensation, which witnessed the appearance of Christ, and the seventh or last dispensation, in which Christ will return to establish the millennium. Dispensationalists therefore view the Church Age as only a "great parenthesis" between God's sending Christ to earth and the cataclysmic events that will precede the final judgment. The corruption of the church is a signal that we are near the close of this dispensation and that things on earth will only get worse until Christ returns.

The most distinctive teaching associated with dispensationalism is that of the secret rapture. The doctrine of the rapture was an expansion of 1 Thessalonians 4:17, which states that all believers in Christ, both living and dead, "shall be caught up together with them in the clouds to meet the Lord in the air." The second advent will thus initially be secret, discernible only to those who experience the rapture of rising in the air to meet Christ. Those who participate in this rapture will thereby temporarily disappear from earth and so be spared the terrible tribulations that the Antichrist will visit on the citizens of earth during his seven-year rule of tyranny. Following this period of tribulation, Christ will return in a public second advent in the manner described in Matthew 24 and Revelation. Most previous Bible interpreters had viewed the "catching up" to be a part of the Second Coming, not a precursor to it. Darby was evidently one of the first to advance the idea that the rapture would take place before the period of tribulations rather than at their end. His views spread throughout the United States, giving American fundamentalists a sense of watchful expectancy and pride in being members of the millennium's vanguard.

Dispensational authors prepared scientific-looking charts to enable readers to see precisely how God has divided the time line of history into seven distinct epochs. These charts graphically place contemporary events in the larger sweep of cosmic history. Historian Martin Marty observed that by providing such ideological tools for interpreting the true significance of human history, dispensationalism has given American premillennialists the excitement of knowing more about the news being reported in the media than their neighbors do.[32] It also provides consolation in the face of continued defeat by the multihorned beast of modernity. The dispensational view of history, after all, predicts that evil must reach unprecedented levels before God will finally take the decisive actions necessary to wipe the Antichrist from the face of this earth. To this extent, dispensationalism even encouraged the premillennialists' tendency to separate themselves from the intellectual and social currents of the era. Knowing that the "church age" is destined to end in failure and can be redeemed only with the destruction described in detail in Revelation, dispensationalists are confident that no amelioration of the human condition is possible and that their religious duty is to separate from, not to seek the improvement of, the world about them.

On this point, dispensationalists were—and still are—emphatic. Commitment to social reform was no longer considered a natural outgrowth of personal conversion to Christ. The social gospelers were, as one premillenialist put it, playing right into Satan's hands:

> Sociology, or social service as generally emphasized is, in its final outworking, a black winged angel of the pit. . . . Satan would have a reformed world, a beautiful world, a moral world, a world of great achievements. . . . He would have a universal brotherhood of man, he would eliminate by scientific method every human ill, and expel by human effort every unkindness; he would make all men good by law, education and social uplift; he would have a world without war. . . . But a premillennialist cannot cooperate with the plans of modern social service for these contemplate many years with gradual improvement through education as its main avenue for cooperation rather than the second coming of Christ.[33]

The core ideas of twentieth-century fundamentalism soon found institutional expression in the form of prophecy meetings, urban revival meetings, premillennial publications, and a host of new denominations and related organizations.[34] Beginning in the 1870s and 1880s, several of the new advocates of dispensationalism organized a series of "Bible and Prophecy Conferences" that were destined to give the fledgling fundamentalist cause its first semblance of being a cohesive, unified movement. The most famous of these, the Niagara Conference, began in 1875. Similar conferences were held in Allegheny, Pennsylvania, in 1895, Boston in 1901, Chicago in 1914, and subsequently in both New York and Philadelphia. Such conferences allowed laity and clergy to gather and reinforce one another's strengthening adherence to biblical inerrancy and premillennialism. These conferences further disseminated Darby's dispensationalism and reacquainted the attendees with biblical prophecies concerning the Antichrist and the latter days. The piety that these conferences generated made the Second Coming seem all the closer. It was thus natural for one participant to be vexed by the apparent decline in enthusiasm that he observed at one of the last Niagara conferences. Complaining of the "evident absence of fervor and depth of conviction which marked the teaching of former years," he asked, "Is it the calm before the storm; or is it a lapse from the first warm fervor of a great spiritual movement and life; or is it the gradual withdrawing of the Holy Spirit from the Christian assemblies preparatory to the Apostasy, the Antichrist and the Advent?"[35]

The resurgence of revivalism in the 1880s and 1890s was yet another institutional means by which premillenialist belief continued to gain adherents among conservative evangelicals.[36] The flow of the nation's population into the cities alarmed most church leaders, as the mobility of urban residents tended to weaken the ties of habit, social pressure, and fellowship that had traditionally bound persons to the church. Although Charles Finney and Lyman Beecher had experimented with revivals in large urban areas, it was Dwight L. Moody (1837–1899) who fully systematized the urban revival meetings that later provided a forum for such renowned millennialists as Billy Sunday, Billy Graham, Jack Van Impe, Jimmy Swaggart, and Pat Robertson. Moody was in many ways the principal progenitor of fundamentalism. He promoted the separatist mentality and the forms of moral perfectionism that would become hallmarks of the fundamentalist identity. He also believed in biblical infallibility and was an unquestioning advocate of dispensationalist premillennialism.[37] A close friend of such noted premillennialist writers as Reuben Torrey, C. I. Scofield, William Erdman, and A. C. Dixon, Moody did more than any of them to blend apocalyptic ideology into middle-class American piety. One of his most noted sermons, "The Second Coming of Christ," dramatized his conviction that it was the duty of every Christian to be constantly on the lookout for Christ's return.[38] Interestingly, Moody almost nowhere mentions the Antichrist, and his writings characteristically avoid the rancor and hate mongering that before long the urban revivalists perfected into an apocalyptic art form. For the most part, premillennialism was for him another weapon of evangelism, a tactic for urging sinners to repent before they had lost the Kingdom for good. Moody did help establish the place and role of urban revivalism as a recruiting and socializing vehicle for fundamentalism. Eventually, urban revivalism became a highly influential medium through which millions learned about the eschatological significance of the "signs of the times."

Perhaps the signal events in the formation of a self-conscious fundamentalism were the publication of a twelve-volume series entitled *The Fundamentals* and C. I. Scofield's *Reference Bible*. The former had its origins in the premillennial piety of millionaire Lyman Stewart. The president of Union Oil Company of California, Stewart understood his true vocation to be that of underwriting premillennialist enterprises. He contributed substantially to the republication of W. E. Blackstone's popular tract *Jesus Is Coming* and donated a thousand dollars to help get the Scofield Reference Bible going. It was important, he wrote Scofield, that works be written that offer "warning and testimony to the English-speaking ministers, theological teachers and students."[39] Stewart knew only too well that enemies of the gospel were everywhere. Infidel professors at the Divinity School of the University of Chicago, the well-known agnostic lecturer Robert Ingersoll, Mary Baker Eddy, and evolutionary scientists were favorite targets of his apocalyptic wrath. In the effort to combat the inroads that these and other such culprits had made on American religious thought, Stewart approached Rev. A. C. Dixon to edit a series that would help reset the nation's theological bearings. Dixon carefully selected sixty-four authors whom he could trust to write articles on topics reinforcing biblical inerrancy and premillennial expectations. Between 1910 and 1915, twelve volumes appeared that collectively defined the fundamentalist cause. Thousands of copies were distributed free, compliments of Lyman Stewart and his brother Milton. By 1920 these volumes solidified the name and ideology of the century's most vocal religious sentiment.

No single book has had more influence on the American Antichrist tradition than the *Scofield Reference Bible*. First published in 1909, Scofield's annotated Bible sold over 5 million copies before 1967; a new edition released in 1967 has sold an additional 2.5 million copies. Unique to this edition of the Bible are copious references in the margins that, to the average reader, appear to be part of God's original text. Scofield predictably disclaimed any originality in his editorial work and marginal references; he was simply elucidating the constant and true interpretation of Christian scripture. But what readers actually got was a wholesale imposition of fundamentalist assumptions on the text. Scofield's marginal notes connected passages in one book of the Bible with passages in different books of the Bible as though God himself had dictated this system of cross-referencing. Scofield had, furthermore, invited a number of scholars to assist him in this exercise, premillennialists all. The end result was a text that made the convoluted machinations of these premillennialist editors indistinguishable from the original word of God.

As if his marginal notes were not sufficient to help readers understand the "literal meaning" of the text, Scofield also added footnotes at
the bottom of each page, whose principal goal was to place both biblical history and contemporary events into Darby's dispensational system. Scholarly-sounding prose explicated the complex details of salvation history. Readers are told that their own age, the sixth and next to
last, is destined to end in ruin because the churches have fallen into
utter apostasy and humanity's erring ways will go unchecked until the
return of Christ. They stand at the brink of the "Fullness of Times," awaiting God to "restore the Davidic monarch in His own person, re-gather
dispersed Israel, establish His power over all the earth, and reign one
thousand years."[40] It is important to note that millions of American fundamentalists, armed with the *Scofield Reference Bible*, are prepared to make
apocalyptic sense of the world about them. As they watch the apostasy
unleashed by modernism and the continued movement of modern
culture away from biblical categories, they can confidently place these
events in their proper cosmic context and be certain that biblical prophecy is coming to pass.

Nowhere are Scofield's biased renderings of the Bible more apparent than in his appendages to the two books that underlie the dispensationalist, premillennial views that distinguish twentieth-century fundamentalism: Daniel and Revelation. His systematic cross-referencing
of passages imposed a theological order on biblical materials that in
themselves are disparate and opaque. His ability to fashion these ambiguous texts into a scientific-sounding chronology have deferred readers from attempting to interpret these cryptic texts in terms of their
authors' historical situation. Instead, subsequent generations have relied
on the *Scofield Reference Bible* to buttress their belief that Daniel and Revelation are the primary sources of "Bible prophecy" and contain intricate timetables forecasting events in their own impending future.

Scofield's ability to forge these apocalyptic materials into a consistent brand of premillennialism depended, however, on his willingness
to exercise considerable editorial license. In his footnotes to Daniel, for
example, he thought nothing of stating as indisputable fact that any
biblical reference to weeks actually means "sevens of years." It seems
that the Bible is inerrant and to be read literally, but only after having
reworked it to make sure it will support the kinds of conclusions dispensationalism supports in the first place. Thus Scofield could confidently assert that the Old Testament prophets lived in a different dispensation and that their writings therefore needed to be reinterpreted
in accordance with Darby's insights into the differences between their
dispensation and our own. Scofield consequently thought himself justified in giving a new interpretive slant to their writings because he was
bringing them into line with the premillennial system that "was hidden from the Old Testament prophets."

From the vantage point of present-day premillennial thought, Scofield was able to help his readers understand how the Book of Daniel cast light on their own immediate future. One such piece of information contained in Daniel is its description of the period of tribulations and destruction that people on earth must endure between the time of the rapture to the moment of Christ's victory over the Antichrist. This period of tribulation will last exactly seven years: "To make it more violates the principle of interpretation already confirmed by fulfillment." Scofield also instructs readers that the "little horn" of the beast in Chapter 7 refers to the Antichrist who will covenant with the Jews at the beginning of this seven-year period but, midway through this period, will break the covenant and bring about great destruction, persecution, and tribulation before his final defeat at the hands of the "prince that shall come."[41] Scofield's chronological scheme, though not entirely original, nonetheless dominated the twentieth century's obsession with identifying Antichrist figures.

A second and quite revealing way in which Scofield imposed a distinctive ideological gloss on fundamentalist interpretations of Bible prophecy was his further reworking of the notion of the Antichrist. In Daniel, for example, Scofield appends a footnote to the description of the "little horn" of the beast, shifting the usual emphasis on the beast's political despotism to his religious apostasy. He then clarifies any possible confusions his readers might have, by instructing them that "the 'little horn' is an apostate, but from Christianity, not Judaism."[42] The importance of this distinction becomes clearer in his footnotes explaining Revelation 13's references to the Beast from the sea and the Beast from the land. He begins by summarily dismissing I and 2 John's explicit references to "many antichrists" and their definition of the Antichrist as one who denies the divinity of Jesus. Without explaining just how a biblical author could be so misleading on such an important topic, Scofield sets the Bible straight by explaining what any good dispensational premillennialist knows:

> The "many antichrists" precede and prepare the way for *the* Antichrist, who is "the Beast out of the earth"; of Rev. 13: 11–17, and the "false prophet" of Rev. 16:13; 19:20; 20:10. He is the last ecclesiastical head, as the Beast of Rev. 13: 1–8 [the Beast from the sea] is the last civil head."[43]

For centuries Christians had linked the Antichrist with the Beast from the sea, which was clearly a reference to Nero and the Roman authorities and which consequently depicted Christians' most feared worldly enemy. The Beast from the land had originally referred to those citizens of the area who participated in Rome's economic and political orders, thus doing the bidding of the Beast from the sea. But to Scofield, true Christianity was only secondarily threatened by the government. Rather, it was religious apostates who most threatened the viability of

the gospel faith. In one fell swoop Scofield gave twentieth-century fundamentalists the biblical foundations to support what they knew all
along: Modernists and all who shared their views were the many
antichrists who are even now preceding and preparing the way for *the*
Antichrist. Although most fundamentalists have not followed Scofield
on this point of identifying the Antichrist with the Beast from the land,
they surely agree with him in making apostasy the Antichrist's chief
identifying trait. The fact that their biblical conclusions are molded by
motives extraneous to any straightforward reading of biblical history
does not seem to matter. The important point is that Antichrist has been
properly named and that fundamentalists can now get on with the
business of doing battle royal.

Dispensationalism, Bible conferences, urban revivalism, and the
issuing of doctrinally authoritative literature combined to create a widespread and self-conscious fundamentalist movement. The central features of this movement proved to be its evangelism, commitment to
biblical inerrancy, social and moral separatism, and premillennialism.
Disputes were still possible on the last point, premillennialism. A few
fundamentalists believe, for example, that Christians will not be spared
the tribulations in the last days. This view, known as *posttribulationalism*,
maintains that the rapture will not take place until after the seven-year
period of tribulation. The majority of fundamentalists, however, believe
in *pretribulationism*; that is, they believe that the rapture will occur before
this catastrophic period on earth and thereby spare the righteous from
having to endure the torment justly visited on unbelievers.

Although there are significant differences in the details or the precise order of events, it is nonetheless possible to summarize the rough
outlines of twentieth-century fundamentalism's apocalyptic expectations: A ten-nation confederacy will come to power on earth, headed
by a powerful ruler.[44] This ruler will be none other than the Antichrist—
the Beast (at least to those who identify the Antichrist with the Beast
from the Sea) prophesied by John in Revelation and by Paul in his references to the "man of sin." As head of the revived Roman Empire, the
Antichrist will wield tremendous power over the world and will be the
central figure in all the events that transpire in the earth's final days.
The Antichrist will at first be viewed as a great moral and political leader
and will be received warmly by all except those whose eyes have been
opened by scriptural prophecy. Early in his rule the Antichrist will seem
a friend to the newly restored nation of Israel, regathered in Palestine
for the first time since its captivity by Nebuchadnezzar in the sixth century B.C.E. The Antichrist and Israel will make a mutual defense pact,
which will permit the Jews to reconstruct their ancient temple.

About this time, however, the true nature and identity of the Antichrist will be revealed. After three and a half years (half the seven-year

tribulation period), he will break the treaty with Israel, enter the temple, suspend all sacrifices, declare himself to be God, and demand worship. From this point forward, all hell will break loose on earth as the Antichrist wields his tyrannical power over the entire globe. Just when in all of this the rapture will take place is a matter of disagreement. The majority of fundamentalists, however, are pretribulationists and are confident that the "catching up" of the saints will occur before the Antichrist's true nature is revealed and hence before the tribulations begin in earnest. Many of those left on earth will realize that the saints have been rewarded for their faith and will at last accept Jesus as their savior. Both a multitude of Gentiles and 144,000 Jews will convert to Christianity at this time but, unfortunately, will be marked for persecution by the Antichrist.

In order to carry out his blasphemous rule, Antichrist will delegate much of his authority to a false prophet (the beast from the land) who will compel worship of the Beast through clever utilization of miraculous powers as well as by sheer force. He will see that all who wish to participate in the worldwide economic order have the "mark of the Beast" on their arm or forehead. Those who refuse to accept this mark will be slain or will risk starvation because they cannot buy food. Those who do accept it will eventually be cast with Satan and the Antichrist into a lake of fire for all eternity. For the next three and a half years, the Antichrist and the false prophet will oversee a reign of terror against all those who refuse allegiance to them. The Antichrist's reign will be challenged by a confederacy of northern nations headed by a commander that the Book of Ezekiel calls "Gog, of the land of Magog" (interpreted by most prophecy experts as Russia). The northern confederacy, assisted by a king of the south (probably Egypt), will threaten Israel before being devastated by earthquake and pestilence. Huge earthquakes will level mountains and cities, and a two-billion-member army from the east (probably China) will begin an assault on all those who survive these disasters. When the army of the east assembles outside Jerusalem for a final assault on the Holy City, Christ will seize the opportunity to return in glory to the earth to join the final battle of history, the Battle of Armageddon. Christ's armies will wreak such destruction that blood will flow as deep as a horse's bridle for a distance of two hundred miles. Christ will then slay both the Antichrist and the False Prophet and cast them into a lake of fire. Satan will be captured and bound in a bottomless pit, thereby inaugurating the long-awaited millennium.

Because most fundamentalists expect to be raptured, they do not plan to be present on earth to see this prophesied scenario unfold. Instead, their reward for knowing about the Antichrist in advance is that they will be permitted to escape the torture and cruelty that is certain to come to apostates of every kind.

The 1920s and After

By 1920, fundamentalism had emerged as a remarkable strand of American popular religion. American Protestantism had always had a core faction that was theologically conservative. But previously in American history, church leaders had articulated their faith in ways that might contribute to the "Christianization" of the wider culture. Religion, even conservative religion, was expected to embrace the social order, identify its most promising elements, and contribute to its gradual amelioration. By the second decade of the twentieth century, however, it was clear that those committed to an unyielding conservative theology had been displaced from center stage. Now at society's margins, they required a new theological strategy that would name those responsible for their displacement and assure them of their ultimate triumph. Fundamentalism was just such a strategy, as it articulated their collective judgment that the existing sources of authority and prestige in American culture were now beyond redemption. True Christians thus had no recourse but to separate themselves intellectually and socially from the defilements of apostate culture. Fundamentalism consequently distinguished itself from earlier forms of evangelical faith by putting less emphasis on what Bible-believing Christians should be *for* than on what they are to be *against*.

It is precisely this "over and againstness" that prompted historian George Marsden to insist that fundamentalism is as much a social phenomenon as it is a theological one. Marsden observed that fundamentalists reacted to their continued displacement from the cultural center of American life by creating their own equivalent of an ethnic identity:

> An overview of fundamentalism reveals them building a subculture with institutions, mores, and social connections that would eventually provide acceptable alternatives to the dominant cultural ethos. As in immigrant communities, religion played a central role in shaping their identity.[45]

Fundamentalism is, in this sense, an ideological resource on which white Protestants might draw as they seek to define themselves over and against all those who have stripped them of their former power base in American culture. Marsden pointed out that when their social base was badly eroded, something else had to give cohesion and define membership in the group. Lacking social, geographic, or ethnic measures of belonging, fundamentalists placed greater stress "on personal commitment and belief as the basis for solidarity. Certain key beliefs—inerrancy, anti-evolution, often premillennialism—gained importance as touchstones to ascertain whether a person belonged to the movement. Exactly correct belief then became proportionately more important to the movement as its social basis for cohesiveness decreased."[46]

From the time that the author(s) of 1 and 2 John addressed this beleaguered community, emphasis on "exactly correct belief" has frequently become the principal means of distinguishing between insiders and outsiders, followers of Christ and minions of the Antichrist. The list of those outside these theological boundaries continued to grow. In his popular tract *Jesus Is Coming*, William Blackstone identified the various popes in history and all Muslims as "types of Antichrist." He also believed that the atheistic and lawless trio of socialism, nihilism, and anarchy were the "immediate precursors of Antichrist."[47] William Riley's *The Menace of Modernism* added college professors to the lineup. Having served as a campus minister at the University of Minnesota, Riley knew only too well how many young persons fell into "soul danger" because of their intellectual tutelage under brilliant but irreverent professors. College professors, particularly those in the humanities and sciences, were bringing an entire generation to the brink of apostasy: "Almost without exception the biology professor in the present-day denominational college is a devotee of Darwinism. In nine cases out of ten, his opposition to Moses is in direct proportion to his defense of evolution; and his boast in the name of 'Science' commonly contains a sneer at Scripture."[48] Nor did the "againstness" of fundamentalism stop with criticism of popes, Muslims, and college professors. Jews, Catholics, blacks, socialists, and various stripes of secular humanists all were destined to join the growing circle of precursors of the Antichrist.

The Scopes Monkey Trial in Dayton, Tennessee, came to symbolize to most Americans just how far removed the fundamentalists were from the nation's cultural center. John Scopes, a young biology teacher fresh out of college, was put on trial in July 1925 for violating Tennessee's statute making it unlawful to teach "any theory which denies the theory of the Divine creation of man as taught in the Bible, and to teach instead that man is descended from a lower order of animals." The trial lasted for eleven days and attracted worldwide attention from the press, who used more than two million words to cover it. The judge barred any testimony on constitutional questions of civil liberties or on the validity of the Darwinian theory of evolution. The sole question at issue was whether Scopes had, or had not, actually taught the theory of evolution, a fact that should have taken only a minute or two to ascertain. The trial is often said to have resembled a prize fight more than a legal process, with famed criminal lawyer Clarence Darrow defending Scopes and squaring off against the equally famed politician William Jennings Bryan, who assisted the prosecution. The climax of the trial was Darrow's articulate cross-examination of Bryan, during which he revealed that Bryan was profoundly ignorant of biological science and even the Bible. Scopes was found guilty and fined $100, but public sentiment went resoundingly against the fundamentalist cause which came across to the nation as backward and intolerant. Efforts to restrict the teaching of evolution did not abate, however. At the annual convention of the World's Christian Fundamentals Association in 1927, William Bell Riley led the effort to push for antievolution laws in every state. This movement was supported by George Washburn's Bible Crusaders of America and Gerald B. Winrod's Defenders of the Christian Faith. Only two other states, Mississippi and Arkansas, ever adopted antievolution laws, but it was clear that fundamentalism had stirred up a grassroots sentiment against modern science that seemed incompatible with either Christian doctrine or moral decency.

Many Americans, especially those with a college education and who were more likely to occupy prestigious positions in American society, assumed that fundamentalism had disappeared after its somewhat comical stand against science and freedom of expression in 1925. Nothing could be further from the case. Far from being confined to the backwoods of Kentucky or Tennessee, fundamentalism has had a major influence on the restructuring of Americans' religious affiliations throughout the rest of the twentieth century. Internal dissension created splits within the nation's Baptist and Presbyterian churches early in the century. Lutherans eventually divided sharply along ideological lines as well. All three of these denominations have seen more than their share of bitter infighting and have endured the emergence of splinter groups that permanently polarized their constituencies along liberal–conservative lines. A host of new denominations have also appeared, each self-consciously aligned with fundamentalist principles and each ranking among the century's most rapidly growing organizations: Assemblies of God, Church of the Nazarene, Seventh-Day Adventists, Jehovah's Witnesses (who, frequently called the Russellites, were sharply rebuked by other fundamentalist groups for their distinctive renderings of apocalyptic teachings), as well as innumerable locally and regionally organized "Bible churches."[49] Numerous Bible colleges and seminaries were created to combat modernism's dominance in higher education. The Moody Bible Institute in Chicago, Bible Institute of Los Angeles, Fuller Theological Seminary in California, and Dallas Theological Seminary all became centers for dispensationalist, premillennial religious belief. Fundamentalism also entered publishing and the airwaves. Magazines such as *Moody Monthly, The Sword of the Lord, End-Times News Digest, Bible Prophecy News,* and *Rapture Alert Newsletter* have kept Americans updated on state-of-the-art understandings of the nature and identity of the Antichrist. Countless radio programs and televangelist productions from the likes of Billy Graham, Rex Humbard, and Pat Robertson have similarly helped millions place the "signs of the times" in cosmic context. All told, fundamentalism has proved resilient over the long haul of the twentieth century and has clearly managed to galvanize resistance to the forces of modernism.

A word of caution is in order against any simplistic identification of apocalyptic name-calling with members of fundamentalist-leaning denominations. Most persons who have chosen to belong to religious groups on the far right of the American theological spectrum have done so for what might be called "prophetic" rather than apocalyptic reasons. They have been drawn to the clear articulation of Bible-based teachings in an era that otherwise seems to lack a moral or spiritual compass. Preserving inherited values, not focusing hate on others, has been the dominant tone in the homes of most religiously fundamentalist American homes. Historians of American fundamentalism, such as George Marsden, Ernest Sandeen, and Nancy Ammerman, are certainly correct in identifying premillennialism (and the accompanying emphasis on separatism) as the single theological doctrine that most distinguishes fundamentalism from other forms of religious conservativism. The premillennial categories of fundamentalist thought have not only encouraged its adherents to interpret their lives in mythic terms but have also given distinct form and identity to the mythic beast who is responsible for every worldly frustration they encounter. To this extent, then, we can also assert that fundamentalism has provided a theological home for the apocalyptic world view out of which naming the Antichrist has developed.

Fundamentalist literature of the 1920s and after reveals just how well the movement succeeded at creating a subculture at odds with the nation's democratic heritage. The movement's commitment to biblical inerrancy, separatism, and premillennial apocalypticism simultaneously disenfranchised it from traditional American ideals. In his summary of the evangelist Billy Sunday's theological outlook, historian William McLoughlin captured the increasing discrepancy between fundamentalism and American democratic values. As McLoughlin put it, Sunday had proclaimed

> freedom of religion applied to all—except to Unitarians, Universalists, atheists, Mohammedans, Hindus, Confucianists, Mormons, Christian Scientists, theosophists, Russellites, and Modernists. All men were born equal—except Negroes and foreigners. Church and state must be separated—except that Christianity should be written into the Constitution, no Roman Catholic should be eligible for the Presidency, there should be a Bible in every schoolroom, all teachers should be converted Christians, and anything contrary to the most literal interpretation of the Bible should be prohibited by law from the curriculum of the public schools.[50]

The "over and againstness" that gave fundamentalism its *raison d'être* would require the continuing presence of enemies both real and imagined. Now that fundamentalism had succeeded in creating a widespread theological subculture steeped in premillennial convictions, the American obsession with the Antichrist was destined to enjoy a renaissance.

Five

Crusades of Hate

This crusade . . . is a call to all the lovers of Jesus Christ to stand against the onslaught of the anti-Christs.

Gerald L. K. Smith, 1948

❧

No form of hatred is as cruel or unmitigating as religious hate. Unfortunately the middle decades of the twentieth century experienced more than their fair share of religious strife. The period roughly between World War I and the start of the Cold War spawned a number of pious crusades designed to exterminate the enemies of Christ. New threats to fundamentalist Christianity's claim to the nation's cultural center kept coming from every possible direction: continued immigration, the northward migration of black workers, the rise of unions and socialist organizations, the Bolshevik revolution in Russia and the consequent threat of worldwide Communist insurrection, the Depression, Roosevelt's expansion of the powers of government through his New Deal programs, international political organizations such as the United Nations, and the sustained infiltration of "modernist" ideas into the nation's schools and churches. In the eyes of Christian fundamentalists, the Antichrist was marching right through the country unopposed. More and more territory was being lost to the forces of chaos with each passing day. Reaction was called for: Enemies needed to be properly identified; strategies of resistance defined, and for this, the apocalyptic tradition of "naming the Antichrist" proved an invaluable resource.

Conservative Christianity contains a strongly prophetic dimension. That is, it offers a source of revealed truth that can be brought to bear on the interpretation of society's moral and spiritual failings. Writers and preachers committed to biblical inerrancy have time and again called their followers to take stock of the nation's current commitments and to rededicate themselves to the religious values of their forefathers. Writing in 1920, the editor of the ultraconservative tract *The Presbyterian* offered precisely such an interpretation of what he called "the American Crisis." His essay typifies the conservative religious community's assessment of the moral and spiritual challenges facing twentieth-century life. It is at once prophetic and reactionary, calling for an examination of conscience and a return to a worldview in jeopardy of being left behind:

> It must be remembered that America was born of moral progenitors and founded on an eternally moral foundation. Her ancestors were Christian of a high order, purified by fire, and washed in blood. Her foundation is in the Bible, the infallible Word of God. . . . There has been some weakening of this moral standard in the thought and life of America. This is the result of an age of luxury within and freedom from conflict from without. There is but one remedy: the nation must return to her standard of the Word of God. . . . She must restore the Bible to its historic place in the family, the day school, the college and university, the church and Sabbath-school, and thus through daily life and thought revive and build up her moral life and faith, or else she might collapse and fail the world in this crucial age.[1]

This call for a return to simple Bible truths is characteristic of the conservative evangelical response to the modern world. It is in many ways a timeless and universal mode of religious exhortation. Its admonishments and encouragements have their counterparts in almost every time period and every region of the world. Most twentieth-century evangelicals, however, have retained intellectual allegiance to these categories while simultaneously adjusting themselves to the more pluralistic and secularist forms of American life. That is, most American religious conservatives have managed to find themselves at home in the modern world. The message they hear in exhortations such as the passage just cited is thus largely prophetic in nature. It calls for them to witness to religious values while actively participating in the world. Apocalyptic categories of separatism and world denunciation, insofar as they attended to at all, are consequently relegated to a theological back burner.

What distinguishes fundamentalists from other conservative evangelicals is their refusal to adjust to the modern era. Their commitment to biblical inerrancy and to premillennial categories leads them to adopt a stridently separatist attitude. Rather than accommodating the world about them, fundamentalists are suspicious of it. Armed with an apocalyptic reading of history, fundamentalists are certain of ultimate victory and are thus emboldened to denounce their adversaries in the severest terms. Fundamentalist thought is anchored on millennialist beliefs that

divide the world into two contrasting groups: the forces of Christ and
the forces of the Antichrist. This apocalyptic understanding of its enemies creates what historian Martin Marty terms the "crisis mentality"
underlying modern fundamentalism: "Such dramatic and dualistic readings of sacred texts and renderings of metahistory provide fundamentalists with a cosmic enemy, imbue fundamentalist boundary-setting
and purity-preserving activities with an apocalyptic urgency, and foster a crisis mentality that serves both to intensify missionary efforts and
to justify extremism."[2]

As distinct from other forms of conservative religion, fundamentalism requires confrontation and opposition. It requires a worthy adversary. As Marty points out, "Fundamentalists name, dramatize, and
even mythologize their enemies. . . . Indeed, the identification and elabo-
ration of the enemy is often the initial step in the fundamentalist rhetoric
of negation and the development of a contra-acculturative orientation."[3]
The act of naming the Antichrist is thus central to twentieth-century
fundamentalists' identity as a separate people. It has helped explain the
"true" source of the social dislocation and cognitive dissonance that
many Americans have endured since the onset of modernity while being
assured that the tables will soon be reversed.

The story of the twentieth-century Antichrist is thus in large part
the story of naming, dramatizing, and mythologizing the enemies of
ultraconservative Protestantism. It is, for this reason, intimately connected with the "nativistic" strain of American social history. As John
Higham and others demonstrated, American history reveals a recurrent
nativistic response to any "foreign influence" that leads to conflicts over
power, status, or resources.[4] Struggling to define and preserve a distinct
national identity, White Anglo-Saxon Protestants have constantly felt
threatened by the appearance of foreign institutions (e.g., Roman Catholicism), foreign ideologies (e.g., socialism), or foreign immigrants. Nativism represents the attempt to define American identity in opposition
to such foreign elements. Nativism is not only inherently reactionary
but also characteristically "conspiratorial" in outlook. That is, there is
in American history a certain legacy of conceptualizing the world in
conspiratorial terms, a tendency to perceive continuing and even diabolical threats to the nation's political and moral order.[5] Typical of such
conspiratorial thinking is the conviction that foreign powers pose an
imminent danger to the security of the nation, if not by outright invasion, then through immigration and other means of infiltration. Also
associated with the conspiratorial outlook are the belief that only
American Protestants can guarantee the preservation of individual
liberty or public virtue, the fear of betraying the priceless heritage of
the founding fathers, and grave concerns over the possibility that
Americans' superiority might be diluted through interracial or inter-
religious contact.

Twentieth-century efforts to name the Antichrist have been prime carriers of this nativistic and conspiratorial strain of American intellectual tendencies. Jews, labor unions, blacks, socialists, Catholics, and liberal government leaders all have been implicated in the grand plot of the Antichrist to dissolve America into a lawless, immoral state. To be sure, fundamentalist theology did not itself create twentieth-century nativism. However, many of those white Protestant Americans who were most likely to fear dislocation were culturally linked to a scriptural heritage that provided metaphors for the chaos to be unleashed against the faithful in the final days. These metaphors, once applied to events and persons in the surrounding world, easily take on a life of their own. Thus Richard Hofstadter found that the apocalyptic categories of fundamentalist thought have historically accentuated what he termed the "paranoid style" of nativist American thought. The distinguishing characteristic of the paranoid style, according to Hofstadter, is not that its exponents see conspiracies or plots here and there in history. It is, rather, that "they see conspiracy as the motive force of history itself. History is a conspiracy, set in motion by demonic forces of almost transcendental power."[6] The paranoid style of conceptualizing the world is one that identifies and characterizes enemies in apocalyptic terms. As Hofstadter put it, "This enemy is clearly delineated: he is a perfect model of malice, a kind of amoral superman: sinister, ubiquitous, powerful, cruel, sensual, luxury-loving."[7] Events that affect us adversely are thus not understood as part of the give-and-take of socioeconomic existence but as the consequences of a demonic will directed precisely at those who would resist it. Since what is at stake is nothing short of the struggle between absolute good and absolute evil, no compromise is possible. The enemy—the Antichrist—has plotted the overthrow of all that is good and holy and the forces of good must rally in obedience to thwart him at every turn.

Nativist sentiment in the middle decades of the twentieth century produced a host of hate-filled campaigns to name and exterminate the Antichrist in all of his clever disguises. Leading these campaigns were several "apostles of discord" adept at identifying the Antichrist during the era's socioeconomic unrest. Among those who flamed the fires of American religious paranoia in this era were Gerald B. Winrod, Gerald L. K. Smith, and Carl McIntire.[8] Winrod was a Baptist evangelist who organized the Defenders of the Christian Faith to combat the spread of evolutionary teaching in the schools. In the mid-1930s he traveled to Europe where Hitler's initiatives against the Jews earned his sympathy. Upon returning home he redoubled his efforts to expose the Jewish menace in the United States and to reveal Roosevelt's "Jewish New Deal" as the satanic threat he knew it to be. His *Defender Magazine*, which reached more than a hundred thousand households by the late 1930s, fed anxious readers with what historian Sydney Ahlstrom called "a diet

of bigotry and fear, as well as Fundamentalist theology, rugged indi-
vidualism, and anticommunism."[9]

No less a hate monger and anti-Semite was Gerald L. K. Smith.
Smith used his *Cross and the Flag* to alert Americans of conspiracies to
abolish Christian civilization, erect Jewish Communism, mongrelize the
white race, and dilute American national traditions through immigration. To combat these forces of disruption, Smith launched the Christian Nationalist Crusade, which resonated clearly with the resentments
and "over and againstness" of so many twentieth-century premillennialists. In his periodical *The Cross and the Flag*, Smith explained that "this
Crusade is in no sense denominational or sectarian. It is a call and a
challenge to all lovers of Jesus Christ to stand together against the onslaught of anti-Christs."[10]

Meanwhile, Carl McIntire founded the fundamentalist weekly *Christian Beacon* which eventually gained a circulation of over 120,000.
McIntire also used his *Twentieth Century Reformation Hour* radio program
to condemn fellow Christians who chose a theology of affirmation and
love over his own brand of condemnation and hate. Denouncing liberal, ecumenically minded Christian clergy as "atheistic, communistic,
Bible-ridiculing, blood-despising, name-calling, sex-manacled sons of
green-eyed monsters," McIntire helped clarify the battle lines in the war
against an enemy who was often invisible to the uninformed.[11]

Defined and embellished by such demagogues of the Christian far
right, the Antichrist has loomed as a prime symbol of religious hate
throughout the twentieth century. It has helped transform the Jew living across town, the college professor teaching evolutionary biology,
the politician seeking social justice, and the minister urging interfaith
unity into treacherous agents of the devil. Going beyond any prophetic
attempt to return the nation to simple Bible teachings, the naming of
the Antichrist has instead fostered an obsession for eliminating conspiracies of every stripe. It has, in short, been the rallying cry for crusades of
hate.

The Antichrist as a Jew

Anti-Semitism has roots long predating the settling of the American
colonies. The very emergence of Christianity as a Jewish sect was destined to evoke Christian antipathy toward nonconverting Jews. Jews
have provided convenient scapegoats throughout the entire course of
Christian history. During the Middle Ages Jews were held responsible
for virtually every famine, war, or epidemic that threatened Christian
communities. Made to live in urban ghettos, Jews have rarely been
welcome participants in Western society. Chapter 3 of this book mentioned the early history of nativistic anti-Semitism in the United States.
Before the late 1870s, Jews still accounted for less than 1 percent of the

nation's population and therefore were not sufficiently threatening to be serious candidates for the mantle of the Antichrist. But this changed quickly with the immigration of more than 2.5 million Eastern European Jews between 1877 and 1924. Workers quickly came to fear their economic competition. Small businessmen feared their entrepreneurial acumen. Capitalists feared their unionism and radical ideologies. Rural folk feared their urban ways. And most of all, fundamentalists feared their stubborn commitment to apostate teachings. The Antichrist was about to reveal himself in new garb.

It is not difficult to understand why immigrant Jews evoked nativistic reactions. Eastern Europeans were "foreign" from the perspective of Americans descended from the British Isles. They looked different, spoke differently, and even ate food that smelled different. Most gravitated to the inner cities, which were already suspect in the eyes of those Americans with rural roots. Having been excluded from European agriculture, many Jewish immigrants turned to developing America's commercial sector. This flood of new business competition naturally led to a resurgence of the stereotype of the greedy, amoral, materialist Jewish businessman. Other Jews became skilled or unskilled laborers in America's notoriously exploitive industries. A discontented Jewish labor force responded to appalling work conditions by both developing a dynamic trade union movement and becoming involved in the growing socialist movement.[12] Jewish-led unions campaigned for improved work and safety conditions, higher wages, and sick benefits. They responded to factory owners' resistance to their requests by organizing effective strikes. For example, when members of the International Ladies' Garment Workers Union voted in favor of a general strike in 1909, twenty thousand workers walked off their jobs. Jewish involvement in the early union movement thus located them in the middle of the most volatile part of the nation's industrial economy.

The traditional Jewish emphasis on education combined with the typical immigrants "drive" to help Jews in their quest for upward economic mobility. Slowly but surely Jews entered the professions of law, banking, higher education, and medicine. The percentage of Jews in these fields eventually grew to two or three times the percentage of Jews in the overall population. Many Americans predictably begrudged Jews their success and became alarmed by the amount of "Jewish influence" in the United States. Somewhat compounding matters was the fact that many Jews also prospered in the entertainment industry. Music, comedy, radio, and film all benefited from the pioneering contributions of Jewish artists and producers. But with these successes came a backlash. The movie industry and modern jazz were frequently singled out as contributing to a libertine moral environment. The media and arts seemed to many to promote sensuality, glamour, and licentious lifestyles. All of this, of course, could be explained as part of a Jewish conspiracy to subvert American morality. Jewish business, economic, and political leaders were no less exempt from the conspiratorial obsession. Roosevelt, for example, called on the technical expertise of several Jewish leaders to help the nation out of its crippling depression. As the New Deal took shape, Jews were frequently blamed for the expansion of government powers and the unfamiliar political philosophies that sought to deal with the realities of modern life.

Anti-Semitic prejudice in the United States reached its historical peak in the quarter century following World War I. Ranging from informal daily bigotry to organized political campaigns expressly designed to suppress Jewish rights, Americans in unprecedented numbers had begun a crusade of hate. Policies to restrict Jewish immigration were enacted; colleges established quotas for Jewish enrollment; and everywhere intolerance became more socially acceptable. In all of this, fundamentalist Christians led the way. After all, there was a biblical warrant for hating Jews. The Bible records in detail how Jews repeatedly sinned against the Lord. They rejected and killed Christ. Bible prophecy is explicit that Jews are destined to make a pact with the Antichrist and assist this false Messiah in deceiving the world. Gerald Winrod explained that "because they rejected God's Christ, they will accept the Devil's Christ during the closing years of this age . . . they will accept the world's greatest Liar as their Messiah."[13] True, Bible prophecy explains that some Jews will finally recognize the true Messiah and convert to Christianity during the time of tribulations. But most will not find their names written in the Lamb's Book of Life and will be cast with the Antichrist into the lake of fire and brimstone. Because of their stubborn apostasy, little time need be wasted feeling sorry for the sufferings of Jews past, present, or future. They are simply receiving their just deserts. "The Jews as a nation," wrote premillennialist Henry Parsons, "were rejected and dispersed abroad, according to the threatened penalty of their refusing and slaying their King."[14] Or as Winrod put it, "the law of exact retribution placed the Jew nation under a curse, nineteen hundred years ago."[15] A people cursed by God were hardly fit for citizenship in a nation destined to emancipate the entire globe for Christ.

Students of the Bible had little difficulty convincing themselves that Jews were responsible for the social, economic, and political chaos that threatened many Americans in the 1920s and 1930s. Winrod was again a leader in finding proof of the Jewish plot against America. In his *The Jewish Assault on Christianity*, Winrod explained that from the time they assassinated Jesus and persecuted the apostles, Jews have sought to destroy Christianity and Christian civilization.[16] One particular group of Jews, the Tribe of Dan mentioned in the Bible, is particularly dangerous and has been entrusted by Satan to bring anarchy to the nation. According to Winrod, "While all Jews who reject Christ are in apostasy, yet the sons of Dan are farthest down the scale."[17] Winrod maintained that many Jewish immigrants to America were descendants of this infamous Tribe of Dan and that their seditious influence was already having an effect on the nation's moral fiber. He explained at length how Jews were doing everything in their power to create fear, envy, hatred, lust, drunkenness, vice, and all other forms of immorality. What is more, this conspiracy had already crept into the highest ranks of American society: "President Roosevelt may be of this tribe. It is now generally known that he comes from Dutch Jewish stock. At different times in the history of his ancestors, such family names as Rosenblum and Rosenberg have been used."[18]

Winrod, like other nativist Americans, knew that Jews were only semiautonomous beings, that Satan had linked their minds together so that they would act collectively in ways that would further his conspiracy against the forces of Christ. Of this Winrod had proof: Soon after becoming president, Roosevelt established diplomatic relations with Soviet Russia.

> Every thinking person knew, from the standpoint of true Americanism, that this was an unwise and foolish step to take. There was no reason, logic or common sense in the move. There is but one way to explain the fatal step which Roosevelt took and that is—his mind, and the mind of Moscow, must have flowed together as two drops of water.[19]

Gerald L. K. Smith preached a similar view of the Jewish plot to turn America over to the rule of Satan. What he referred to as "Franklin Roosevelt and his Jew advisers" were conspiring with Jewish bankers to destroy the American economic and political systems, thereby paving the way for the rise of the Antichrist.

Among the other conspiracies attributed to Jews was the dissemination of liberal philosophical and theological thought. Winrod's *Defender Magazine* maintained that Jews were the root of "Modernism, Higher Criticism, Rationalism, Evolutionism, Behaviorism, Freudianism, Communism, and Atheism [and] all other illegitimate children of so-called liberalism."[20] Jewish influence could also be detected in the Revised Standard Version of the Bible, the "modernistic" version of the Bible through which liberal Protestants were leading the nation into apostasy. Second only to such apostasy, however, the gravest of all Jewish plots against the people of God was Communism. As Winrod instructed, "All communism is of Jewish origin, financed by Jewish money and directed by Jewish minds."[21] Perhaps the zenith of this paranoia over the Jewish plot to enslave the world through Communism was the panic created by the infamous *Protocols of the Learned Elders of Zion*, a collection of forged documents that purported to expose a plot by "international Jewery" to rule the world. The *Protocols* were brought to the West by a group of exiles from Bolshevik Russia who claimed to possess documents proving that the revolution in their land had been a plot hatched by Jewish capitalists to seize control of every government in the world. Later proven to be forgeries, these documents were written with the hope of inciting the world to action against the Bolsheviks. To those who took the *Protocols* at face value, however, they offered "proof" of a Jewish masterplan to use both intellectual and political liberalism as a means of overthrowing Christian societies:

> By the severity of our doctrines, we shall triumph and shall enslave all governments under our supergovernment. . . . Do not think that our assertions are without foundation: note the successes of Darwinism, Marxism and Nietzcheism engineered by us. The demoralizing effects of these doctrines upon the minds of the Gentiles should already be obvious to us. . . . We will present ourselves in the guise of saviours of the workers from oppression when we suggest that they enter our army of Socialists, Anarchists, Communists, to whom we always extend our hand under the guise of the rule of the brotherhood demanded by the human solidarity of our social masonry.[22]

The *Protocols* appeared in a number of newspapers across the country but received the greatest attention in the Ford Company's publication the *Dearborn Independent*. Henry Ford, who had come to believe that Jewish bankers were responsible for the failure of his efforts in 1915 to achieve a cease-fire in Europe, was one of many Americans who found the *Protocols* to be proof of what he had already instinctively known: that all the world's ills were the result of Jewish machinations. Ford's four-volume compilation of these materials, *The International Jew*, provided a comprehensive theory of how recent immigration had brought this Jewish conspiracy right to America's own shores. Although Ford eventually became convinced that the *Protocols* were forgeries and apologized profusely, his efforts helped fixate hundreds of thousands of Americans on the notion of Jewish conspiracy. Arno Gaebelein, a premillennialist who otherwise denounced overt anti-Semitism, found *The International Jew*'s evidence "unimpeachable" and consistent with Bible prophecy.[23] Another premillennialist, Charles C. Cook, conceded that Roman Catholics might have forged the documents. But, Cook reasoned, the *Protocols* taught valuable lessons nonetheless:

> The Jewish race is morally fully capable of doing all that is charged against it. It is at present rejected of God, and in a state of disobedience and rebellion. . . . As a race Jews are gifted far beyond all other peoples, and even in their ruin, with the curse of God upon them, are in the front rank of achievement; but accompanying traits are pride, overbearing arrogance, inordinate love for material things, trickery, rudeness, and an egotism that taxes the superlatives of any language. . . . the unregenerate Jew usually has a very unattractive personality. There is a reason for his being *persona non grata* at resorts and in the best society: who can deny it?[24]

Winrod knew that forgery or not, the *Protocols* were consistent with what the Bible predicts would happen in the end time of this age: "The

Bible says that the Jews will return to their homeland. They will leave the nations in chaos, and take the wealth of the world with them. They will eventually accept a Superman as their Messiah, who is known to Bible students as the Antichrist."[25] Even as he wrote, Jewish capitalists were ruling Russia and despised the poor and struggling masses over whom they exercised supreme authority. Citizens of the United States must be alert, however, because the secret leaders of the worldwide Jewish conspiracy plan to use different methods in different nations. "Thus, in Italy, England and the United States, where the nations are friendly, they would use entirely different tactics than they did in Russia."[26] With this in mind Winrod thought it ominous that Franklin Delano Roosevelt had just been installed as president, pledging to help America enter a new period of liberalism that would require unity of purpose. More directly to his point, he suggested that

> it is also significant to note how many Jews he has appointed to the powerful offices of government. His revolutionary farm bill, which has been condemned for its Communistic principles, is said to have been prepared by a Jewish member of his "Brain Trust" who acquired the basic ideas for it while in Soviet Russia. If these suspicions are grounded in truth, it is not difficult to see in which direction the leading nations are drifting. The movements of current history seem to confirm what the prophecies indicate, namely, that prior to the Second Coming of Christ the Jewish nation will emerge holding the position of dominant power.[27]

Christians are to be exceptionally cautious, for "the plan provides for the killing of preachers and the bombing of churches when the hour of revolution comes, and the signal is given for the conspirators to strike, here in the United States."[28]

For centuries the symbol of Christians' archenemy, the Antichrist was naturally the most befitting designation for Jews. Although scholars had often vacillated between the Jewish or Roman heritage of the end-times "beast," the matter was less murky for mid-twentieth-century fundamentalists. Gerald Winrod's *Antichrist and the Tribe of Dan* unequivocally declared that "there is no question but what Antichrist will be a Jew."[29] Arno Gaebelein, a much-respected premillennial writer, weighed the evidence and also concluded that Bible prophecy offers unmistakable proof that the Antichrist will be a Jew.[30] Not all premillennialists would agree on this technical point, but all certainly know that Bible prophecy is clear that Jews will at the very least make a pact with the Antichrist and thereby participate in his confederacy of evil. It was thus plausible to mid-century premillennialists that Jews were fostering almost every conceivable form of radical and subversive activity that would pave the way for the Antichrist's reign. The United States was under the control of the Jewish brain trust. Russia was governed by secret Jewish leaders. Great Britain and France were ruled by the international Jewish money power. The handwriting was on the wall:

A Jewish Antichrist, in the end of this age, presupposes an international system of Jewish government. There can be little doubt that such a system, based upon the Jewish money power, has already been created—and is ready to step into the open and assume control of world affairs as soon as the time is ripe.[31]

The entanglement of Jews with the Second Coming has had profound consequences for Americans' attitudes toward foreign policy and, in particular, toward the modern nation of Israel. Students of Bible prophecy have known for centuries that the entire end-times scenario hinges on the existence of a restored Jewish state in Palestine. Without such a restored Israel, the day of triumph and revenge will never come. Premillennialism consequently gave rise to what might be called Protestant Zionism, the intensely pro-Israel stance among precisely those rightist Protestants who in other contexts were anti-Semitic.[32] Prominent dispensationalists such as William Blackstone assumed leadership in the advocacy of Zionism and were jubilant at every step leading to the final creation of Israel in 1948. Such commitment to Bible prophecy, incidentally, has on many occasions tempered or even wholly eliminated anti-Semitism among premillennialist Christians. Winrod, Smith, and McIntire all at one time or another publicly denounced anti-Semitism, as do most fundamentalist leaders today.

Such pro-Israeli sentiments and public disclaimers of any anti-Semitism notwithstanding, however, premillennialist belief is inherently laden with condescension and prejudice. Judgments about Jews are not made on the grounds of just or moral reasons but on whether Bible prophecy is being confirmed. For example, Israel's persistent militarism and its inhumane treatment of Palestinians have been tacitly endorsed as integral to the fulfillment of Bible prophecy. But these kinds of judgments cut both ways. Over and beyond being rejectors of Christ, Jews are in the final analysis not really persons to be understood or valued in their own right. They are pawns in God's salvation history, a history that assigns them significance only as actors in preparatory dispensations, not as persons to be redeemed in the final dispensation. Premillennialist Dave Hunt, for example, wrote that

> modern Israel has many faults, which we do not excuse and for which she will yet taste God's judgment. She is back in her land not because of her own merit, but because God is fulfilling His promises to Abraham, Isaac, and Jacob as He swore that He would in the last days.[33]

Even more illustrative of fundamentalism's tendency to view Jews in mythological categories is Arthur Bloomfield's contention that Hitler's policies toward the Jews were perfectly in keeping with God's use of this race. That is, the Holocaust was a just chastisement of a wayward race and a divinely directed step toward effecting the next dispensation. After all, Palestine could not support twenty million Jews, and therefore God had to see that the number of Jews was reduced before returning them to their homeland. Hitler helped make it clear to the Jews that they could be happy and live in peace only if they had their own nation, thereby helping create the restored Israel that would make it possible for Gentiles to receive their deserved eternal rewards.[34] Christians should help protect Jews, Bloomfield warned. The reason for doing so, however, is not that it is morally noble or even politically prudent, but because their possession of Israel is a necessary precondition of the Second Coming.

Apocalyptic belief, then, may take the form of patronizing "affection for our Jewish friends," but it continues to perpetuate ancient prejudice and spite.

Stalking the Papal Beast

Nativism goes beyond prejudice aimed at a particular ethnic group. It consists of a more generalized opposition to any "foreign element" perceived as unworthy of being assimilated into the American cultural order. Such nativist sentiment has existed throughout American history and has been directed at many racial and ethnic groups.[35] To be sure, Roman Catholicism has been its most steady target. The roots of this intense anti-Catholicism go back to more than a century before the first wave of Puritans immigrated to New England in an effort to rid themselves of every last vestige of papist influence. Beginning with the Reformation, Protestants have historically viewed Catholicism as a hopeless amalgamation of heresies and superstitions. American Protestants are thus linked with a historical heritage that has consistently portrayed the Roman Catholic Church as a rival to the "true gospel faith" of the Reformers and, consequently, as part of Satan's conspiracy to delude innocent souls.

A respected historian of American nativism, John Higham, suggested that there have been four particularly acute episodes of anti-Catholic nativism.[36] The first such episode took place roughly in the years just before the American Revolution when the cry of the "papal Antichrist" rallied colonists against Catholic France and, later, against the king of England (who, after all, was the head of the papal-like Anglican Church). The second period of intense anti-Catholicism came in the 1850s when the massive Catholic immigration from Ireland and Germany incited fears of subversion from foreign powers and stimulated the emergence of the Know-Nothing Party. In the late 1880s a third period of anti-Catholicism began when the social strains accompanying modernism exacerbated latent resentments against all things new or foreign. This era, that of the American Protective Association, once again witnessed apocalyptic renderings of the Catholic Beast.

The fourth outbreak of nativist sentiment, according to Higham, was

the decade after the Bolshevik revolution in 1914 when socioeconomic
strains in American life led to a resurgence of the Ku Klux Klan. Not
coincidentally, this fourth episode of anti-Catholic nativism emerged as
part of the resurgence of apocalyptic, premillennial thinking in fundamentalist circles. Premillennialist imagery concerning Satan's conspiracies against the faithful has enabled twentieth-century Protestants to keep
the Catholic menace in proper cosmic perspective. Writing for one of the
many prophecy conferences early in the formation of modern fundamentalism, Henry Parsons made sure that no premillennialist would misun-
derstand the true nature of the Catholic menace: "Without doubt the
Roman Church is an illustrious and conspicuous and continued repre-
sentation of the spirit of Antichrist manifesting itself through the age."[37]

Apocalyptic categories have helped twentieth-century fundamentalists see that Roman Catholicism is more than a heresy. Catholicism
is destined to be intimately associated with the revived Roman confederacy that will arise in the end times to tyrannize the globe and persecute
loyal followers of Christ. Bible prophecy, it seems, predicts the emergence of an all-powerful, one-world religious system that will impose
apostasy on the world as part of the tribulation period. Variously referred
to as Babylon, the Scarlet Woman, or the Great Harlot, premillennialists
from Cotton Mather to Hal Lindsey have insinuated that Roman Catholicism is the nucleus around which this colossal abomination will emerge.
Arno Gaebelein, for example, contended that Revelation's references
to the apostate Babylon could have no other meaning than papal Rome.
A champion of biblical inerrancy, Gaebelein's anti-Catholicism was
strong enough to justify an important exception to his otherwise unre-
lenting insistence on the literal interpretation of the Bible. Reminding
us that "there is another Roman revival predicted," Gaebelein explained
that "it is a grave error for anyone to go to Revelation, a book so decidedly symbolical, and say that the symbolical term Babylon means the
literal Babylon. . . . The Babylon of Revelation is Papal Rome."[38]

Other apocalyptic writers connected with the fundamentalist cause
have associated Catholicism with the "scarlet woman" or great harlot
mentioned in Revelation 17. As the "harlot" that persists in infidelity
to Christ and sells out to all the false religions of the world, the Catholic
Church is destined to be revived as a source of world power and to play
an integral part in the Antichrist's last stand against the followers of
Christ. The premillennialist preacher I. M. Haldeman delivered a sermon, "The Scarlet Woman," just before World War I, in which he expressed the modern era's apocalyptic account of the Catholic Church:

> It is the prophecy that the Roman Catholic Church will again be car-
> ried and supported by nations of the Roman earth, and will once more
> rule and reign with temporal power.
> It is the divine forecast of the revival of Romanism.
> THIS REVIVAL HAS ALREADY BEGUN.[39]

The revival of the Ku Klux Klan in 1915 carried nativist hatred to new extremes. Whereas the first Klan, founded in 1866, was small and exclusively antiblack, the revived Klan was more widespread and included strong elements of anti-Semitism and anti-Catholicism.[40] With many informal links to the fundamentalist ministries of persons such as Gerald L. K. Smith, the Klan was a principal voicepiece of the ultraright's religious disdain for Catholicism. In his infamous 1926 essay "The Klan's Fight for Americanism," Hiram Wesley Evans vented the widespread belief that "the Roman Church is, fundamentally and irredeemably, in its leadership, in politics, in thought, and largely in membership, actually and actively alien, un-American and usually anti-American."[41] Old-stock Americans, he explained, see the Roman Church as a dangerous alien power with a foothold inside American boundaries. Catholics, led by foreign-born priests,

> vote almost as a unit, under control of leaders of their own faith, always in support of the interests of the Catholic Church and of Catholic candidates without regard to other interests, and always also in support of alienism whenever there is an issue raised. They vote, in short, not as American citizens but as aliens and Catholics![42]

Obsession with Catholics' unpatriotic voting patterns continued in earnest through the election of John F. Kennedy in 1960. Throughout this period, premillennialist literature kept alive the legacy of the "papal Antichrist."[43] To be sure, overt anti-Catholicism among Protestant fundamentalists has waned in recent decades, with other "modernist" foes supplanting the preoccupation with Catholics. The large numbers of Catholics in the United States have also made them seem less subversive, even if no less objectionable. Yet premillennialist literature speculating on Rome's role in the end-times scenario keeps these ancient prejudices alive and within easy intellectual reach of millions of contemporary Americans.

For example, David Webber's 1976 volume published by Southwest Radio Church, *Countdown for Antichrist*, explicitly listed Pope Paul VI as likely to be revealed as the awaited Antichrist.[44] More recently, Southest Radio Church's Noah Hutchings focused prophetic attention on Pope John Paul II. Hutchings was impressed by the fact that the pope had survived an assassination attempt, thereby fulfilling the prophecy in Revelation concerning the Beast's surviving a mortal wound. (Revelation 13: 3 reads, "One of its heads seemed to have a mortal wound, but its mortal wound was healed, and the whole earth followed the beast with wonder.") From this obvious connection with Bible prophecy Hutchings concluded that

> in Pope John Paul we see a man who is rising in international stature, a man who will be increasingly called upon to bring peace to a troubled world. His recovery from a deadly wound directed world attention and

admiration to his personage, and he, like those before him, would seemingly like to establish authority over the Holy Hill of Zion.[45]

Bible prophecy experts John Ankenberg and John Weldon similarly linked the pope with the message of the Antichrist.[46] In his *One World Under Antichrist*, Peter Lalonde instructs his readers that "the Roman Catholic Church is indeed at the core of Mystery Babylon."[47] Other end-times writers such as Dave Hunt suggest that the Roman Catholic Church will rise as the "false prophet" who will assist the Antichrist in his quest to be worshiped by the entire planet. The pope, Hunt writes, is "the ideal partner for the Antichrist in ruling what will be a worldwide kingdom of darkness."[48] Thus whether insinuated to be the Scarlet Woman, the False Prophet, or the Antichrist himself, Catholics have by no means lost their privileged status in Protestants' prophetic interpretations of the world.

The Menace of Socialism

Modernism confronted the "old pioneer stock" with much more than a set of new ideas.[49] It was also an economic revolution caused by the maturing of the Industrial Revolution in the United States. The nation's gross national product was six times higher in 1900 than it was at the end of the Civil War. Basic industry grew, with the production of rolled iron and steel increasing more than twelvefold in the last three decades of the nineteenth century, leading to the rapid expansion of such industries as transportation, construction, and manufacturing. A new class of capitalist emerged in America; small in number but with fortunes unimaginable just a generation earlier. What historians call the "Gilded Age" was, however, gilded for only an elect few. The great profits earned by those with investment capital were not shared with the unskilled workers, usually immigrants, who had little to show for their hard labor. The wages for unskilled laborers were generally below the subsistence level for a family. Working-class families thus needed the incomes of women and often even children just to survive. In 1890, for example, one out of every five children held a job. Working conditions were notoriously poor. Long hours, poor wages, and unsafe machinery made the plight of even skilled workers difficult, but for unskilled workers it was often a nightmare.

To make things even worse, the economy underwent wild fluctuations. Accompanying the boom periods were major contractions and depressions that almost instantly gobbled up fortunes and added whole households to the ranks of the unemployed. Stock markets, cartels, and cyclical downturns of varying duration were beyond the understanding of those reared in a predominantly agrarian economy. No one really knew how to explain, much less control, this new economic order, but there was always someone who could be blamed.

The rifts among different socioeconomic groups grew larger. The industrial economy seemed to have a centrifugal effect on the social order, forcing groups further and further apart from one another. Even in colonial times the differences between rural/agrarian and urban/mercantile were capable of launching witch hunts. But none of this prepared Americans for the great gulf between the wealthy capitalists and the impoverished workers or, for that matter, even the great discrepancy in the working class between skilled craftsmen and unskilled laborers. In general, members of the "old pioneer stock" were better situated to take advantage of business opportunities and to situate themselves well compared with recent immigrants. Rivalries and fierce competition ensued not only between enfranchised WASPS and immigrants but among immigrant groups as well. Each new wave of Jewish, Irish, Italian, Chinese, and Hispanic immigration helped transform the national "melting pot" into a steam cooker under great pressure.

The formation of unions and the rise of socialism as a viable force in American politics were largely rooted in the working class's efforts to adapt to the modern industrial order.[50] Skilled craftsmen were attracted to the craft-labor movement known as the Federation of Organized Trades and Labor Unions which was formed in 1881 and reorganized as the American Federation of Labor (AFL) in 1886. The AFL was strongly influenced by socialist philosophy and gradually helped organize local craft unions into a national labor network. It might be added that many leading labor organizers were Jewish, furthering the impression, in many Americans' minds, of the union movement's "foreignness" and "conspiracy." A competitor of the AFL, the Knights of Labor, flourished among the Irish American population and even included a large number of African-American workers, with its membership soaring to over 500,000 in the 1880s.

With unionization came workers' strikes, many violent. The nationwide railroad strike of 1877, the Pullman strike of 1894, the coal miners' strike of 1902, and the Chicago packinghouse strike of 1904 sent shock waves throughout the country and became symbols of the tensions inherent in the nation's economic structure. Whereas the AFL and Knights had confined their efforts largely to craft workers and had been reticent about entering politics directly, the Industrial Workers of the World (IWW) emerged in 1905 with more explicitly socialist goals. Appealing to unskilled workers, the IWW led its members in a series of confrontational and violent strikes. In 1919 there were more labor strikes than in any other year in American history. Government at all levels began to intervene in these strikes, beginning a backlash by the enfranchised population against upstart immigrant radicals and their left-leaning philosophies.

Socialism grew up alongside the union movement as yet another "foreign" threat to the existing American order. In one sense, socialism had long roots in the American experience. Various kinds of utopian communes had sprouted throughout the nineteenth century, each espousing some kind of idealistic philosophy that might be termed socialistic. Brook Farm, the Amana colonies, Oneida, New Harmony, and the philosophical teachings of Robert Owen and Charles Fourier all spread the seeds of such idealistic socialism in American soil. Yet the new, more Marxist socialism of the industrial era was largely an immigrant response to the realities of American economic and political life. This new kind of socialism, often referred to as *scientific socialism*, was based on the overt recognition of class conflict. The socialist labor movement headed by the immigrant Jewish intellectual Daniel de Leon was one of the first institutional expressions of such a socialist outlook. De Leon believed that all political structures were oppressive to workers and espoused anarchical views that gave the labor movement a radical tone. In 1902 the Socialist Party of America emerged under the leadership of Eugene Debs and, by 1910, had a membership of over 60,000. In the decade between 1902 and 1912 American socialism enjoyed its so-called golden age. The fact that the socialist weekly *Appeal to Reason* reached a national circulation of 500,000 during this period offers some idea of the movement's popular appeal. In 1912 more than 2,000 socialists served in public offices, and the future of the movement seemed bright.

By the onset of World War I, however, nativistic reactions began to mount against the labor movement and socialism. The Bolshevik revolution in Russia in 1917 symbolized fears of the socialist presence in America, and the nation swung dramatically against leftist influences of every kind. Strikes had crippled the economy, and the government acted swiftly to curtail the power of unions to organize workers in ways that would lead to open conflict with company management. Socialism, from the start riddled with internal dissensions over philosophical issues, went into rapid decline as popular opinion changed and various agrarian and mining groups withdrew their support. The emerging Communist Party picked up some of the remaining leftist sympathizers, including many children of Jewish socialists drawn to the idealistic and intellectual dimensions of the Communist agenda. The Communist Party carried forward the radical political outlook spawned by the early union movement and had some success recruiting members in the 1920s and, during the 1930s, had considerable influence on the labor unions (particularly the CIO). But the Communist movement also dissipated quickly because of both the continued hostility toward union strikes and the general economic and social turmoil caused by the Great Depression of the 1930s.

When President Franklin Roosevelt expanded the powers of government in order to get the country out of the Depression, he incorporated many socialist conceptions, thereby eliminating the perceived need for a separate socialist or communist party. His "New Deal" programs, including the National Recovery Act (NRA), rescued America from economic chaos and brought a new level of social conscience to American government. It also confirmed the worst fears of the "paranoid-style" of American nativist thought; that is, to many it appeared that foreign conspirators, probably Jews, were seizing hold of the country's highest offices and molding the country into an unrecognizable form. The "radical right" soon began voicing its resentments against unions, socialism, communism, and New Deal politics. As Seymour Lipset notes in his analysis of the radical right, political movements that successfully appeal to status resentments typically do so by identifying a scapegoat.[51] Unionists, socialists, communists, and liberal politicians all came under fire in this new round of status politics, and all were revealed by the premillennialists as agents of the Antichrist.

In the eyes of dislocated "pioneer stock" businessmen, the unions represented a united front of opposition. Dispensationalist writer Arno Gaebelein understood well the threat to WASP freedom and independence, explaining how the Antichrist's economic system was already taking shape in "the great trades-unions to which all will have to belong on pain of death."[52] Albert Sims also believed that the trade union movement was an obvious plot to inaugurate the Antichrist's world economic system. Sims noted that Revelation prophesied that during the tribulation, no one would be able to buy or sell without the mark of the Beast. He wrote that "union-made" labels were to be found in increasing number, indicating the beginning of "the worldwide influence of Antichrist's mark."[53] Sims charged that because unions were clearly precursors of the Antichrist's rule, Christians must avoid joining or having any association with unions.

Charles Hudson, editor of the weekly *America in Danger*, similarly played on the middle class's fears of being edged out of their jobs by unions. Hudson also warned of the possibility of a union-led socialist revolution that would confiscate their private property. In a 1938 editorial he wrote,

> CIO and radical A F of L unions . . . can and will, when "Der Tag" (sometime prior to 1941) is decided upon by the Hidden Hand, plunge cities into darkness, shut off water, gas, phone, telegraph, radio, food, and transportation generally, so that in terror imposed by fear, thirst and starvation, the weak-kneed NEW DEAL politician, businessman, and labor leader in most large cities are expected to surrender to Anti-Christ dictatorship.[54]

Protestant fundamentalists were also capable of seeing the ominous sides of big business and unscrupulous capitalism. Arno Gaebelein, for example, criticized the labor unions for being in league with the Antichrist at one moment but at other times chastised the rich for their extravagant and frivolous misuse of wealth while the poor starved.[55] Historian Paul Boyer observed that anticapitalist themes surfaced in many

Depression-era prophecy treatises. One writer proclaimed that "God hates Big Business [and the] spirit of commercialism." He went on to warn that a rebuilt Babylon would emerge as the world's "commercial center" in the last days, but—modern capitalists should take heed—the destruction of this commercial center would be "quick and complete and terrible." Another pointed out that "the great prophecy against capitalism in the epistle of James" symbolized "the whole idea of commerce."[56] Jehovah's Witnesses, meanwhile, preached that Satan was working his evil will in the world through a "triple alliance" of conspiracy. These three vehicles of the devil—the apostate churches, secular government, and big business—were symbols of the tyranny to be exercised against the faithful of God in the last days. Careful to restrict their use of the term *antichrist* to persons "who deny what the Bible says against Christ" as 1 and 2 John use the term, Jehovah's Witnesses have nonetheless aimed apocalyptic suspicion at greedy business practices that exploit society's disenfranchised.[57]

For all the alienation and disenfranchisement that twentieth-century fundamentalists have experienced at the hands of capitalism, socialism and communism have always appeared more sinister. One reason is undoubtedly their foreignness, which alone gives rise to the suspicion of conspiracy. Second, as a social class, fundamentalists have felt themselves to be more integral to, and potentially successful in, the American economy than the immigrants and effete intellectuals whom they associate with socialist politics. Finally, the ultraconservative wing of twentieth-century American religion is heir to the Protestant conviction concerning America's manifest destiny. The American way has been foreordained by God as the instrument through which gospel faith might spread across the globe. As the evangelist Billy James Hargis put it, "I am a Christian conservative today, because conservatism in the United States espouses the philosophy of Christ. . . . Capitalism is the system that is in accord with Christianity."[58] According to premillennial logic, if capitalism is in accord with Christ, then its opposite—socialism—is, of necessity, in accord with the Antichrist.

Premillennial conferences and writings began identifying socialism with the Antichrist as early as the 1870s.[59] It was considered common knowledge in premillennial circles that worldwide socialism was masterminded and financed by Jewish bankers, who schemed to use socialism as a means of destroying the world's economy and thereby setting the stage for Antichrist's rise to power. The worst was that socialism had sneaked right through the back door of American government where it was corroding its democratic system from within. Commenting on the "signs of the times," Arno Gaebelein cited the emergence of Roosevelt's New Deal and the "radical, communistic tendencies" of his Jewish brain trust.[60] One member of William Pelley's anti-Semitic "Silver Shirt" organization took the Jewish connection with the New Deal one step further and made connections between the blue eagle of the National Recovery Administration's logo and the mark of the Beast:

> Now look at the N. R. A. emblem. Count the teeth in the cogwheel. It's fifteen. Five and one. Get it? Five and one is six. Count the tail feathers on the bird. Six. That's six and six. Now how many bolts of lightning are there (on the Eagle's claw)? Six! And that makes 666—the mark of the beast.[61]

Gerald Winrod devoted an entire monograph to a discussion of "The NRA in Prophecy and a Discussion of Beast Worship."[62] Winrod acknowledged that the Depression had caused an economic emergency that appeared to make necessary the creation of new programs such as the NRA. Students of Bible prophecy, he countered, are not fooled by worldly logic or by seeming external appearances: "Prophetic believers . . . are informed concerning the demonism at work behind the scenes."[63] That is, fundamentalists are equipped with apocalyptic beliefs that accentuate their conspiratorial view of the world. Given such a predisposition to suspicion and hate, clues could be found anywhere. The first such clue is the "undisputed fact" that "the present Washington Administration is being controlled by Jews." The Antichrist had selected the members of Roosevelt's Jewish brain trust as the agents through whom he planned to bring the world into one controlled political and economic system. A second clue can be found by examining the blue eagle emblem of the NRA, which is full with combinations of six. The emblem has six claws. There are six bars of lightning. The word *member* located above the eagle's head has six letters, and the eagle has precisely twenty-four feathers, or four times six. Yet another clue is the fact that the NRA was a dictatorship, as expected in the final days. Roosevelt's administration was, to Winrod, a frightening concentration of power into the hands of a Jewish socialist. The government's concern with alleviating poverty was a conspiracy to establish the Beast system that, with the help of the False Prophet, would eventually coerce all citizens into worshiping a newly erected apostate religion.

Socialism, in the form of the New Deal, was upon America. Apocalyptic belief help put into a cosmic perspective both the fears of potential Bolshevik-like revolution and more general confusions about the appropriate role of government. Ambiguity vanished. It was now clear why democratically elected governmental leaders could perpetrate such horrors. They were agents of the Antichrist, part of the diabolical Jewish conspiracy to deliver America to the Beast. Once having named the Antichrist and found him in the contemporary world, distrust and contempt toward one's enemies became religious virtues. Intolerance of Jews, ethnic pluralism, and liberals were transformed into an apocalyptic mandate. Loyalty to the fundamentals of faith seemed to require willingness to participate in crusades of hate, and nowhere was this hate expressed more vehemently than in the crusade against both the Communist Soviet Union and the political liberals who were "soft" against this godless enemy.

Hyperpatriotism and the Soviet Demon

Most hate gradually recedes over time. The wounds that one's enemy originally delivered, whether real or imagined, ordinarily heal, and the sense of threat diminishes over time. But when one's enemy is Satan, the threat never diminishes; the guard can never be let down. For this reason, religiously motivated hate frequently escalates into an obsession, a persistent preoccupation with a seemingly unreasonable idea. Outsiders can never fully comprehend just how this kind of hate identifies its enemies, let alone the intensity with which these enemies are pursued. The "logic" of such hate, however, is not the logic of objective rationality but, rather, that of emotion and the channeling of this emotion by powerful religious symbols.

Protestant fundamentalism's preoccupation with the threat of Communism is an excellent example of such obsessional hate. This threat, personified by the Soviet Union, has induced twentieth-century American fundamentalists to adopt the most curious of attitudes—patriotism. Before World War I, premillennialist preachers portrayed patriotism as idolatrous; a Christian's only loyalty is to the coming kingdom of God. Since World War I, however, premillennialists (with the exception of Jehovah's Witnesses, who refuse to support any militarism not directly commanded by God) have tended to endorse a stridently patriotic anti-Communism. Although it would be a gross oversimplification to argue that Antichrist rhetoric caused this shift to fervent patriotism, it surely helped channel a host of otherwise diffuse resentments and fears into an obsession with the Soviet Beast.

At first glance the development of hyperpatriotism among fundamentalists seems difficult to explain. After all, how could premillennialists, whose sole loyalty is to the coming Kingdom of God, embrace the "American way" to the point of unceasing opposition to the Soviet system that challenged it? Historian George Marsden argues that this merging of the religious and political right resulted from fundamentalists' continued dislocation from the national center. By the end of World War I and the fiasco of the Scopes trial, fundamentalists could no longer avoid the perception that they had "become a laughingstock, ideological strangers in their own land."[64] Modernism had turned them into a cognitive minority whose view of the world was no longer credible to the educated public. What they knew for certain was that the Antichrist must be present in the "cultural elite" whose lifestyles, arrogance, and indifference to religion were eroding the only way of life they trusted.

Those who belonged to this elite, furthermore, were liberals who found old-fashioned patriotism intellectually indefensible. Thus, as R. Laurence Moore maintains, "superpatriotism became the premillennial Christian's way to protest the sophistication of liberal elite groups who no longer found it fashionable to accept the Bible or to wrap themselves in the flag. Those who wore American flags in their lapels recognized the Anti-Christ in those who did not."[65] Patriotism, then, was yet another expression of the "over and againstness" by which fundamentalists could distinguish themselves from the hated Antichrist closing in all around them.

Premillennialist religion has made it a sacred duty to stand up for the American way against its many challengers. The chief of these challengers has, without question, been the Russian-led Soviet Union. Russia was associated with all sorts of evils. It was thought to be run by greedy Jews who were either consciously or unconsciously helping the Antichrist sow the seeds of chaos about the world. It was godless. It was a tyrannical dictatorship. What is more, almost every one of Russia's evil characteristics was connected with themes of Bible prophecy, but not without some confusion.

Although many premillennialists saw in the Communist Soviet Union the embodiment of the Antichrist himself, others identified Russia as Gog, the leader of the great northern confederation prophesied to fight *against* the Antichrist. The latter view was championed by Scofield before the Bolshevik revolution and for this reason has dominated dispensationalist thinking in the twentieth century. The Book of Ezekiel speaks of "Gog, of the land of Magog, the chief prince of Meschech and Tubal" who will war against Israel and eventually be defeated by the Lord. Following Darby and a host of other nineteenth-century prophecy students, Scofield summarily stated that all prophecy experts agree that "the primary reference is to the northern (European) powers, headed up by Russia."[66] To this day, followers of Scofield's dispensationalist rendering of the Bible equates Russia with the biblical Gog. Hal Lindsey's *The Late Great Planet Earth*, which sold approximately nineteen million copies in the last three decades of the twentieth century, informs readers without hesitation or qualification that "Russia is Gog":

> We have seen that Russia will arm and equip a vast confederacy. This powerful group of allies will lead an attack on restored Israel. However, Russia and her confederates will be destroyed completely by an act that Israel will acknowledge as being from their God. . . . The attack upon the Russian confederacy and the resulting conflict will escalate into the last war of the world, involving all nations. Then it will happen. Christ will return to prevent the annihilation of all mankind.[67]

As historian Paul Boyer notes, "When the Bolsheviks seized power in October 1918 and the new regime repudiated Christianity and espoused atheism, history and prophecy seemed to converge; the identification of Russia as Gog took a powerful new lease on life."[68] For the rest of the century, prophecy writers found new roles being played out by this most sinister of America's enemies. In 1933, for example, Gerald Winrod published a monograph entitled *The United States and Russia in Prophecy and the Red Horse of the Apocalypse*. He explained that Communist Russia, inspired by "Jewish hatred for Christianity," had emerged with the sole intention of wiping the Christian faith off the face of the earth. Linking Russia with the biblical Gog, Winrod concluded that "considering that Communism is atheistic it is not difficult to understand why God should address himself as being against Russia."[69] Another premillennialist treatise published in 1934 similarly maintained that Bible prophecy points directly to the Soviet Union: "Satan is mobilizing for the last battle of this age, he has indeed established his headquarters in Moscow."[70]

From books written in the 1940s with titles such as *The Red Terror and Bible Prophecy* and *Russian Events in the Light of Bible Prophecy* to books from the 1980s such as *The Coming Russian Invasion of Israel* or *Apocalypse Next!* Americans have been amply alerted to the Soviet role in bringing the world to the brink of utter ruin.[71] The apocalyptic division of humanity into forces of light and darkness contributed greatly to the Cold War ideology that dominated the United States from the end of World War II to the late 1980s. Premillennialists such as Hal Lindsey and his Dallas Theological Seminary professor John Walvoord issued tracts that translated the political tensions of the Cold War into religious terms by linking the Soviet Union and China to the demonically inspired kings of the north and the east prophesied in Ezekiel and Revelation.[72] Meanwhile, Charles Taylor, author of *World War III and the Destiny of America*, informed readers of his *Bible Prophecy News* that the initials of three prominent Soviet leaders fulfilled Ezekiel's prophecy: "For the first time in history, GOG has a meaning: qualifying the chief leaders of the Soviet Union, the land of Mesech and Tubal as GOG: *G*romkyo, *O*garkov & *G*orbachev."[73]

Other spokesmen of the religious right have seen the Soviet Union not as Gog but as the Antichrist himself. Writing in the *Moody Monthly* in 1923, O. R. Palmer maintained that the Bible had predicted all along that "Russia would develop into the kingdom of the Antichrist and with this development would come a personal Antichrist as ruler."[74] The president of the Christian Freedom Foundation, Howard E. Kershner, voiced what a good many Americans thought about the Soviet threat when he explained that

> World War III, in which we are now engaged, is not simply a struggle of Russia against America, it is a battle between lies and honesty, hooliganism and integrity; unprincipled gangsterism against sound worth and accomplishment; anti-Christ against Christ. The lowest slime that ever crawled out of the pit now challenges all that honest God-fearing men have builded (*sic*).[75]

No twentieth-century evangelist has been more zealous in his efforts to warn Americans about "godless anti-Christian Communism" than Billy James Hargis. Founder of the Christian Crusade, an interdenominational anti-Communist ministry, Hargis battled tirelessly against Communist infiltration into American schools and churches. His writings took great care to show how the liberal press, leftist school teachers, unions, the Supreme Court, and ecumenical religious organizations such as the National Council of Churches of Christ participated in the conspiracy to turn over the United States to Satan's most sinister agent. In the bluntest terms, Hargis charged that the "the battle against Communism is Christ versus anti-Christ."[76] To Hargis, loyalty to the gospel and patriotism can hardly be distinguished: "Would to God [America] were falling upon its knees to God rather than falling upon its knees before its wicked enemies. America must revere its patriots—not help smear them—or patriotism in America will die alongside freedom."[77]

Not surprisingly, Soviet leaders have ranked among the century's prime targets in fundamentalists' game of "pin the tail on the Antichrist."[78] Stalin and Khrushchev both were early candidates for Antichrist speculation. In more recent years Gorbachev dominated the Antichrist spotlight. His attempts to bring about peace had the appearance of apocalyptic conspiracy written all over them, and the birthmark on his head surely could not be overlooked as an indication of his beastly identity. In his *Gorbachev! Has the Real Antichrist Come?* Robert Faird detected apocalyptic significance in the spelling of Mikhail S. Gorbachev. Faird was able to create a scheme for assigning numerical values to each letter of his name in several different languages and, with sufficient manipulation of the method by which numbers are assigned, arrive at results that could be further divided or multiplied to reach 666.[79] Faird's and other such efforts to discern the subtle disguises of the Beast make it clear that a nation that understands itself in the mythic terms of salvation history is likely to find itself forever confronting demonic enemies.

Americans who have sought rapprochement or détente with the Soviet Beast have also come under premillennialist suspicion. Gerald Winrod, for example, fairly fumed when Franklin Roosevelt established diplomatic relations with Soviet Russia. Reminding readers of Roosevelt's suspected Jewish ancestry and connection to the Antichrist's "Tribe of Dan," Winrod suggested that Roosevelt's mind was subconsciously linked with the Antichrist and therefore was either consciously or unconsciously executing the Antichrist's conspiratorial plans.[80] The architect of détente between America and the former Soviet Union, Henry Kissinger, frequently occupied the seat of the Antichrist during the 1970s and 1980s. His name in Hebrew was said to add up to 111, which when multiplied by 6 surely designated him as the feared beast. Kissinger's role as a peacemaker in Middle East diplomacy also fit the Antichrist tradition, as, of course, did his Jewish heritage.[81]

   Americans favoring disarmament and the reduction of nuclear
weapons are also suspect in the premillennialist camp. According to Hal
Lindsey, the "Bible supports building a powerful military force," including a potent nuclear arsenal.[82] Bible prophecy establishes beyond dispute that the United States will shortly become involved in the war of
all wars; it would thus be suicidal to let down its guard against godless
Communism. As Lindsey pointed out, the world is choosing Antichrist
rather than Christ: "The military capability of the United States, though
it is at present the most powerful in the world, has already been neu-
tralized because no one has the courage to use it decisively."[83] Dave
Hunt devoted an entire text, entitled *Global Peace and the Rise of Antichrist*, to the thesis that "the Antichrist is almost certainly alive" in every
traitorous cause promoting global peace, world government, or cultural
toleration.[84] A 1985 prophecy novel, Dan Betzer's *The Beast: A Novel of
the Future World Dictator*, explains how the Antichrist will take over the
world by pushing for nuclear disarmament."[85] Or in the somewhat less
fictional world of televangelism, preacher James Robison warns that
"any teaching of peace prior to [Christ's] return is heresy. . . . It's against
the Word of God; it's Antichrist."[86]
   The "naming" of the Soviet Union as either the Antichrist or Gog
fit neatly into the American legacy of demonizing enemies, both foreign and domestic. Just as Catholic France, King George of England, or
the philosophers behind the French Revolution had earlier symbolized
threats to the American order, the Soviet Union struck most Americans,
including President Ronald Reagan, as the "evil empire" against whom
any act of aggression is politically, morally, and religiously justified.[87]
   The motives that lead to such demonizing of the United States'
national enemies are perhaps too numerous and complex to be summarized here. But it appears that any nation, or subculture within that
nation, that wishes its members to adhere strictly to a single religious
vision must perpetuate a sense of being threatened from without by the
"beast of chaos." The sense of external threat helps accentuate the need
for internal cohesion and dramatizes the danger of straying too far from
trusted sources of authority. Indeed, much of the "Soviet Union as Gog
or Antichrist" rhetoric seems to have been intended not to describe a
foreordained and inevitable sequence of future world events so much
as to cajole listeners into renewed commitment to "the American way."
Thus, for example, such anti-Communist crusaders as Gerald Winrod,
Billy James Hargis, Hal Lindsey, and Pat Robertson all have concluded
their end-times scenarios involving the Soviet Union with impassioned
reminders that Americans still have a chance to rescue themselves indi-
vidually or even as a nation if they heed the call to repentance. As
Winrod explained at the conclusion of his rendering of the prophetic
role to be played by the creature called Gog:

The United States is situated geographically, economically, and prophetically, where she can be spared much of the suffering that is certain to visit other nations. But she must give God a chance. She must remain true to the great principles of Christian Democracy. . . . The Country must have a new spiritual baptism of its national conscience. This can only be accomplished by a great spiritual awakening.[88]

The existence of the foreign Soviet enemy thus helps marshal new resolve to counteract the forces of the Antichrist that lie much closer to home, such as permissiveness in the schools, Darwinism, situation ethics, biblical scholarship, new sexual moralities, and liberal religious thought.

The end of the Cold War and the demise of the Soviet Union have temporarily put a damper on prophetic calculations concerning Ezekiel's "Gog." Many premillennialists have predicted that a sure sign of Antichrist's rise would be false promises of peace, and accordingly, the apparent dismantling of the Soviet Union may be only a ruse to lull the world into complacency just before history's bloodiest hour.[89] But many prophecy students are also exploring the possibility that the Antichrist has found Russia too economically impoverished to serve as a vehicle for spreading chaos and destruction throughout the world. It appears that the Antichrist is contemplating a strategic return to a political base long proven as a source of Christian vexation: the religion of Islam and the Arab nations. Christian scholars have known for nearly fourteen hundred years that the Antichrist was especially present among "Mohammedans." Whether identified as Turks, the Ottoman Empire, or Arab States, Muslim political powers also existed to the "north" of Israel and hence have always been understood as at least part of Gog's endtime alliance.

John Walvoord first published his *Armageddon, Oil, and the Middle East Crisis* in 1973, eventually selling over 700,000 copies.[90] Walvoord's analysis of the Middle East's strategic role in all things anti-Israel and anti-Christian helped bring Muslims back into the focus of contemporary Bible prophecy. A 1990 revised edition makes it clear that the Antichrist, who will emerge as ruler of the ten-nation revived Roman Empire, will be a "Mediterranean leader"—that an Arab might be such a Mediterranean leader purporting to bring peace to the region cannot be ruled out.

Hal Lindsey followed Walvoord's lead and devoted considerable attention to what he called "the Islamic Peril" in his 1980 sequel to *The Late Great Planet Earth, the 1980s: Countdown to Armageddon*.[91] Lindsey specifically identified the Ayatollah Khomeini, Anwar Sadat, and Yasser Arafat as potential bringers of "false peace" and hence likely candidates for the title of Beast. Meanwhile, in 1982 prophecy teacher Mary Stewart Relfe shortened her list of Antichrist candidates to Henry Kissinger, King

Juan Carlos of Spain, Pope John Paul II, and Anwar Sadat: "After giving much time to studying the scriptural qualifications, characteristics,
and prerequisites, my prudent assessment is that President Anwar Sadat
of Egypt is either history's nearest prototype or the real Mr. '666.'"[92]
Relfe's "prudent assessment" notwithstanding, Sadat was assassinated
before her book reached the market. But other Arab candidates soon
came to the forefront.

Shortly after the Ayatollah Khomeini directed the revolution against
the shah of Iran in 1979, the stage was set for a new round of musical
chairs in the attempt to identify the Antichrist. As Paul Boyer chronicled,
American hostility toward Arab Muslims continued to escalate throughout the 1980s, and as a consequence, the Arab world was increasingly
seen by premillenialists as fraught with apocalyptic portents.[93] In 1980,
for example, Wim Malgo was certain that Khomeini was "a demonically appearing forerunner of Antichrist."[94] In 1982, Southwest Radio
Church's *Gospel Truth* settled on Libyan leader Mu'ammar Gadhafi, stating that Gadhafi's "messianic credentials qualify him in many respects
as a candidate for Antichrist."[95] Premillennialist James McKeever described the larger picture that justifies these and other such identifications of Muslim leaders as the Antichrist: "The Muslims have declared
war on the West, the United States and especially Christians. . . . The
Muslim faith could turn out to be the 'beast system.'"[96] Interest in linking Saddam Hussein with the Antichrist peaked during the Gulf War.
Although most established premillennialist authors held back from any
explicit or unqualified identification of Hussein as the expected Beast,
most hinted strongly at the possibility of some connection. Charles Taylor, for example, released a book and cassette, *Saddam's Babylon the Great*,
and Charles Dyer of the Dallas Theological Seminary sold over 300,000
copies of *The Rise of Babylon* with Saddam's picture on the cover.[97]

The quick defeat of Saddam Hussein in the Gulf War has tended to
make Muslim Antichrist identifications a bit more cautious, but it has
hardly brought them to a halt. A host of new prophecy books appeared
in the early 1990s prominently featuring the "Middle East crisis" as an
ominous portent of the Antichrist's imminent rise to world power.[98] It
appears that Muslim fundamentalists are almost certain to remain the
bête noire of Christian fundamentalists in the next few decades.

Denouncing World Peace and Interfaith Unity

The Antichrist has used many clever disguises in his effort to sneak by
the vigilant eyes of prophecy students, but none has gone undetected.
Knowing the essential character of the two beasts of Revelation—the
tyrannical dictator and the false prophet—premillennial scholars have
been quick to discern the Antichrist's presence in political institutions
such as the League of Nations or the United Nations and in ecumenical

religious organizations like the National Council of Churches of Christ. Beginning in the 1920s, the threat of Russia loomed sufficiently to set prophecy writers working overtime in their efforts to identify just who would soon emerge to fill the role of the Antichrist and oppose Russia (Gog) in the final days. The chief contenders for the role were the fascist Italian leader Mussolini and the League of Nations created by Woodrow Wilson and others to bring peaceful resolutions to international conflicts. Mussolini was suggested principally because of his association with Rome, the center of the Antichrist confederation that will rise to dominate the world in the end times. As early as 1925, premillennialist publications such as *Prophetic News* and *Evangel* alerted their readers that they should be on the lookout for the revival of the old Roman Empire. Mussolini, Evangel warned, was "the strongest character in world politics today," and his rise to power could mean nothing else than that "the climax is near."[99] Gerald Winrod's *Mussolini's Place in Prophecy* (1933) reviewed all the biblical clues concerning the identity of the Antichrist and concluded that they "all point to Mussolini."[100] Prophetic interest in Mussolini died, however, with the onset of World War II and the demise of the Axis powers. Besides, the League of Nations and its successor, the United Nations were much closer to home and thus directly associated with the drift of American culture toward the kinds of tolerance and pluralism despised by the Christian right.

The formation of the League of Nations provoked an immediate response from premillennialist writers. Whereas most Americans viewed the League as a rational attempt to find peaceful resolutions to world political crises and thereby prevent a recurrence of the devastation unleashed by World War I, prophecy students knew otherwise. Writing in the *Evangel*, James McAlister summarized their feelings:

> The World War thus originated by demon teachings has produced the result predicted in Revelation 16:14. It has gathered together all the kings of the earth and of the whole world. It has gathered them into a league of nations which will become the preparation of the nations for Armageddon. The gathering or leaguing of the nations together is the signal that the end is in sight. The Peace Conference at Paris had unconsciously set the stage for Antichrist and Armageddon.[101]

Another fundamentalist tract, *The King's Business*, elaborated on the many ways in which the League of Nations fulfilled the prophecies of Daniel and Revelation. After learning that the League embodied the figure of "iron and clay" described in Daniel, readers were helped to understand that "the man who will finally dominate the World League of Nations will be the Politico-Beast described in Daniel, and in the Book of Revelation. He is the Anti-Christ."[102] Other writings of the era speculated that the two contenders for the throne of the Antichrist—Mussolini and the League of Nations—might soon converge, with the League providing the political institution through which Mussolini would grab hold of "the despotic power of the Anti-Christ."[103]

After World War II, the United Nations assumed the Antichrist mantle formerly worn by the League of Nations. Like the League of Nations, the United Nations represented a cosmopolitan outlook that tried to embrace all of the world's diverse cultures. Although tolerance and pluralism may be useful traits for international diplomacy, they have fared poorly in the eyes of premillennialists. Separatism and loyalty to a narrowly defined cultural outlook are critical to the fundamentalist critique of modernism and all that it stands for. Thus the ultraconservative wing of American religion viewed the formation of the United Nations as an evil destined to end in the Antichrist's rule and its accompanying false religious order. In his article "How Antichrist Will Rule," Wilbur M. Smith maintained that the effort to create an international alliance of nations was destined to lead to the Beast's dictatorship prophesied in Revelation 13.[104] Writing for *The King's Business*, Louis Bauman predicted that "when the Antichrist shall attain this 'power' over the 'nations,' then the whole world will become indeed 'United Nations,' united in one great super-government."[105]

Part of the fear of the United States' participation in the United Nations was that its national autonomy would be lost. Such a relinquishment of political independence would be nothing short of a betrayal of its mission as God's chosen nation. As Gerald L. K. Smith remarked, anyone who favored the United States' membership in the United Nations was at once betraying the priceless heritage of the founding fathers and the true gospel of Christ. Unfortunately, Smith realized, seditious influences had already pushed the nation's leaders in this direction:

> Every member of Eisenhower's cabinet is for the United Nations. . . . Its flag is the same color as the Jew Palestine flag, and is the same design as the Russian military banner. Our new President has paid tribute to this internationalist organization which promises no good for the future of America. It outlaws prayer and forbid anyone to mention the name of Jesus within its halls or within its sessions without the official disapproval of the United Nations as such. It represents the most expensive denial of Christ in an attempt to please the anti-Christs in the history of the world.[106]

Known to premillennialists by such epithets as the "alien, treasonable, anti-American Jewnited Nations," the UN's attempt to foster world peace represented just the kind of liberal rationalism that fundamentalism had emerged to crusade against.[107] To Carl McIntire, for example, even the peace symbol popular among youth in the 1960s and 1970s represented the insignia of the Antichrist.[108] Americans needed to be waked up to the possible consequences of their continued participation in this godless organization. Billy James Hargis challenged all Bible-loving Americans to ask themselves, "Why should the United States, a

Christian nation, take note of the United Nations, an Antichrist institution?"[109] The answer, of course, was that fundamentalist Christians had everything to lose if they abandoned their exclusivism and separatism for the kind of international pluralism represented by the United Nations.

Efforts to promote religious tolerance and interfaith unity have been equally suspect in ultraconservative circles. Throughout the nineteenth century, various Protestant denominations cooperated in the formation of voluntary societies aimed to alleviate social ills and to promote the gospel. In 1908, leaders of most of the major denominations worked collaboratively to establish the Federal Council of Churches, intended to bring churches together to deal with the social problems created by the growth of urbanization and industrialization. As such, the FCC was closely associated with the social gospel movement's concern with ministering to the needs of the poor. Specifics of theology were minimized in the effort to develop programs that could make a concrete difference in the lives of those who were without shelter, food, or proper medical care. In 1950 the FCC was reorganized as the National Council of Churches of Christ. For the last four decades of the twentieth century, the NCC has acted as the nation's largest ecumenical organization, spearheading the churches' effort to identify common theological ground among the major Protestant denominations and to apply Christian principles to contemporary social issues.

All this, of course, has been offensive to fundamentalists, who believe that the winning of individual souls, not the amelioration of society, is the sole duty of Christian ministry. Even more vexing is the general "modernist" spirit that has animates such ecumenical organizations. If Christian unity is to be achieved at the expense of unyielding adherence to important tenets of faith such as biblical inerrancy or dispensationalist premillennialism, then it can only lead to the kind of apostate religion prophesied in Revelation. Gerald Winrod knew that attempts to find common ground in religion are examples of "Antichrist psychology." The "so-called Fellowship of Faiths" he heard modernist preachers calling for could lead nowhere else than to the "World Church, over which the second Beast of Revelation thirteen will preside."[110] Carl McIntire's weekly *Christian Beacon* carried an article by a southern preacher, J. Harold Smith, who saw right through the FCC's facade of Christian love. The Federal Council, he warned, is no dove of the gospel; it is instead a "daemonic vulture":

> The Federal Council of Churches of the Anti-Christ would make prostitutes of your daughters and libertines of your sons. This is the dirty, hellish, gang of sex-mad devils that some of the Knoxville preachers are falling over themselves to defend. Leave this atheistic, communistic, Bible-ridiculing, blood-despising, name-calling, sex-manacled gang of green-eyed monsters and hell-bound devils before God's judgment is poured out on them.[111]

Hatred of the values represented by the Federal Council of Churches continued to build. Denounced for its atheism, immorality, pacifism, and support of civil rights, the FCC was everything that fundamentalists associated with godless communism. To combat the Antichrist apostasy that was being spread under the name of "social Christianity," a group of ultraconservative Protestants under the leadership of Carl McIntire formed the American Council of Churches in 1941. Its mission statement captures well the "over and againstness" for which it was crusading: "To Provide a Pure Testimony for Fundamental Churches; to Facilitate Cooperation Among True Christian Churches; to Project a United Stand Against Religious Modernism; to Expose Communist Infiltration into the Churches; to Oppose Every System Alien to the Bible."[112] It was, in short, intended to expose and oppose the Antichrist rampant in the established Protestant denominations.

The ecumenical mind-set is one of universality, humility, and toleration. As such, it is antithetical to the "true believer" commitment that the Christian right asks from its adherents. When Gerald L. K. Smith called his followers to a crusade against the onslaught of the antichrists, he spelled out the kind of militant piety this would require:

> absolute love for Jesus Christ, one that knows no fear, no compromise, no turning back . . . an absolute recognition on the part of God's children of their destiny in the world . . . an absolute identification of the enemies of Jesus and the willingness to pay the price of death, if need be, in order to resist the power and force and the satanic venom of those who would take the name of Jesus Christ out of this world.[113]

This zealous "identification of the enemies of Jesus" continued throughout the final decades of the twentieth century. These enemies, ultimately controlled and coordinated by the Antichrist, could assume clever disguises and appear in seemingly innocent attire. But the hunt for Antichrist has continued with great success in even the most unlikely places in contemporary American culture.

Six

Camouflaged Conspirators

This person, the Antichrist, is called the "beast" because from God's viewpoint that is exactly what he is. . . . He will have a magnetic personality, be personally attractive, and a powerful speaker. He will be able to mesmerize an audience with his oratory. . . . So we see who will worship the Antichrist. Everyone will worship him who has not put his faith in Christ.

Hal Lindsey, 1970

🔶

The events foretold in Daniel and Revelation concerning a seven-year tribulation period could not begin until Israel was reestablished in the ancient Jewish homeland of Palestine. Nor could the end times commence without the revival of the old Roman Empire in the form of some ten-nation confederacy. It is thus not surprising that the creation of the modern nation of Israel in 1948 and the formation of the European Economic Community (EEC) in the 1980s helped make the final decades of the twentieth century fertile soil for the prophetic imagination. Hal Lindsey, whose *The Late Great Planet Earth* sold somewhere in the order of nineteen million copies during this period, summarized his review of world events by declaring, "It is happening. God is putting it all together."[1] Lindsey and other Bible prophecy experts sat in amazement as the pieces of the apocalyptic puzzle all seemingly fell into place: the restoration of Israel, the formation of the EEC among many of the nations formerly constituting the Roman Empire, the emergence of Russia as Ezekiel's Gog, the rise of menacing powers from the east (China), and the general decay of human culture. Given the lateness of the hour, it was urgent that students of Bible prophecy redouble their efforts to locate the Antichrist.

Greece became the tenth member of the European Economic Community in 1979, thereby completing the ten horns of Daniel's beast. Lindsey reasoned that the Antichrist must therefore already be in our midst. It is inevitable, he wrote, that the European Economic Community "will be headed by the anti-Christ. And I believe that leader is alive somewhere in Europe; perhaps he is already a member of the EEC parliament."[2] Lindsey's certainty of the Antichrist's imminent appearance was widely shared among fellow premillennialists. Televangelist Pat Robertson boldly proclaimed that "there is a man alive today, approximately 27 years old, who is now being groomed to be the Satanic messiah."[3]

In 1974 Charles Taylor surmised that "the person who will become 'the beast' of the Tribulation Period *must be alive* today because the signs show we are rapidly approaching the day of his revealing. Furthermore, the Antichrist must be a man who already has considerable status."[4] Although Taylor suggested a number of world leaders who fit the general description of the Beast, he has been especially wary of Spain's King Juan Carlos. Other prophecy pundits have added scores of names to the list of possible suspects, including Kurt Waldheim, Willy Brandt, Prince Bernhard of the Netherlands, Jimmy Carter, Ronald Wilson Reagan (who has six letters in each of his names and who "miraculously" recovered from a gunshot wound), Henry Kissinger, Mikhail Gorbachev, Anwar Sadat, Muammar Gadhafi, and Saddam Hussein. As Peter Lalonde put it in his *One World Under Antichrist*, regardless of just which of these persons might be revealed as the nefarious beast and regardless of just how he manages to rise to world dominion,

> we know he will accomplish three main objectives. First, he will convince the Jews that he is their long-awaited Messiah. Secondly, he will convince the false church that is left behind after the rapture that he is the true church. Finally, he will convince everyone that he is the beginning of the millennial period.[5]

All this, of course, is standard premillennial fare. The Antichrist tradition builds on a literary corpus that is more than two thousand years old. Nearly every generation in the history of Western civilization has produced its scholars to inquire into the scriptural foundations of the Antichrist concept. Ours is no exception.[6] Discussions concerning the Antichrist grow out of a theological tradition that in certain respects transcends the vicissitudes of cultural history. On the other hand, however, we cannot overlook the fact that the term *antichrist* appears in scripture nowhere outside 1 and 2 John, where it is used to explain the various theological opinions in the author's own day. For this reason, every subsequent attempt to connect the concept of the Antichrist with present-day events invites historical, sociological, and psychological interpretation. Put differently, efforts to "name the Antichrist" usually reveal less about the transhistorical consistency of scriptural exegesis than about the universality of the "apocalyptic mentality."

Contemporary Americans, no less than the authors of Daniel or Revelation, have a peculiar propensity to mythologize their world. The symbol of the Antichrist permits persons to view even the most common events in their lives against a cosmic background. It encourages them to believe that behind the "seen" world lie hidden, deeper forces. Human history is thereby transformed into a drama of universal proportions in which events are not caused by a simple commingling of physical, social, or economic forces, as many mistake it to be. It is, rather, a strategic battleground in the universal struggle between God and Satan, Christ and Antichrist. We have already seen how the symbol of Antichrist has enabled twentieth-century Americans to interpret their social dislocation in terms of a conspiracy set in motion by a demonic force. By giving mythic expression to the nativist fears aroused by the gradual pluralization of American culture, the symbol of the Antichrist has helped create an "ethnic" identity for many white, religiously ultra-conservative Americans. Belief in the Antichrist has fostered group loyalty by dramatizing the satanic nature of every enemy facing the faithful community. It has, furthermore, alerted individuals to the insidious tactics that this enemy might use to attract them to apostate ideas or lifestyles and in this way has encouraged a self-consciously separatist stance toward the surrounding world.

The concept of the Antichrist, then, has helped fundamentalists establish and maintain boundaries between themselves and the wider culture. To understand the many forms in which the Antichrist has appeared in the late twentieth century, it is important to remember that these boundaries are often more psychological than social. That is, vigilance against the Antichrist not only legitimates hatred toward those outside one's own tribe, but it also helps "wall off" one's own unacceptable thoughts and desires. As Freud showed long ago, a culture's taboos invariably reveal hidden or unconscious desires.[7] Taboos serve to prohibit actions that are deemed socially unacceptable but for which strong inclinations nonetheless exist. To this extent, modern images of the Antichrist provide important hints about the "apocalyptic war" between good and evil being waged within the believer. Richard Hofstadter picked up on precisely this point when he observed that "the enemy" against whom so many Americans struggle is invariably depicted as embodying total evil. "The enemy seems to be on many counts a projection of the self: both the ideal and the unacceptable aspects of the self are attributed to him."[8] This observation helps us understand why the Antichrist is characterized as an attractive individual (i.e., confident, eloquent, possessing a magnetic personality and yet simultaneously treacherous and deceitful. Hatred vented at the Antichrist thus seems to reveal a deeper level of anxiety concerning the believer's own unacknowledged tendencies toward errant ways of thinking and living.

This insight into the apocalyptic method of construing reality is critical to understanding the many forms that the Antichrist has assumed in the last few decades. The Antichrist has recently been discovered in modern computer systems, supermarket bar codes, fiber optics, the feminist movement, rock music, the ecological movement, and—of course—almost every form of nonbiblical modern philosophy. The preoccupation with these faces of the Antichrist is not so much a nativist obsession with foreign social forces as it is a continuing struggle against "unacceptable aspects of the self." Many efforts to name the Antichrist appear to be rooted in the psychological need to project one's "unacceptable" tendencies onto a demonic enemy. It is the Antichrist, not oneself, who must be held responsible for wayward desires. And with so many aspects of modern American life potentially luring individuals into nonbiblical thoughts or desires, it is no wonder that many people believe that the Antichrist has camouflaged himself to better work his conspiracies against the faithful.

The Seduction of Ideas

A Jesuit priest, Father Vincent Miceli, wrote a book in 1981, entitled *The Antichrist*, that captures almost perfectly the late twentieth century's fearful obsession with the prophesied Beast. The book includes a foreword by the journalist and social critic Malcolm Muggeridge, who acknowledges how difficult it is for believers to discover every camouflage under which the Antichrist operates in the world. Muggeridge was grateful that books such as Miceli's are available to help alert "Christ and his Church Militant." He maintained that we cannot effectively wage war against the Antichrist unless we have first studied his characteristic strategies and tactics:

> That a crucial campaign is already upon us cannot be doubted. I thank God that there are priests and teachers like Fr. Miceli to act as His intelligence officer, and ensure that the soldiers of Christ may *know who are their enemies, however camouflaged, and where are the booby-traps and ambushes*, and take heart in the knowledge that, seemingly outnumbered and out-gunned as they may be, with God on their side victory at last is certain.[9]

Fr. Miceli lives up to his billing as God's vigilant staff officer by providing thorough descriptions of the dangerous terrain and deceptive enemies awaiting obedient Catholics. Although apocalyptic thinking is somewhat rare in American Catholic thought, Miceli knows full well that the Beast of apostasy has begun ambushing the faithful from every side of modern culture, that it is high time that he called the "Church Militant" recognizes just how outnumbered and outgunned it is in danger of becoming.

"The world," Miceli warns, "has a death-wish to be dominated by the Antichrist."[10] That is, both our everyday common sense and our natural tendencies are to be distrusted; they lead us away from the ranks of the steadfastly loyal. Those who hope for salvation must learn to recognize and forcefully resist all that prompts them to "wish" for the Antichrist. Toward this end Miceli gives readers a full account of the "types, precursors, shadows, and earnests" of the Antichrist that might otherwise catch them off guard. The "shadows" of the Antichrist that most worry Miceli are fellow priests and other self-proclaimed Christians who are undermining the church from within. The death wish to be dominated by Antichrist has reared its head right in the church in the form of modernist priests and theologians who have been among the first to champion "progressivist" understandings of faith. Both in parish and university settings, "intellectualism is preferred to Catholicism, scientism to faith, relativism to truth, immanentism to transcendence, subjectivism to reality, situationism to moral integrity, and anarchism to authority."[11]

Miceli noted that theologians such as Paul Tillich, Teilhard de Chardin, David Tracy, and Charles Curran have been popular among intellectual Catholics who seek ways of bringing Christianity into dialogue with the main currents of modern thought. The theologians that Miceli singles out have inspired thousands of modern Christians to emphasize those elements of their theological heritage that welcome the insights of modern science and that will orient individuals to responsible social action on behalf of the poor or oppressed. The ideas of these apostate intellectuals are, however, precisely the kind of booby trap or doctrinal camouflage by which the Antichrist leads them astray. The effect of all such modernist theology, Miceli warns, is to encourage ways of thinking that will "rob God forever of the allegiance of men's minds." Miceli's point is that the Antichrist snares millions of souls through their fascination with novel doctrines. In particular, the Antichrist hides in any intellectual system that promises to bring liberty, equality, higher standards of living, illumination, knowledge, or science. Those whom Miceli calls the "fighting faithful" must therefore resist any temptation to stray from the orthodoxy that can alone preserve the purity and infallibility of the church.

The secret to the phenomenal success of Hal Lindsey's *The Late Great Planet Earth* is that it, too, alerts anxious readers to the booby traps and ambushes that lie in wait for unsuspecting souls. Lindsey served as a missionary and preacher for Campus Crusade for Christ in the late 1960s. While counseling young Christian adults about the doubts that emerged in the course of their university studies, he gradually became adept at helping persons wall off ideas that would otherwise create cognitive dissonance for those previously committed to such notions as biblical inerrancy or premillennialism. Lindsey learned at first hand that for many modern believers, doubt is not just something that confronts them in the form of "unbelieving outsiders" who refuse to be assimilated into the true church. Rather, even self-identified believers must occasionally face up to unbelief within themselves. Contemporary Christians cannot avoid daily mental contact with a culture that is at once pluralistic and grounded in scientific reasoning. It is thus almost impossible to protect themselves from being subtly assimilated into the cognitive outlook that has produced the technological advances, forms of entertainment, and passing cultural fads that define participation in the modern world. As Lindsey and other premillennialist writers learned, this is precisely what makes the symbol of the Antichrist such an important homiletic tool. Belief in the Antichrist invokes a mythic framework for interpreting the cognitive dissonance and vacillating intellectual commitments that believers, particularly the young, often find themselves struggling against. The concept of the Antichrist reinterprets their divided loyalties by explaining them in terms of the cosmic struggle between cosmic good and cosmic evil. In this way, the fight against seductive ideas is externalized; unacceptable doubts are explained away as the tactics of a treacherous enemy. And more important, the apocalyptic framework helps people protect themselves against further temptation by maintaining rigid intellectual and psychological boundaries.

Lindsey remarks that while writing *The Late Great Planet Earth*, he envisioned himself addressing a youthful, questioning audience who vacillated between belief and disbelief:

> As I wrote, I'd imagine that I was sitting across the table from a young person—a cynical, irreligious person—and I'd try to convince him that the Bible prophecies were true. If you can make a young person understand, then the others will understand too. A young person isn't hesitant to call you on something, and it forces you to come to grips with people who aren't in the religious club.[12]

Lindsey's way of coming to grips with people who were not in his "religious club" was to point out the nature of the company they keep. He reminds his readers that those who continue in their cynical, irreligious ways are destined to be left behind on the day of the rapture and will consequently be among those to come under the tyrannical rule of the Antichrist. Lindsey's advice for those who wish to join the religious club before it is too late is to begin distrusting academic authorities, suppress their natural curiosity, and submit reason to unquestioning acceptance of biblical authority:

> How do we know in what direction we should go? How can we separate truth from opinion? In whom can we trust?

> On one side we hear that the answer to our dilemma is education. Build bigger and better schools, hire more teachers, develop a smarter generation. Has the academic community found the answers? There are many students who are dissatisfied with being told that the sole purpose of education is to develop inquiring minds. They want to find some of the answers to their questions—solid answers, a certain direction.[13]

Lindsey assured his readers that both solid answers and certain directions can be found in the Bible. The academic community, meanwhile, lacks the kind of absolutes that alone can separate biblical truth from all impostors. Because universities foster the pursuit of relative truths and reasoned approximations, they are the perfect medium for the Antichrist's promulgation of his perverted gospel. It consequently comes as no surprise that Lindsey's description of the Antichrist sounds precisely like the college professors who had helped the students he counseled develop "inquiring minds." He warns that the Antichrist "will have a magnetic personality, be personally attractive, and a powerful speaker. He will be able to mesmerize an audience with his oratory."[14] Lindsey adds that the Bible calls the Antichrist "'the beast' because from God's viewpoint that is precisely what he is."[15] Lindsey cautions his readers to avoid the snares of the Antichrist by avoiding the kinds of intellectual processes that undermine unquestioning faith. After all, the Antichrist snatches innocent souls from the safety of salvation and sets their inquiring minds loose in the wilderness of academic thought: "So we see who will worship the Antichrist. Everyone will worship him who has not put his faith in Christ."[16]

Distrust of secular education is hardly new to fundamentalist circles. Early fundamentalist tracts such as William Blackstone's *Jesus Is Coming* (1908, republished in 1989) and William Riley's *The Menace of Modernism* (1917) were equally concerned about the Antichrist's inroads into the public educational system. For nearly one hundred years, fundamentalist writers have decried the religious cynicism they believe permeates "modernist" intellectual thought. Closer to our own day, Tim LaHaye's *The Beginning of the End* (1972) focused the apocalyptic spotlight on the nature of modern education: "The molders of our educational and philosophic thought today are predominately scoffers, acting exactly as the Bible predicted they would in the last days."[17] By placing our era's intellectual currents in the context of apocalyptic history, premillennialists etch in their readers' minds the Antichrist-character of rival positions and assure them of the rewards that are ordained for all who remain loyal.

Parents committed to fundamentalist principles are understandably concerned about the educational influences that surround their children on every side. Studies of fundamentalist Christian schools by scholars like Alan Peshkin and Susan Rose have discovered a world in which children must be taught to distrust their own inclinations and rely instead on scriptural authority. As one parent told Peshkin, "We look around us and see Satan. He's prince and power of this age and he has stronger involvement with this world than Christians do."[18] In her *Keeping Them out of the Hands of Satan*, Susan Rose observes that

> evangelicals are not the only ones who feel that the social fabric is disintegrating, that they are being assailed by forces beyond their control. What is distinctive is how they identify and cope with these forces. Evangelicals identify them as satanic; therefore, their response is framed differently from some other Americans who may blame the hegemony of a corporate elite or mass, commercialized culture as the culprit.[19]

By framing modern intellectual thought in the context of Satan's or the Antichrist's plot against the faithful, fundamentalist Christians have created a pious justification for their efforts to push the cultural clock backward to an era when pluralism and relativism were not yet necessary elements of a democratic worldview.

The founder of the American Association of Christian Schools described the frustration that many Christian parents feel:

> There are two major things we must do if our country is to continue as a free nation. . . . Christians must join hands in stopping the floodtide of socialistic–communistic legislation that is now being introduced and we must rescue our Christian youth from the brain-washing, socialistic, amoral, and often atheistic public school system to educate them in a Biblical philosophy of life.[20]

Thousands seem to agree. Enrollment in conservative Christian schools grew to over 450,000 in the 1980s. The "Biblical philosophy of life" that students encounter in these schools extols traditional sex roles, the submission of women to men, the virtues of a free-market economy, creationism, and anti-Communistic patriotism. The parents of these students told Susan Rose that before their commitment to fundamentalism, they were often confused, uncertain, and at a loss about how to bring up their children. The decision to "keep their children out of the hands of Satan" by educating them into biblical absolutes reassured them and encouraged them about their socializing roles. Although these parents are now "quick to tell you that they do not have all the answers, they have the essential one. By surrendering their lives to Christ and faithfully following the Scriptures, they find themselves much more secure in their parenting."[21] Put differently, by reinforcing the very doctrines that establish fundamentalist boundaries, they feel confident they have exorcised the Antichrist and thus helped free their children from the kinds of doubts that even most adult believers can never fully expunge.

The pluralistic, rationalistic, and humanistic aims of American education have, in short, been found to be camouflage for Antichrist's campaign to dominate the world. It is difficult to raise the next generation within the narrow intellectual boundaries of fundamentalism when at every turn the Antichrist seeps into their minds and lures them into forbidden territory. The militant faithful have pressed their school boards to adopt textbooks that skimp on evolutionary biology, to remove "amoral" literature from their libraries, and to censor teachers who believe that the goal of education is to empower young minds to explore the world without inhibition. When their efforts have failed, they have simply withdrawn to create an alternative system of schooling whose boundaries are impervious to the seductions of Antichrist.

The Lure of Contemporary Culture

Twentieth-century American culture has evolved in ways that have proved to be a nightmare for the nation's premillennial population. The "baby-boom" generation in particular has been raised in an era that glamorizes all that dares to call traditional religious values into question. Humanistic psychologies have made self-actualization the goal of individual existence. Existential philosophies have boosted the virtue of self-gratification over communal commitment. The media have glorified promiscuous sexuality. The advertising and film industries have made both alcohol and drugs seem sophisticated. Rock music has voiced defiance of authority and glorified unreflective spontaneity and impulse-driven behavior. The feminist movement has undermined traditional authority structures and stripped males of their once unrivaled access to the sources of social power. All in all, the Antichrist has prospered in popular American culture.

Apocalyptic writings understandably give vent to virulent denunciations of apostate culture. But within these critiques it is frequently possible to detect a hint of envy. The author of 1 John himself was acutely aware that "the world listens" to the dissident members of his community who had given up separatism to embrace the world. This in itself was sufficient proof to him that the nonconformists were animated by the spirit of the Antichrist. He counseled those who were tempted to join the renegade group that it is far better that the world "does not listen to us," for the world is the abode of the Antichrist. The author of Revelation also wrote to a community that was envious of those in their midst who cooperated with the Roman Empire and prospered for doing so. He warned that those who traffic in the beast's kingdom carry his mark and will suffer the consequences at judgment day.

Contemporary premillennialists are no less envious of the fact that the world listens to the cultural elite. It is thus incumbent on premillennialist writers to follow in the footsteps of 1 John and show fellow believers how far the cultural elite have strayed into the path of the beast. Tim LaHaye, for example, tells his readers that the chief "spirit of error" in the world today is the humanistic philosophy through which the Antichrist leads persons to amorality, permissiveness, and belief in evolution. In his aptly titled *Battle for the Mind*, LaHaye writes that "most of the evils in the world today can be traced to humanism, which has taken over our government, the UN, education, TV, and most of the other influential things of life."[22] In a novel depicting the Second Coming, Ernest Angley goes a step further and argues that every status symbol is a mark of the Beast. A follower of the Antichrist tells a reluctant holdout whom he is trying to lure into apostasy, "It's the most popular thing of the day, you don't want to be behind the times."[23] Angley and LaHaye know that the world about them does not listen. The battle for the mind is thus not so much about changing the world as it is about preventing further defections. Fellow believers, particularly the young, must be helped to recognize the true source of all that beckons them to participate in the world about them. They must learn to distrust and combat much of what seems to be common sense. Failure to check such inclinations and to preserve unyielding boundaries will almost certainly lead to unwitting acceptance of the mark of the beast.

The cultural elite's conspiracy to entice people into doing the bidding of the Beast can be found everywhere. Peter Lalonde, for example, found it in art work sponsored by the National Endowment for the Arts. He charges that the NEA has deliberately promoted art that promotes the Antichrist's hatred of Christians.[24] Lalonde also found the Antichrist's gospel in the Teenage Mutant Ninja Turtles, He-Man cartoons, Walkman stereos, and MTV.[25] Encouraged by the passage in Daniel and Revelation describing the beast as having "a mouth speaking great things," other prophecy writers have connected the Antichrist with the influential power of television and the electronic media in general. Not only do current television programs promulgate Antichrist's gospel of amorality and licentiousness, but when he soon rises to a position of world dominion, television will give him the means of reaching into every home on earth. Whatever the precise medium of his camouflage, prophecy writers tell us that the Antichrist will have the power to influence unsuspecting souls with the sheer brilliance of his communication skills. Hal Lindsey, as noted, depicted the Antichrist as one who "will have a magnetic personality, be personally attractive, and a powerful speaker. He will be able to mesmerize an audience with his oratory."[26] In other words, any convincing or alluring person in American culture is almost by definition a vehicle of the Antichrist's apostate influence.

One of Antichrist's least camouflaged hideouts over the past several decades has been rock music. Lalonde's concern with adolescents' immersion in the world of "Walkman" stereos and cassette players has been shared by vigilant stalkers of the Beast. The counterculture spawned by rock music is, after all, a perfect vehicle for disseminating apostasy and anarchy. The adulation of rock stars and their instant rise to world popularity can hardly be anything else than a precursor to the rise of the Antichrist. These fears were confirmed when the Beatles' press agent reportedly characterized the group's influence as, "They're completely antichrist," and John Lennon mused that the group was more popular than Christ. Rock lyrics abound in references to the destruction of the human race and occasionally invoke the spirit of the Antichrist by name.[27] Surrounded by such flagrant examples of the world's "death wish to be dominated by Antichrist," Father Miceli became convinced that dirty jeans, wild rhythms, and electrified music create the perfect medium for spreading the ideals of the Antichrist. The "angel of flashing light and thundering music," the Antichrist is nowhere more alive than in the rhythm and lyrics of rock. Citing the Rolling Stones' hit singles "Sympathy for the Devil" and "Street Fighting Man," Miceli warns of the seduction of youth into an apocalyptic revolution: "The result is that today millions of youth will 'groove' with rock music, but tomorrow they will be passively submissive to the cadences of some demagogue behind whose tyranny will be the controlling power of the puppet masters, Satan and all the forces of hell."[28]

Some Christian fundamentalists have focused on the ideological dimensions of rock lyrics. David Noebel, an associate evangelist in Billy James Hargis's Christian Crusade, devoted an entire book to the subject of how modern music was being used to subvert young Americans. In *Rhythm, Riots and Revolution*, he charged that "the damage already done to this country through his [Pete Seeger's] influence is *impossible to calculate*."[29] Noebel noted that the Communists had contrived an elaborate scheme to render an entire generation of Americans neurotic through the nerve jamming and mental deterioration that comes from listening to rock music. "It is our studied opinion that the Communists and the pro-Communists have an *unbelievable influence* in the folk realm *far grater than most would dare imagine*."[30]

Noebel's conspiratorial paranoia is restrained in comparison with Jacob Aranza and other contemporary fundamentalists who worry about the "backward masking" techniques used to produce rock albums through which the Antichrist surreptitiously recruits new followers. Backward masking, explains Aranza, is a technique that rock groups use to convey satanic and drug-related messages to the subconscious minds of their audiences. In support of his thesis, Aranza cites quasi-academic studies of subliminal perception such as the often-cited example in which the flashing of the words POPCORN and COCA COLA across a movie screen allegedly contributed to an increase in the theater's concession sales. Aranza does not describe just how such "backward masking" techniques have actually been used, but his books are filled with profiles of rock stars that highlight their histories of substance abuse and interest in non-Christian philosophies. He also reminds us that to persuade people to serve Satan, rock music need not get them to fall on their knees and worship him. It is sufficient to get them thinking about and serving themselves. Although Aranza's argument may be muddled, his conclusion is crystal clear: "Many anti-Christian statements can be found backmasked into songs, effectually attacking the faith of masses of young people."[31]

The feminist movement is another of Antichrist's bastions in the battle for American culture. The Bible is quite clear about the ontological status of women. The Book of Genesis tells us that woman was created to be a helpmate to man. In the New Testament, Paul explains that women are to acquiesce to male authority, particularly in matters of religion. Paul counsels women to be quiet in church and to obey their husbands, because this was ordained by God and is embedded in the very nature of creation. Scripture clearly depicts institutional religion as something to be entrusted to males. On the Catholic side, no less a canonical authority than Thomas Aquinas declared that "woman was made to be a help to man. But she was not fitted to be a help to man except in generation, because another man would prove a more effective help in anything else." As for Protestants, Martin Luther himself perpetuated belief in the scriptural foundations of the hierarchical relationship between man and woman. Luther asserted that "women are on earth to bear children. If they die in child-bearing it matters not; that is all they are here to do." The twentieth century's most formidable conservative Protestant scholar, Karl Barth, put the matter succinctly and unequivocally: "Women are ontologically inferior to men."

Spokesmen for ultraconservative Christianity can hardly avoid viewing feminism as yet another source of the cultural dislocation they have continued to endure in recent decades. Condemnation of the Equal Rights Amendment and tirades against female subversion of traditional family structures have consequently been common fare in conservative pulpits across the country. But a few prophecy students discern something more ominous in the cultural ascendancy of feminism. Colin Deal, for example, knows that only one entity is both malevolent and powerful enough to turn God's ordained system of gender inside out: the Antichrist. Deal picked up quickly on the apocalyptic significance of the United States government's decision to mint the Susan B. Anthony coin. Deal urged Bible-believing Christians to look carefully at the potential role this beastly coin might have in fulfilling biblical prophecy concerning the end times:

> Will this coin signal the end. . . . Will it also signal the beginning of a "new order of the ages" as predicted by John (Revelation 13)? Watch for the replacement of the American dollar and its symbolic meaning. Isn't it odd that this new coin, minted in a God-fearing nation, has the bust of Susan B. Anthony, a renowned atheist and the instigator of the present unrest with women's liberation?[32]

Feminism has had even more serious implications for Catholicism's understanding of what might be understood as an assault on Christ's church. Fortunately, however, Father Vincent Miceli has served faithfully in his role as Christ's "intelligence officer" in the battle against the Antichrist and has alerted the church to this treacherous booby trap set by the Beast to ensnare the unsuspecting. Miceli charges that by aiding and abetting the feminist cause, Catholic universities have themselves become "soldiers of the Antichrist." No other conclusion is possible in an era "when a woman lecturer, with no particular qualifications as a theologian, is invited to address large student bodies at many Catholic universities and during her lecture ridicules Christ, the holy mother of God, and attacks the Church's teaching on contraception and abortion."[33] It is scary enough that the Antichrist has used women to subvert proper church authority. But Miceli also warns that women are the tools with which he will also destroy the family and undermine male identities: "Women, in ever growing numbers, are despising and abandoning families. Men, frightened by the blazing fury of the women's liberation movement, are surrendering male roles and positions to psychologically desexualized women."[34]

It should be pointed out that popular culture has produced its own peculiar fascination with the Antichrist. It would be hard to overestimate the influence that the American scriptural heritage concerning the Antichrist has had on Western culture's images of incarnations of evil, false messiahs, satanic influence, or catastrophic endings of the world.[35] To some extent, evangelical Christians themselves have aided the translation of biblical topics into the vernacular of popular culture. Televangelists have popularized Christian eschatology over the same electronic media that bring science fiction into American homes. Evangelical movies such as *A Thief in the Night*, *Image of the Beast*, *The Late Great Planet Earth*, and *The Road to Armageddon* have also helped disseminate apocalyptic themes to wide audiences but have done so at the great risk of losing the message to the medium. Months after viewing Bible-prophecy films, viewers have difficulty sorting out which images of evil are accurate depictions of biblical passages, which are dramatic embellishments, and which have subsequently blended in their memories with scenes that were depicted in similar but nonbiblical films produced by Hollywood.

Hollywood long ago discovered Americans' appetite for apocalyptic thrillers. David Seltzer's novel *The Omen* was successfully transformed into a box-office success. *The Omen* (1976) and its sequels *Damien-Omen II* (1978), *The Final Conflict* (1981), and *The Awakening* (1991) are the story of the birth and gradual rise to power of the end-time ruler. Biblical accuracy, of course, gives way to directorial license. As Peter Malone shows in his book *Movie Christs and Antichrists*, Hollywood's Antichrist figures stray far afield of scriptural authenticity and connect inherited biblical images of evil with all sorts of popular fantasies concerning the incarnation of evil (*Dracula*, *Frankenstein*, *Rosemary's Baby*), demonic possession (*The Exorcist*), openings to the gates of hell (*Amityville Horror*), malevolent expressions of nature (*The Birds, Jaws*), angels of darkness (*Psycho*), and the technology of destruction (*Dr. Strangelove, The Day After, The Terminator, 2001: A Space Odyssey*).[36]

Much modern fiction is concerned with what critic W. Warren Wagar calls "terminal visions."[37] Beginning with the works of Mary Shelley, Edgar Allen Poe, and H. G. Wells, Western literature has displayed a preoccupation with the impending doom to be unleashed by biological, geological, or nuclear disaster. This literature, however, is usually less a product of biblical exegesis than a creative act of the secular imagination. Wagar argues that the secular doomsday imagination reflects what might be termed a "stratigraphy of fear." Secular visions of the end, he says, express at least three separate layers of human fear. The first and most primitive layer contains fears of separation, powerlessness, sexual rivals, loneliness, failing, and dying. According to Wagar, these most primitive human fears provide the dominant themes in religious apocalyptic writing because they are the most universal and hence least tied to conditions peculiar to any one specific historical era. Apocalyptic writing originating from this level of primal emotion satisfies the hunger of its readers for violence and death. As Wagar explains,

> Psychoanalytic theory suggests that such a hunger is no less part of the human condition than the desire for life, love, and fulfillment through useful work. Destructive impulses are related organically to the same fears of powerlessness that nourish fantasies about heroically saving the world or surviving its end. A sense of powerlessness can invoke all the devils of Thanatos: uncontrollable rage, bitter hatred, insatiable gluttony and lust, the desire to destroy supposed enemies and oppressors, self-loathing, and cravings for humiliation and death.[38]

We will have more to say about this in the epilogue of this book. We note now only that contemporary apocalyptic thinking, both religious and secular, is rooted in primal desires and fears expressed in the mythopoetic language of evil adversaries, reigns of lawlessness and terror, catastrophe, and final victory over one's enemies.

For Wagar, a second layer in the stratigraphy of apocalyptic fear is the dread of nature. Although fears of nature can be projections of psychological conflict, they are just as often prudent concerns about real menaces to life and health. Dangerous animals, violent storms, and destructive plagues are part of almost every generation's mythic imagination. The natural sciences have added a host of new fears to our own generation's sense of the precariousness of the human condition. From astronomy's discovery of the inevitable death of suns and their solar systems to microbiology's detection of deadly diseases, secular apocalypses abound with new end-times scenarios. Added to all this are the fears attending the growing awareness of the consequences of environmental recklessness. Fears of the exhaustion of our natural resources, the depletion of the ozone layer, and the irremediable pollution of our water supplies have found their way into modern novels, films, and song lyrics. In fact, Wagar conjectures, scientifically grounded theories of human vulnerability have largely transmuted older fears of the super- natural and the wrath of God into new, secular forms.

A third cluster of fears found in contemporary visions of the end center on what humans do to themselves. The modern apocalyptic imagination is easily inspired by stories of the mad or reckless scientist, accounts of the lethal effects of technology on the environment, or theo- ries concerning the escalation of class, economic, or racial tensions into global war. The possibility of nuclear holocaust has given recent gen- erations a vivid image around which to envision their imminent self- destruction. Unlike the time of Daniel or Revelation when only an act of God could terminate the whole of creation in the twinkling of an eye, contemporary Americans know full well that somewhere along the line they assigned this dreadful power to themselves. Barry Maguire's 1965 hit record "The Eve of Destruction" may have lacked explicit scriptural references, but it did express the contemporary secular fear that the end may indeed be imminent and that the only Antichrist to be named is ourselves.

Scientific and Technological Portents

Neither scientific nor technological progress is likely to be an unalloyed blessing. Nearly every humanly engineered "victory" over nature has brought with it unexpected potentials for abuse. Real possibilities exist for the irreparable disruption of the planet's ecological balance, the un- leashing of a genetically engineered "virus" that could prove lethal to untold numbers of species, or the subtle suppression of the human spirit through the progressive ordering of society along technological lines. Such portents of human self-destruction have not only remained in the secular apocalyptic imagination but have also factored into the late twentieth century's religious eschatologies. There are, however, slightly different agendas at work in the premillennialists' incorporation of sci- entific and technological imagery into their end-times speculations. Since the early twentieth century, premillennialists have found them- selves in the vortex of a turbulent cultural change. First, they have experienced at first hand the gradual demise of their own "cultural clout." As the natural and social sciences undermined the cognitive sta- tus of biblically based beliefs, ultraconservative religion was placed on the permanent defensive. Immigration, the mass media, and general social mobility made the United States one of the most culturally plu- ralistic societies in human history, further displacing fundamentalists and their biblical worldview from the nation's symbolic center. At the same time, fundamentalists have been forced to witness the ascendancy of a new cultural outlook; one that is rational, secular, and technological in nature. Everything from school curricula to the organization of government bureaucracies reflects the nation's tacit acceptance of a worldview that banishes the supernatural from everyday thinking. Surely the miracle-working wonders of science and technology must be yet another of the Antichrist's desperate tricks to deceive the world as we enter the final hour.

Largely because of its success in generating medical and other technological breakthroughs, scientific reasoning threatens to ensnare an entire generation in infidelity. Prophetic books can therefore ill afford to ignore what Mary Stewart Relfe refers to as the "elite but secular groups of scientists" who have become the virtual Pied Pipers of the Beast.[39] Indictments of the scientific Antichrist have grown increasingly specific in identifying the ways in which he has tried to perpetrate his ideological deceptions. It appears, for example, that Antichrist had the ingenuity to inspire the creation of both the microchip and the computer. In their book *Computers and the Beast of Revelation*, David Webber and Noah Hutchings escalated paranoia about the potential uses of computers into an apocalyptic frenzy: "Comparing the rapid turn of world events today with biblical prophecy is more thrilling than reading the best-seller in fictional books. Satan, through man, finally does have almost god-like omnipresent power. Satan is making his final push to exalt his throne above the stars of God."[40]

What makes computers so threatening to Webber and Hutchings is that they seem to constitute the quintessential expression of humanity's cardinal sin—the quest for knowledge of the world independent of God's revelation. They caution us to "remember that Satan promised Eve that knowledge in itself leads to God-likeness."[41] If there is anything that modern premillennialists are committed to abhor, it is "knowledge in itself." Somewhat predictably, Webber and Hutchings' book is short on details as to just how Antichrist has embodied himself in computers, but it is long on the dangers of the secularist education that children receive in schools. Computers seem a poignant symbol of the kinds of knowledge that remain foreign to those who think only in biblical categories. Seeing their children learn to think in computer-driven, technological ways has obviously raised anxiety about how far one can stray into the modern world without being permanently scarred by the "mark of the Beast."

Peter Lalonde gave this fear of computer-age technology an even more grotesque expression when he conjectured that soon the government or large corporations might begin implanting computer microchips directly into human flesh, possibly even on the right hand or forehead, as Revelation long ago predicted: "It could well be that what [John] was referring to almost 2000 years ago was what is known today as the computer microchip."[42] Lalonde warned that once we have received the "microchip" mark of the Beast, the Antichrist will have the techno-logical capacity already in place for regulating even the most minute details of our lives.

Expanding on this fear of the "Big Brother" powers associated with new technology, other prophecy writers have given currency to the rumor that a giant supercomputer is being created in Brussels for the purpose of taking over the world's banking system and creating a cash-less economic system, as was prophesied in Revelation. As early as 1975 the Southwest Radio Church reported that this supercomputer, dubbed "the Beast," would link banks throughout the world and gradually force "a socialistic economic leveling and a new money system in the 1980s."[43]

In the same year Colin Deal informed his readers that

> Common Market leaders during a crisis meeting in Brussels, Belgium, were introduced to the "Beast," a gigantic computer that occupies three floors of the Administration Building at the Common Market Headquarters. The computer is capable of assigning a number to every person on earth in the form of a laser tatoo. Then, through infared scanners, this invisible tatoo would appear on a screen.[44]

Rumors about "the Beast" and its ability to track our every movement escalated in premillennial publications. William Alnor noted that, for some, this mythical computer took on demonic characteristics and was perceived as the center of a massive conspiracy. He cited a 1979 issue of the *Awakeners Newsletter*, which charged this supercomputer with plotting to enslave and ruin the human race (not to mention impersonating the pope):

> The European Common Market Computer at Brussels, Belgium . . . [is] prefixed by the numbers 666. It is called the Beast by those who built it and work on it. . . . The Beast has many tentacles in the Mafia, the CIA, the Knights of Malta and other sinister organizations which have been working for many years together to bring this enslavement about. Those who accept the "Mark of the Beast" will spend time in Hades after passing over in death. This alone is worth thinking about. In January of 1979 we were told that the current Pope in Rome is an actor, a look-alike for the real Pope who was murdered in this World-Wide conspiracy. Also recently Jimmy Carter was injected with cancer [leukemia] by agents of the Beast who need him replaced by one more obedient in this worldwide plan to enslave humanity.[45]

This conspiratorial link between computers and the events foretold in the Book of Revelation was further embellished by Emil Gaverluk and Patrick Fisher in their 1979 book, *Fiber Optics: The Eye of the Antichrist*. With straight faces, Gaverluk and Fisher maintained that the Antichrist is monitoring us even now through our television sets. The technological innovation that sends electronic digital signals gives the Antichrist a peephole into each of our living rooms.

There is a pinhead-sized camera lens on the end of the fiber optic which can watch anything taking place in the room. . . . This data is recorded on computers which can collate all remarks pro or con, to implement dictatorial control by any group or individual. The startling thing is that this fish-eye camera lens can still see and record everything, EVEN WHEN THE TELEVISION SET IS NOT TURNED ON. This means that every family will be under 24-hour surveillance. What a perfect setup for the Antichrist![46]

Computers, microchips, and fiber optics are not the only technological disguises assumed by the Antichrist. He has also had an uncanny presence in the nation's space program. Mary Stewart Relfe reported that the *Apollo* mission was rife with the digits 666. She noted that the word *Apollo* has six letters; each of the astronaut's names had six letters; the spacecraft had six sections; the journey lasted sixty-six hours; and so on.[47] In an even more imaginative vein, David Webber and Noah Hutchings latched onto UFO sightings as positive proof that we are in the latter days. The Bible, they say, refers to UFOs in several places (e.g., Ezekiel's visions of metallic objects in the sky and the passage in Genesis that describes how God took up Abraham in "a smoking fire pot and a flaming torch") and suggests that beings will come from outer space and intervene in human affairs. More to the point, these prophecy experts suggest that the Antichrist himself may use UFOs to force his people into an outer-space exile.[48]

These and other such flights of the apocalyptic imagination continue to return to the theme enunciated by Webber and Hutchings. Behind every potential scientific and technological "danger" lies humanity's inherent tendency to seek knowledge of the world independent of God's revelation. Premillennialists' fantasies that science and technology will someday usher in a "Big-Brother" government that will force them to do the bidding of Antichrist reveal a deeper fear of finding themselves in an increasingly alien world. All about them are those who willingly seek "knowledge in itself" and willingly participate in the Beast's cultural order. Moreover, these persons who have put secular rationality ahead of God's revealed truths seem to be prospering from their very apostasy. Apocalyptic denunciations of a world dominated by new technologies are thus more than efforts to slow down the "depersonalization" of our society; they are calls to name the Antichrist, to guard against intellectual impulses that propel persons beyond the boundaries of fundamentalist faith.

Political and Economic Beasts

Premillennial books and newsletters have relentlessly stalked the Antichrist over the past few decades. Most sightings have taken the form of foreign leaders. The principal targets have continued to be Soviet politicians, Arab statesmen, or European aristocrats deemed likely to become leaders in the European Economic Community. All such efforts to ferret out the Beast share Dave Hunt's assumption that

> somewhere, at this very moment, on planet Earth, the Antichrist is almost certainly alive—biding his time, awaiting his cue. . . . Already a mature man, he is probably active in politics, perhaps even an admired world leader whose name is almost daily on everyone's lips. Or he could be the head of a multinational corporation, or a little-known international banker.[49]

They also share Hunt's intuitive feel for the key quality or identifying trait that will reveal the Beast's sinister nature: His public profession of tolerance, pluralism, one-worldism, global peace, and ecological purity. All of these, Hunt insists in his *Global Peace and the Rise of Antichrist*, are the hallmarks of the Antichrist. All belie an antipathy for the theological absolutes and rigid social boundaries that have demarcated American fundamentalism since its emergence nearly a century ago.

Hunt's identification of globalism, peace, and tolerance as "the horrifying image of the Antichrist" tells us much about what motivates the continuous naming of world leaders to the status of the Beast. Each Antichrist candidate has in some way been connected with the kinds of late-twentieth-century political, economic, and cultural trends that premillennialists find objectionable. Hunt, for example, concedes that there are sound economic and political reasons for promoting a more global outlook. He also concedes that are reasons to think that a new sense of world unity is necessary to rescue the entire planet from ecological collapse. But, Hunt warns, these are the reasons of Antichrist: "Unless one is a Christian and really believes that either Christ or Antichrist must rule the world, nothing makes better sense than a one-world government in some benign form."[50] Hunt shudders to hear that the National Education Association seeks to implement educational programs designed to help students embrace the ideals of global community or the equality and interdependence of all peoples. Even worse is that American citizens have largely applauded statements by such likely Antichrists as the pope or Mikhail Gorbachev when they urge tolerance and multicultural unity. Hunt and his fellow fundamentalists know that tolerance and belief in the equality of all cultures are steps toward surrendering belief in Christian superiority. They are, therefore, steps that inevitably lead toward the rule of the Antichrist. As Hunt puts it, "It is an easy step, especially in a child's mind, from tolerance to acceptance."[51] It is imperative that vigilance be maintained against any political leader or political institution that might promote such work of the Antichrist.

Economic forces have also pulled the world in directions that threaten to leave behind many middle-class Americans. Consider, for example, that computerization and the introduction of bar-code technologies have disadvantaged "mom and pop" retailers from coast to coast. New and more cosmopolitan forms of commerce have flourished at the expense of those who either lack access to new capital reserves or prefer to remain loyal to the older ways in which they were reared. Instances of economic disenfranchisement such as these are, of course, hardly new to the Western world or its heritage of interpreting worldly distress in apocalyptic terms.

The author of Revelation was acutely aware that those who participated in the cosmopolitan Roman world prospered while separatist Christians endured both poverty and scorn. His apocalyptic rendering of the situation was clear in its moral judgment and assured believers that triumph over outsiders was only a matter of time. In the order of the Antichrist, John warns, "no one can buy or sell unless he has the mark, that is, the name of the beast or the number of its name . . . on the right hand or the forehead." But those who bear this mark "shall drink the wine of God's wrath, poured unmixed into the cup of his anger, and he shall be tormented with fire and brimstone." It has therefore been incumbent on Bible prophecy writers to identify just how and where these predictions are manifested today as the world moves further away from the political–economic forms with which they are familiar. We have already seen how the European Economic Community's computerized headquarters has provided premillennialists with a terrifying symbol of a one-world economic system capable of "marking" every person within its omniscient economic mind:

> It has been written in the Biblical Book of Revelations [sic] what is beginning to happen in today's world, that a vast conspiracy by certain banking interests in the U.S. and abroad are deliberately wrecking the economy of the U.S. and planning a world-wide depression . . . that will culminate in this laser "Mark of the Beast." . . . The European Common Market Computer at Brussels, Belgium . . . [is] pre-fixed by the number 666. It is called the Beast by those who built it and work on it.[52]

Alert students of Bible prophecy have detected other clever schemes to institute the Antichrist's one-world economy. In 1986 David Webber and Noah Hutchings realized that there could be only one reason that the U.S. Post Office wanted citizens to begin using a nine-digit zip code. A nine-digit zip code coupled with a nine-digit social security number means that each of us will be marked by the government with a total of eighteen digits; this, of course, is combination of three sixes.[53]

Charles Taylor, who for years has been identifying Spain's King Juan Carlos as the most likely person to emerge as the Antichrist, is one of many prophecy writers who has circulated the rumor that the U.S. government inadvertently revealed its intention to turn over the nation to the Antichrist when it prematurely issued social security checks that required a mark on the forehead or hand in order to be cashed. Although never having seen one of these checks himself, Taylor explained:

Scores of Social Security checks were accidentally mailed to recipients that required a special and unusual process for cashing. . . . The instructional paragraph [that had been developed for future use and was not to be implemented yet] of these particular checks was changed to read that the party cashing the check MUST HAVE THE PROPER IDENTIFICATION MARK IN THEIR RIGHT HAND OR FOREHEAD. . . . The technology is here. Bible prophecy is ready for fulfillment. The time is at hand.[54]

Mary Stewart Relfe's *When Your Money System Fails . . . The "666 System" Is Here* has sold over 600,000 copies. This book and its sequel, *The New Money System 666*, warn of the Antichrist's newest device, the bar codes on almost every product at the grocery store. Everywhere Relfe looked, she could find one or more sixes on these bar codes. Persistent effort confirmed her fear that consumer products, bank checks, government documents, and credit cards alike have at one time or another used some kind of numbering codes in which combinations of six were alarmingly visible to the discerning eye. Relfe is convinced that the ubiquity of sixes on bar codes is proof that a system is already in place awaiting the orders of the Antichrist. She is careful not to blame any one corporation for complicity with the Beast: It "is not these organizations which are evil, it is a World Wide Satanic Conspiracy (begun in the Garden when Eve was deceived) that is culminating in the alignment of all commerce today toward accommodating Satan's plan."[55] Relfe has little advice to offer concerning just how Christians might combat this cosmic conspiracy. Until the Rapture occurs, whisking them away to a life unfettered by secularist economies, they should be on the lookout for further activities of the Antichrist wherever they find such "behavioral traits as deception, flateries [*sic*], and much talk about Peace."[56]

Apostasy Running Rampant

Since its inception in 1 John, the symbol of the Antichrist has signaled a wariness of religious beliefs that venture beyond the confines of orthodoxy. Each new generation must account for the fact that otherwise decent human beings become attracted to apostate views. Religious conservatives historically have been quick to find the Antichrist wherever "false teachings" find particularly lively or sensible expression. As Billy Graham instructs, "The Bible teaches that Satan can transform himself into an 'angel of light,' adapting himself to every culture and every situation, even at times deceiving the believers. This is how Satan operates today."[57] An intelligence officer for the church militant, Father Vincent Miceli, reports, "We know that Satan and the Antichrist snare millions of souls through their fascination for novel doctrines and their enthusiasm for revolutionary morals."[58] Today, as never before, novel doctrines and progressive conceptions of morality attract educated Americans. Prophecy students find themselves saddled with a tremendous responsibility to locate this Beast of apostasy and ward off his incursions into contemporary Christian life.

For his part, Miceli can hardly be accused of slackening his vigilance against the possibility that many people in our culturally pluralistic era might be tempted to seek out new understandings of faith and morality. To his horror, proposals for progressive understandings of faith have been championed by laity and clergy alike: "All the enemies of God, but especially the 'New Church' Catholics, as heretics and rebels against God and His church, bear the characteristic mark of the Antichrist."[59] Miceli, furthermore, has a good idea of just which moral and doctrinal tendencies bear the Antichrist's characteristic mark. Among the Beast's most blatant assaults on the church have been his ability to induce people to favor permitting divorced couples to receive communion, allowing women the power to preach with authority, countenancing the use of birth control, teaching pacifism, and urging the creation of a more democratic, nonhierarchical church.

Hal Lindsey has perhaps been the most successful of all premillennialists in alerting readers to the inroads that the Antichrist has already made in American culture. Lindsey particularly singles out those church leaders who deny or minimize the apocalyptic teachings that have earned him such a handsome profit. Addressing the choice between premillennialism and the nonmillennialist teachings prevalent in most churches, Lindsey looks for biblical guidance:

> Peter writes that in the "last days" there would be "mockers" who would say: "Where is the promise of His coming?" (2 Peter 3:4 NASB)
> John, the apostle of love, spoke strongly about false teachers who deny the fact that Christ will return bodily to earth the second time. He wrote: "For many deceivers have gone out into the world, those who do not acknowledge Jesus Christ as coming in the flesh. This is the deceiver and the antichrist" (2 John 7 NASB).
> We need to be alert. When we hear church leaders, teachers, or preachers questioning the visible return of Christ, this is a doctrine of apostasy.[60]

As Stephen O'Leary observes, "one can hardly imagine a better strategy for inoculating an audience against counterarguments than to dub one's opponents as 'deceivers and antichrists.'"[61] Lindsey's rhetorical strategy in naming the Antichrist is in this sense reminiscent of the Millerite preacher Charles Fitch, who a century earlier proclaimed that "whoever is opposed to the PERSONAL REIGN of Jesus Christ over this world on David's throne, is ANTICHRIST."[62] The message in either case is clear: It is high time to cease intellectualizing about Bible prophecy and separate ourselves from all those who persist in inhabiting Antichrist's apostate churches.

Lindsey also shed apocalyptic light on the religious sensibilities of today's college-educated youth. The students he met on campuses had been exposed to evolutionary biology, non-Western cultures, and philosophical critiques of claims to intellectual certainty or absolutism. These students have consequently gravitated to more liberal or ecumenical forms of religious thinking. He talked with many who yearned for a more intense form of spiritual experience than their churches could provide and, already dissatisfied with theological orthodoxy, looked to alternative forms of spirituality. Some were curious about exploring mysticism, even if it meant looking beyond biblical religion to non-Western religious traditions. Lindsey realized, of course, that once persons begin to follow their own spiritual sensibilities, they may stray far beyond the doctrinal boundaries that demarcate the ranks of the faithful. His interpretation of such pluralistic and ecumenical kinds of spirituality was predictable and sounded a warning to potentially wayward souls: "We believe that the joining of churches in the present ecumenical movement, combined with this amazing rejuvenation of star-worship, mind-expansion, and witchcraft, is preparing the world in every way for the establishment of a great religious system, one which will influence the Antichrist."[63]

Detroit attorney Constance Cumbey also stumbled across the Antichrist's influence in various forms of alternative American spirituality. In her 1983 book, *The Hidden Dangers of the Rainbow*, Cumbey sought to educate unsuspecting Christians about the organized conspiracy being perpetrated by the many kinds of spiritual interests that are frequently characterized as "New Age":

> It is the contention of this writer that for the first time in history there is a viable movement—the New Age Movement—that truly meets all the scriptural requirements for the antichrist and the political movement that will bring him on the world scene. It is further the position of the writer that this most likely is the great apostasy or "falling away" spoken of by the Apostle Paul and that the antichrist's appearance could be a very real event in our immediate future.[64]

The kinds of religious groups that Cumbey has in mind are those exploring metaphysical ideas concerning the potential unity between humans and the spirit of God. Cumbey found that many New Age groups use the rainbow as a symbol of the spiritual bridge connecting individual souls with the Over-Soul or God. She warns that this concept of a direct link between individuals and God is antibiblical, and for this reason alone, the symbol of the rainbow is fraught with "hidden dangers." Cumbey's point is not simply that such contemporary interest in metaphysical ideas is naive or unscriptural. Instead, she contends that New Age religious organizations have concocted an organized conspiracy to turn our nation into a Nazi-like regime. Cumby claims that reliable sources have informed her that New Age operatives are planning a political overthrow of the U.S. government and have already infiltrated orthodox medical, religious, governmental, and business organizations.

Cumbey is not clear about what New Agers hope to do with all these institutions once they have taken them over. But she is certain that they have already succeeded in deceiving thousands into accepting the fraudulent notion that humans are able to become inwardly closer to God. She notes that New Age groups have prompted Americans to become interested in such blatantly non-Christian topics as Jungian psychology, Yoga meditation, the coscientific spirituality of Teilhard de Chardin, and the metaphysical interpretations of humanity's "higher spiritual nature" found in such occult sources as theosophy, Edgar Cayce, and trance channeling.

Many scholars interpret this interest as a search for forms of spirituality befitting a scientific and culturally pluralistic age.[65] New Age religion promotes forms of religious thinking that encourage people to find inner harmony with God. Understanding God as immanent throughout the universe, New Age movements tend to endorse lifestyles that revere all life and are therefore nonracist, nonsexist, and sensitive to environmental concerns. Cumbey finds these contemporary forms of spirituality abhorrent and believes that they are the fulfillment of the prophecy in Daniel 11:21 that warns us of false prophets who will "obtain the kingdom by flatteries. . . . I believe the central flattery the antichrist and his followers will employ is the same as that consistently employed by Satan in the past: 'Thou shalt be as god.'"[66] Cumbey has, in fact, identified one New Age writer, Matthew Fox, as in all likelihood the Antichrist himself. Cumbey claims that Matthew Fox is a pen name and that his original name can be reworked in ways that yield the mark of 666: "Whether he is or is not, however, his net effect is just as deleterious. If people buy the perverted gospel of Matthew Fox, their souls will be just as eternally lost as if they take the mark of the beast from the actual antichrist!"[67]

Dave Hunt offers yet another insight into the Antichrist's rise to power through contemporary religious tendencies. Hunt realizes that "the environmental movement could play a significant role in bringing the unity essential to the rise of Antichrist."[68] Conceding that there is a global ecological crisis, Hunt is true to his premillennialist commitments and acknowledges that humans will never solve the problems of this earth. Rather than seeking to use frail reason to improve this world, they should instead repent their sins and await the return of the Lord who—in the twinkling of an eye—will rejuvenate this earth and all who are fit for eternal life.

The environmental movement is bereft of such Christian vision. Instead, it is laying the foundation for the coming world religion by fostering pantheistic ideas about the presence of God in nature. Hunt is quick to defend the literal reading of the Bible that establishes a cosmic hierarchy ruled by a male supreme being. In practice, this hierarchical model of the universe has encouraged many in the United States to view white male Americans as highest on the divine scale of things, thereby justifying various forms of sexism, racism, nationalism, and environmental exploitation.[69] The notion of an immanent God, equally accessible by people of all nations, genders, and races, consequently has threatening implications. Hunt sees them all. He warns, "Laying the foundation for the coming world religion, ecological concerns are being expressed increasingly even by atheists in spiritual pantheistic/New Age terms, as though the universe were a living and even conscious entity (the Gaia hypothesis) with whom we must make peace and live in harmony."[70] Hunt correctly notes that for those in the environmental movement, spirituality has to do with learning to become connected with cosmos as a whole. He cites then-Senator Al Gore as a prime spokesman for this gospel of the Antichrist and quotes him declaring— in Moscow no less—that "I do not see how the environmental problem can be solved without reference to spiritual values found in every faith." The problem, of course, is that Gore was not referring to exclusively Christian values but, rather, to values that derive from what Gore called "a new faith in the future of life on earth . . . [providing] higher values in the conduct of human affairs."[71] Hunt is emphatic about the connection of this kind of spirituality with the imminent rise of the Antichrist. It suggests, after all, that global peace is a spiritual imperative when any Bible-reading premillennialist knows that Christ will not return until the goriest battle of human history, the battle of Armageddon, is in full swing. It also suggests that every religion possesses insights into how people can find harmony with God when fundamentalists are already certain of their monopoly on religious truth. Perhaps worst of all, such pantheistic/New Age language encourages people "to love and accept themselves and to recognize their inherent 'self-worth'" when it is obvious that this message would lead to the dissolution of a community based on absolutist authority.[72]

The Antichrist, it seems, has found many effective disguises in which to operate in the late twentieth century. Secular intellectual thought, popular culture, technological advances, economic innovations, and even the environmental movement all have threatened to persuade Americans to adopt lifestyles that leave the world of premillennialism far behind. No person or family can escape coming into contact with these main currents of contemporary life. The risk of finding oneself or one's children seduced by these wayward influences is great. The battle against unbelief is thus no longer restricted to discovering and thwarting groups of unbelieving outsiders (Jews, Catholics, Socialists), as it was earlier in the century. In the late twentieth century, the battle against unbelief has become increasingly focused on finding and defeating one's own internal impulses to affiliate with the surrounding world. Contemporary symbols of the Antichrist have therefore been less concerned with portraying external groups as the feared disbelievers than with identifying those aspects of people's own thoughts and desires that are vulnerable to wayward influences. The Antichrist is, in the final analysis, a projection of the "unacceptable aspects of the self." The act of naming the Antichrist thus provides a symbolic vehicle for projecting disloyal—and hence loathsome—tendencies onto a cosmic backdrop against which people might gain a more acceptable understanding of this internal war between good and evil. In this way, many Americans have found it possible to exorcise themselves of disbelief and to remain among the ranks of those who will be vindicated on the day of final reckoning.

Interpreting the Obsession

History is both a descriptive and an interpretive discipline. As an academic discipline belonging to the humanities, history is expected to enrich our understanding of all that it means to be human. To do this, historians frequently need to go beyond what is objectively reported in the historical record and try to reconstruct layers of meaning, motivation, and significance that have perhaps never been fully clear to the participants in a particular historical tradition. For this reason, good historical scholarship must be cautious. Ascribing motivations to other persons is a precarious enterprise, fraught with opportunities to impose our own interpretive biases on actions of the past or present. Many contemporary historians are so acutely aware of the potential for interpretive bias that they refrain from judgments of any kind. The result often is history of the blandest sort. We are left with historical narratives in which every cause is just, every group noble, every belief as sincere and as intellectually credible as any other belief. History of this sort might help us know the past, but it does little to help us understand or learn from it.

The story of the "American Antichrist" contains far too many glimpses into our nation's religious psyche to allow flinching from the task of historical interpretation. The subtitle of this book, "The History of an American Obsession," is intended to make it clear from the outset that I have tried to help readers understand Americans' enduring proclivity for "naming the Antichrist." By using the word *obsession* I have tried to draw attention to the ways in which apocalyptic name-calling resembles popular conceptions of an obsession as a persistent preoccupation with an irrational idea or feeling. The word *obsession* also is intended to alert us to the ways in which certain kinds of repetitive behavior lead us away from healthy functioning. My goal throughout this chronicle of the American Antichrist has been to provide some insight into the social and psychological dynamics underlying this obsessional interest in the mythic beast of Revelation. This is not to say, however, that I believe that there is only one such historical interpretation. Our interpretations of the American penchant for "naming the Antichrist" differ widely depending on how each of us defines what it means to be "rational" or to function in "healthy" ways. Although this fact militates against the possibility of single interpretations of this tradition, it does not diminish the importance of using various interpretive perspectives to shed light on such an important chapter in American religious life.

Many historical works have already sought to clarify the meanings and significance of apocalyptic discourse. One of the best known is Norman Cohn's *The Pursuit of the Millennium*, which maintains that apocalyptic thinking is essentially a "paranoid" response to economic deprivation and political persecution. The original edition of this work uses psychoanalytic theory to help explain the psychological appeal of medieval apocalypticism. Cohn argues that any attempt to explain apocalyptic fantasies such as the concept of the Antichrist

> cannot afford to ignore the psychic content of the phantasies which have inspired them. All these phantasies are precisely such as are commonly found in individual cases of paranoia. The megalomaniac view of oneself as the elect, wholly good, abominably persecuted yet assured of ultimate triumph; the attribution of gigantic and demonic powers to the adversary; the refusal to accept the ineluctable limitations and imperfections of human existence, such as transience, dissension, conflict, fallibility whether intellectual or moral; the obsession with inerrable prophecies—these attitudes are symptoms which together constitute the unmistakable syndrome of paranoia. But a paranoiac delusion does not cease to be so because it is shared by so many individuals, nor yet because those individuals have real and ample grounds for regarding themselves as victims of oppression.[1]

Cohn understandably came under scholarly attack for this facile application of modern clinical categories to records deriving from another historical era.[2] The revised edition of his text wholly omits this analysis and sharply reduces other uses of psychoanalytic theory to explain the meanings and motivations of apocalyptic discourse. Cohn was wise to be more cautious about trying to disclose the "true" nature of historical actors who subscribed to one ideological tradition by applying interpretive categories drawn from an ideological viewpoint that is fashionable in our own era. His original argument nonetheless has merit. Apocalyptic thought is certainly laden with fantasies about evil adversaries. The psychic content of these fantasies must surely hold clues to the functions of millennial thought in the lives of persons or communities. Modern scholars like Cohn thus seem justified in using the best theoretical tools at their disposal to uncover otherwise hidden dimensions of human activity. Every theoretical perspective has its limitations, but historians must seek to advance human understanding, even though their interpretations are themselves products of particular historical forces.

Cohn advanced an additional perspective on apocalyptic thinking: He found that industrial workers in technologically advanced societies typically show little interest in apocalyptic beliefs. Cohn contends that such workers are concerned with improving their own conditions through self-directed efforts and are consequently unlikely to base their hopes for a better future on some supernatural or miraculous change in worldly conditions. He believes that his research demonstrates, however, that technologically backward or economically desperate populations are much more apt to be attracted to fantasies of a final, apocalyptic struggle resulting in the triumph of the faithful. His argument, then, is that apocalyptic beliefs promise a kind of illusionary panacea. Those without real worldly prospects can find comfort in the assurance that the tables will soon be turned, with the last becoming first and the first being destined for a lake of fire.

Michael Barkun offers another version of this scholarly tendency to view apocalyptic thinking as a "coping" mechanism found among the educationally and economically deprived. In his *Disaster and the Millennium*, Barkun contends that natural and human disasters predispose people to an apocalyptic view of the world. Analyzing the historical settings in which apocalyptic movements have arisen in diverse cultures and historical eras, Barkun concludes that "disasters serve to predispose individuals to millenarian conversion."[3] David Aberle's theory of "relative deprivation" is yet another variation on this attempt to link apocalyptic thinking with fragile socioeconomic status or the experience of disaster. Defining relative deprivation as "a negative discrepancy between legitimate expectation and actuality," Aberle argues that apocalyptic belief tends to prevail among people who experience such discrepancy in their pursuit of possessions, status, behavior, or worth.[4] Robert Jay Lifton provides an additional version of this coping theory in maintaining that apocalyptic believers suffer from psychological conditions of "anomie" and "absence of meaning."[5]

More recently, Charles Strozier has written a psychological study of apocalyptic thinking in America in which he asserts that preoccupation with end-times imagery "has roots in trauma in the self."[6] Strozier's concern is not so much that psychological trauma gives rise to magical fantasies about an imminent battle between cosmic good and evil, but that these fantasies tragically lead individuals even further away from satisfactory relationships with the surrounding world. The dualistic categories of apocalyptic thinking mirror the brokenness within the self and thus even further "isolate the fundamentalist individual from complex social interaction."[7] Strozier maintains that apocalyptic thinking undermines personal efficacy by denigrating the present as profoundly evil and shifting the source of agency away from the self to God. As a result, premillennialist thinking "tends to undermine personal efficacy and a commitment to human purposes."[8]

In *Arguing the Apocalypse*, Stephen O'Leary notes that even though each of these theories sheds light on certain features of apocalyptic discourse, none is fully adequate. He notes, for example, that apocalyptic thinking has appealed to persons in a wide variety of socioeconomic classes and in times of prosperity as well as adversity. Just as important, most people experiencing disaster or relative deprivation never end up traveling in apocalyptic circles. O'Leary turns his attention instead to the theodicial functions of apocalyptic belief. Although he agrees that paranoia, disaster, relative deprivation, and anomie all help explain varying predispositions to apocalyptic discourse, O'Leary insists that its central function is that of explaining the persistence of evil. In his assessment, "the unique feature of apocalyptic myth is that it offers a temporal or teleological framework for understanding evil by claiming that evil must grow in power until the appointed time of the imminent end."[9] Apocalyptic thinking, then, is intended to "solve" the problem of evil through its mythic reworking of time. Apocalyptic discourse places believers in the context of cosmic time, providing assurance that by enduring various hardships they are participating in the movement of history toward its ultimate fulfillment.

Readers will find much in the history of the American Antichrist to corroborate each of these interpretations of apocalyptic belief. Indeed, each of these theories alerted me to possible meanings and motivations in this history. To this extent, each of these perspectives has been incorporated into the preceding narrative, though none has emerged as anything approaching a definitive framework for explaining the "true" significance of the Antichrist tradition in the United States. Indeed, I am doubtful that any single meaning, motivation, or significance underlies Americans' varied uses of apocalyptic rhetoric. This is not to say, however, that we cannot make some concluding generalizations about Americans' efforts to name the Antichrist. I have personally found it helpful to approach this historical project from what might be characterized as the perspective of philosophical pragmatism, and its corollary in the natural and social sciences known as *functionalism*.[10] Functionalist interpretations of persons or groups focus not on what they "are" but, rather, on what they do. More specifically, functionalism assesses various actions or ideas in terms of how effectively they facilitate organisms' adaptation to the social, economic, and moral worlds they inhabit. The significance of an action or idea is thus determined by the degree to which it enables organisms to function effectively and healthfully in the larger natural and social environments.

A functionalist interpretation of specific religious beliefs, such as belief in the Antichrist, focuses on the functions of these beliefs in guiding individual or group interaction with the surrounding world. Philosophical pragmatism comes into play as we begin seeking some means of comparing or evaluating competing ideas or beliefs. Pragmatism shifts our attention away from philosophy's traditional interest in judging the truth of an idea, in favor of the task of assessing an idea's functional value. Pragmatism, in fact, is wary of any attempt by humans to discover "ultimate" truth. The radically contingent nature of the universe and the changing character of human history make such truth elusive. Pragmatism is instead concerned with "working truths," ideas that provide effective hypotheses for action that will nourish us as persons and as groups. As William James put it, pragmatism's "only test of probable truth is what works best in the way of leading us, what fits every part of life best and combines with the collectivity of experience's demands, nothing being omitted."[11] From a pragmatist perspective, there are no moral absolutes to guide our conduct. We must instead use the full range of our critical intellects to find courses of action that will fulfill the greatest range of our personal and collective needs. In James's words, we must act in ways that work "always for the richer universe, for the good which seems most organizable, most fit to enter into complex combinations, most apt to a member of a more inclusive whole."[12]

A pragmatist interpretation of the act of "naming the Antichrist" reveals this chapter of American cultural history to contain few heroes, few people who championed ideas that would seem to work for a richer universe. It is important to repeat the caution that appears near the end of Chapter 4. Most persons who belong to the religious institutions associated with premillennial thought are undoubtedly motivated more by the love of family and cherished values than by the kinds of mean-spirited territorialism that factored so prominently in our story of the American Antichrist. To this extent, however, they have emphasized the prophetic dimension of premillennial thought at the expense of the more specifically apocalyptic themes typically associated with the far right end of the theological spectrum.

From a pragmatic perspective, it is when the balance shifts from the prophetic outlook to apocalypticism and separatism that ultraconservative religion is most likely to thwart wholeness-making behavior. From the Salem witchcraft trials to the denunciation of proponents of ecology, the historical record is sufficiently clear that apocalyptic name-calling has served decidedly nativistic and tribalistic functions. The labeling of witches, Catholics, Jews, Masons, Deists, modernists, socialists, feminists, or various forms of humanists as the Antichrist functioned not to promote "more inclusive wholes" but to strengthen the separatism or tribalism that has been integral to apocalyptic communities since biblical times. Naming the Antichrist is a vivid example of such territorialism. Although the separation of clan groups is elementary throughout nature, humans today can ill afford the barriers to communication and

cooperation that territorial and tribalistic behaviors erect. We might here
repeat this important observation concerning tribalism offered by biologist Garrett Hardin:

> Any group of people that perceives itself as a distinct group, and which is
> so perceived by the outside world, may be called a tribe. The group might
> be a race, as ordinarily defined, but it need not be; it can just as well be a
> religious sect, a political group, or an occupational group. The essential
> characteristic of a tribe is that it should follow a double standard of mo-
> rality—one kind of behavior for in-group relations, another for out-
> group.[13]

The act of "naming the Antichrist" has time and again promoted
precisely this kind of tribalistic boundary posturing. It has made it possible to love one's family and religious community while hating all who
are associated with the Antichrist. Belief that Jews, Catholics, socialists, humanists, or feminists are in league with the Beast has made the
most uncivil behavior toward the "social other" a badge of piety and
religious devotion. No doubt the perception of disaster, anomie, relative deprivation, or technological backwardness all have contributed to
the functional value of apocalyptic belief in distinguishing between in-
group and out-group identity. I would like to draw attention, however,
to the fact that all of these factors in predisposing persons to apocalyptic thought share something: Each points to what might be called a "curtailed sense of agency." Western religious thought has, since biblical
times, offered both a prophetic and an apocalyptic outlook on the world.
Whereas prophetic thought places more emphasis on the role of humans
in responding actively and responsibly to God's will, apocalyptic thought
ascribes all decisive activity to God (and his angelic forces) and thereby
offers hope even to a powerless or socially passive group. By its very
nature, apocalyptic thinking grows out of and appeals to the sense of
curtailed human agency. This is undoubtedly part of the reason that
we witnessed such virulent Antichrist naming in the first half of the
twentieth century. Premillennial Christians realized that they were losing hold of the cultural center. No longer possessing the social clout to
hold outside groups at bay, they resorted instead to the only weapon
left in their meager arsenal: apocalyptic name-calling.

Naming the Antichrist created an "ethnic" identity for many white,
religiously ultraconservative Americans. It served the adaptive function
of demarcating all those who are to be considered out-group but did so
by separating premillennialists from precisely those trends of twentieth-
century life that humanist scholars deem most likely to contribute to
the progressive amelioration of human life. The apocalyptic rhetoric of
naming the Antichrist has perpetuated intellectual outlooks that are
functionally counterproductive. That is, the "over and againstness" of
apocalyptic rhetoric has prompted large numbers of Americans to ig-

nore the productive possibilities of "modernist" thought, to remain mired in tribalistic prejudice, and to fail to reach out for a form of civil discourse that would help them become contributing members of a pluralistic and fully democratic society.

The cultural situation for premillennialists changed slightly in the final decades of the twentieth century. Whereas the problem of unbelief had formerly been the growing presence of unbelieving outsiders, the problem of unbelief in the latter part of the century became that of confronting elements of unbelief within themselves. Premillennialists have found themselves engulfed by a foreign world and, at times, have found themselves tempted to "defect" to the technologies, entertainment, lifestyles, or academic standards that this foreign world has produced. It has been important, therefore, that apocalyptic imagery function in ways that erect boundaries that are more psychological than social in nature. That is, vigilance against the Antichrist not only legitimates hatred of those outside one's own tribe, but it also helps "wall off" one's own unacceptable thoughts and desires. This has been particularly true in the last few decades when the Antichrist has been variously located in ecumenical religious thought, modern computer systems, supermarket bar codes, fiber optics, the feminist movement, rock music, the European Economic Community, and the ecological movement. The obsession with these faces of the Antichrist has been a continuing struggle with what Richard Hofstadter termed the "unacceptable aspects of the self." The act of naming the Antichrist has projected onto a demonic enemy the "unacceptable" tendencies that people refuse to recognize in themselves. It is the Antichrist, not themselves, who are responsible for the divided loyalties that plague them. With so many aspects of American life potentially luring individuals away from the premillennialist fold, it is no wonder that the Antichrist has been found camouflaging himself in diverse sectors of modern culture.

A pragmatist interpretation of Antichrist imagery must be concerned with assessing whether this imagery functions to promote or hinder psychological health. It often seems that contemporary schools of psychological thought agree on very little. But on one thing they all are in accord: Psychological health requires the attainment and preservation of a fundamental sense of self-worth. What psychologists such as Erik Erikson, D. W. Winnicott, and Heinz Kohut showed is that this pursuit of self-worth begins early in infancy and is initially acquired through a certain rapport or communion with a nurturing parent. What Kohut terms the universal need for idealization and merger refers to the psychological necessity of finding a "higher" other such as the mother from whom the infant can receive a sense of security and well-being. The infant comes to feel warm and prized largely through its merger with the "higher" being of the parent. This mirrored sense of worth gives rise to a healthy narcissism, that is, the earliest psychological ability to maintain a sense of being a prized, cohesive self. As it grows older and thus more detached from the nurturing parent, it nonetheless continues to have a psychological need for feeling connected to a "Higher Other" in relation to which it might sustain this sense of meaningfulness and self-worth. Religion and other "idealized" cultural values often fulfill this need. Psychologist of religion Peter Homans notes perceptively that classical Protestantism has flourished largely owing to its ability to meet this fundamental psychological need for idealization and merger. The evangelical doctrine of the believer's oneness with Christ—I am in Christ and Christ in me—nurtures the believer's need for merger with an idealized "higher other."[14] In this way evangelical belief satisfies important psychological needs in the lives of millions of contemporary Americans.

Unfortunately, much of modern culture threatens the literal truth value of evangelical Christian belief and therefore jeopardizes many Americans' ability to "idealize" and merge with Christ. Insofar as modern culture may sever people from their source of feeling prized and meaningful, it also may threaten to curtail their sense of agency. Modern culture has inflicted a sense of powerlessness on many Americans that is expressed in a host of emotions linked with apocalyptic rage: hopelessness, self-loathing, bitter hatred, victimization, and a desire to seek revenge on one's oppressors. No person or family can escape coming into contact with aspects of modern culture that entice them into defecting from the community of belief. The battle against unbelief, then, is not so much a battle against external groups who believe differently but against one's own "destructive" inclinations. Any urge to affiliate with the surrounding world is accompanied by an internal battle of ontological proportions insofar as this urge simultaneously threatens to sever the self from its accustomed source of being worthy, valued, and loved. Persons or environmental influences that prompt such inclinations understandably produce a considerable amount of dissonance and anxiety. These external influences are understandably perceived as threatening one's basic safety and organismic well-being. As psychologist Paul Pruyser observed,

> It is extremely interesting to note how frequently any beliefs partake of descriptive or explanatory imagery in which persons, or person-like entities, are conjured up to convey their existential significance or cosmic meanings. The human mind becomes automatically mythopoetic when it has to contend with threatened or actual attack upon a person's organismic integrity.[15]

The apocalyptic heritage to which modern premillennialists are heir is adept at projecting such anxiety onto a mythic villain. The symbol of the Antichrist shapes an ontological reality congruent with these anxieties and in so doing satisfies the believer's need to interpret the sur-

rounding world (e.g., humanistic education, rock music, ecumenical religion, hopes for world peace) as fraught with danger and deceit. The
tyranny and deceit attributed to the Antichrist mirror the anxiety and
self-loathing aroused by one's own continuing inclinations to jeopar-
dize connection with the "Higher Other" of Christ. This is, I think, what
literary critic W. Warren Wagar had in mind when he suggested that
the bedrock of apocalyptic thinking is a primitive level of human emotion containing fears of separation, powerlessness, loneliness, and failing. The mythopoetic language of evil adversaries, reigns of lawlessness
and terror, catastrophe, and final victory over one's enemies is ultimately
rooted in one's own primal fears and hungers. As Wagar put it,

> Destructive impulses [i.e., the urge to destroy the Antichrist] are related
> organically to the same fears of powerlessness that nourish fantasies about
> heroically saving the world or surviving its end. *A sense of powerlessness can
> invoke* all the devils of Thanatos: uncontrollable rage, bitter hatred, insa-
> tiable gluttony and lust, the desire to destroy supposed enemies and op-
> pressors, self-loathing, and cravings for humiliation and death.[16]

The point here is that psychological as well as sociological threats
to our sense of agency and self-worth are likely to dispose us to apocalyptic, as opposed to prophetic, modes of religious discourse. To this
extent, contemporary symbols of the Antichrist function in a way similar
to what psychologist Melanie Klein called "bad objects." Klein's clinical experience led her to conclude that obsessions with evil or hostile
adversaries are typically projections of a person's own anxieties and
impulses.[17] She found that beginning in childhood, many of these emotions and impulses are so threatening that they must be projected onto
the external world. That is, these destructive impulses are projected onto
a variety of external persons or objects that are thereafter perceived as
harsh and either superhuman or extra worldly. In this way, "bad objects"
become the basis of a repetition compulsion involving a constant attempt
to establish external danger situations that will mobilize a person against
his or her own erring or destructive impulses.

Modern images of the Antichrist provide a psychological symbol
capable of constraining those errant tendencies that would otherwise
sever the self from continued merger with Christ. They do so, however,
at a tragic price. Rather than strengthening people's own sense of responsible action, as does the prophetic core of the Judeo-Christian witness, apocalyptic imagery exacerbates the very conditions of curtailed
agency that predispose persons to it in the first place. It turns them away
from the revelations open to the human intellect, away from community with the whole of God's creation, and away from activity designed
to promote peace or good will across the earth.

Those who engage in naming the Antichrist feel themselves exorcised of the demons of disbelief and consequently numbered among

those who will be vindicated on the day of final reckoning. Like all obsessions, however, the naming of the Antichrist seeks to preserve the self by narrowing rather than enlarging its field of vision. The tragedy of this obsession is that it closes off believers from the possibility of finding an idealized or "Higher Other" immanent in the world about them. Obsession with the Antichrist closes off persons from discovering the redemptive and wholeness-making possibilities of the many persons, ideas, and cultural activities that lie immediately before them. In religious terms, the obsession with the Antichrist has channeled many Americans' desire to be loyal to God into hate-filled crusades rather than into efforts leading to a deepened receptivity to, or communion with, the "Higher Other" (whether conceived as transcendent or immanent) in relation to which they can know themselves to be inherently valued and prized.

The history of the American Antichrist has proved to be a varied and fascinating one. It has revealed just how frail human existence can be and how many people frequently cope with this frailty by mythologizing life in apocalyptic ways. It appears that the sea of human insecurities is teeming with beasts that arise to threaten their social and psychological well-being. At times these beasts have threatened the boundaries of their social or theological orthodoxy. At other times they have ravaged the psychological boundaries that protect them from our own wayward inclinations. By mythologizing these threats—by naming the Antichrist—they seek to push back the threat of chaos, restore order, and secure their sense of agency and well-being. The historical record seems to indicate, however, that apocalyptic name-calling has rarely functioned in ways that lead to a productive engagement with life. Seldom have carriers of the Antichrist tradition acted in ways that demonstrably worked for a richer universe, for the good that seems most organizable, most fit to enter into complex combinations, most apt to be a member of a more inclusive whole. In brief, this relentless obsession with the Antichrist appears to have done more to forestall than to signal the realization of the Kingdom of God on earth.

Notes

Introduction

1. Wilhelm Bousset, *Der Antichrist in der Uberlieferung des Judentums, das Neuen Testament und der alten Kirche* (Gottingen: Vandenhoeck & Ruprecht, 1895). Translated into English as *The Antichrist Legend: A Chapter in Jewish Folklore* (New York: AMS Press, 1985), Gregory C. Jenks, *The Origins and Early Development of the Antichrist Myth* (New York: Walter de Gruyter, 1991), and Bernard McGinn, *Visions of the End: Apocalyptic Traditions in the Middle Ages* (New York: Columbia University Press, 1979). Jenks provides a helpful overview of the historical scholarship on the Antichrist legend, including important qualifications concerning the merits of Bousset's influential work.

2. Jeffrey Burton Russell, *The Prince of Darkness* (Ithaca, NY: Cornell University Press, 1988); Richard Kenneth Emmerson, *Antichrist in the Middle Ages: A Study of Medieval Apocalypticism, Art, and Literature* (Seattle: University of Washington Press, 1981); and Christopher Hill, *Antichrist in Seventeenth-Century England* (Oxford: Oxford University Press, 1971). William Alnor's *Soothsayers of the Second Advent* (Old Tappan, NJ: Fleming H. Revell, 1989) is an informative and entertaining work by a contemporary evangelical who wishes to warn against the foolishness in which fellow evangelicals embroil themselves when they seek to set specific dates for the Second Coming or engage in the fallacy of "pinning the tail on the Antichrist."

3. "Beyond the Year 2000: What to Expect in the New Millennium," a special issue of *Time* (Fall, 1992).

4. This overview of Americans' end-times expectations presents the "pretribulation" position that places the rapture before period of the Antichrist's reign of lawlessness. It should be noted that although this has been the predominant belief among twentieth-century Christian premillennialists, there have been those who adhere to the "posttribulation" view that the rapture will occur after Christians have been forced to endure Antichrist's rule. See, for example, Jim McKeever's *Christians Will Go Through the Tribulation* (Medford, OR: Omega Publictions, 1980).

5. Martin E. Marty and R. Scott Appleby, eds., *Fundamentalisms Observed* (Chicago: University of Chicago Press, 1991), p. 820.

6. Ibid.

7. Michael Barkun, *Disaster and the Millennium* (New Haven, CT: Yale University Press, 1974). Barkun's contention that "disasters serve to predispose individuals to millenarian conversion" is perhaps overstated. By his own admission, his thesis holds up only if we believe that disaster "is to some extent in the eye of the beholder" and that "if the world has no disaster to offer, then one must be constructed." Thus Barkun's book, though an excellent study of early nineteenth-century millennialism, does not help us understand why in some circumstances disasters give rise to—and are symbolically managed with—apocalyptic thought, whereas in other circumstances we find no widespread movement to embrace apocalyptic thought.

8. David A. Aberle, "A Note on Relative Deprivation Theory as Applied to Millenarian and Other Cult Movements," in *Millennial Dreams in Action: Studies in Revolutionary Religious Movements*, ed. Sylvia Thrupp (New York: Schocken Books, 1970).

9. Stephen O'Leary, *Reading the Signs of the Times* (New York: Oxford University Press, 1994). O'Leary's book, a rhetorical analysis of the logic of apocalyptic speech, contains an excellent review of recent studies of the social and psychological functions performed by apocalyptic thought.

10. Norman Cohn, *The Pursuit of the Millennium* (London: Secker and Warburg, 1957), p. 309. Capitulating to scholarly criticism of his application of modern psychiatric labels to medieval men and women, Cohn omitted this paragraph from the revised edition (Oxford: Oxford University Press, 1980).

11. See, for example, John Gager's *Kingdom and Community: The Social World of Early Christianity* (Englewood Cliffs, NJ: Prentice-Hall, 1975) for a sociological study of the emergence of apocalyptic thought among the "disinherited" peoples who were among the first to embrace Christianity.

12. Richard Hofstadter, *The Paranoid Style in American Politics* (New York: Knopf, 1965), p. 29.

13. Ibid., p. 32.

Chapter 1. Antichrist: The History of an Idea

1. Readers who wish a general introduction to these epistles or the other biblical materials covered in this book should consult one of several fine introductory-level textbooks such as Stephen Harris's *Understanding the Bible* (Toronto: Mayfield, 1992); Robert Spivey and D. Moody Smith's *Anatomy of the New Testament* (New York: Macmillan, 1989); Walter Harrelson's *Interpreting the Old Testament* (New York: Holt, Rinehart and Winston, 1964); or Morton Enslin's *The Literature of the Christian Movement* (New York: Harper & Row, 1938).

2. Perhaps the most helpful commentary on the epistles of John is Kenneth Grayston's *The Johannine Epistles* (Grand Rapids, MI: Wm. B. Eerdmans, 1984). Readers may also wish to consult Raymond E. Brown's *The Epistles of John* (Garden City, NY: Doubleday, 1982); or Charles Erdman's *The General Epistles* (Philadelphia: Westminster Press, 1966). Brown's commentary is partially colored by his assumption that 1 and 2 John's references to the Anti-

christ are to be linked with other New Testament references to Christ's "eschatological adversary," such as can be found in 2 Thessalonians and Revelation. This may or may not be the case, but it is surely not warranted by the scriptural passages themselves, as Grayston, for example, makes clear.

3. Grayston, *The Johannine Epistles*, pp. 16–20.

4. Ibid., p. 76.

5. Erdman, *The General Epistles*, p. 194.

6. Grayston, *The Johannine Epistles*, p. 79.

7. A more detailed discussion of how contemporary cognitive dissonance theory helps explain the development of early Christian belief can be found in John Gager, *Kingdom and Community: The Social World of Early Christianity* (Englewood Cliffs, NJ: Prentice-Hall, 1975).

8. Brown, *The Epistles of John*, p. 337.

9. Walter Harrelson, *Interpreting the Old Testament*, p. 227.

10. Paul D. Hanson, *The Dawn of Apocalyptic* (Philadelphia: Fortress Press, 1975).

11. A thorough discussion of the history of scholarly attempts to define apocalypticism as a literary genre can be found in John J. Collins's *The Apocalyptic Imagination* (New York: Crossroads Press, 1985). Collins also edited the Society of Biblical Literature's project on apocalyptic literature entitled *Apocalypse: The Morphology of a Genre. Semeia 14* (Missoula, MT: Scholars Press, 1974), which defines apocalyptic literature as "a genre of revelatory literature with narrative framework, in which a revelation is mediated by an otherworldly being to a human recipient, disclosing a transcendent reality which is temporal, insofar as it envisages eschatological salvation, and spatial insofar as it involves another, supernatural world" (p. 9).

12. See Klaus Koch's seminal study, *The Rediscovery of Apocalyptic* (Naperville, IL: Allenson, 1972).

13. David Hellholm, "The Problem of Apocalyptic Genre and the Apocalypse of John," in *Society of Biblical Literature 1982 Seminar Papers*, ed. K. H. Richards (Chico, CA: Scholars Press, 1982), p. 168.

14. Collins, *Apocalyptic Imagination*, p. 205.

15. Ibid., pp. 214–215.

16. An excellent account of the Book of Daniel that connects it directly to the developing Antichrist legend can be found in E. R. Chamberlain, *The Antichrist and the Millennium* (New York: Dutton, 1975). My reconstruction of Daniel follows Chamberlain's account. Readers interested in the history and current status of the literary study of Daniel should consult Shemaryahu Talmon's entry in Robert Alter and Frank Kermode, eds., *The Literary Guide to the Bible* (Cambridge, MA: Belknap Press, 1987), pp. 343–356.

17. See the discussions of early christology in Rudolf Bultmann's *Theology of the New Testament* (New York: Scribner, 1951); Enslin's *Literature of the Christian Movement*; Willi Marxsen's *Introduction to the New Testament* (Philadelphia: Fortress Press, 1970); and Hans Conzelmann's *An Outline of the Theology of the New Testament* (New York: Harper & Row, 1969).

18. A sound discussion of the controversies surrounding the authorship and date of composition of Revelation can be found in Adela Yarbro Collins's *Crisis and Catharsis* (Philadelphia: Westminster Press, 1984).

19. George Bernard Shaw, cited in Bernard McGinn's essay on the liter-

ary study of Revelation in Alter and Kermode, eds., *The Literary Guide to the Bible*, pp. 523–544.

20. See Adela Yarbro Collins, *The Combat Myth in the Book of Revelation* (Missoula, MT: Scholars Press, 1976), p. 33; and Collins, *Crisis and Catharsis*, p. 114.

21. Collins, *Combat Myth*, p. 114.

22. Collins, *Crisis and Catharsis*, p. 160.

23. In about 200 Hippolytus (d. 235) wrote a *Treatise on Christ and the Antichrist*, which is the most complete summary of early patristic traditions on the Antichrist. In his *Visions of the End: Apocalyptic Tradition in the Middle Ages* (New York: Columbia University Press, 1979), historian Bernard McGinn includes a remarkable physical description of the Antichrist written in the third century: "And these are the signs of him: his head is as a fiery flame; his right eye shot with blood, his left eye blueblack, and he hath two pupils. His eyelashes are white; and his lower lip is large; but his right thigh slender; his feet broad; his great toe is bruised and flat. This is the sickle of desolation" (p. 22).

24. See Wilhelm Bousset, *The Antichrist Legend* (London: Hutchison, 1896, reprinted by AMS Press, 1985), p. 140.

25. Ibid., p. 139.

26. See Jeffrey Burton Russell, *The Prince of Darkness* ((Ithaca, NY: Cornell University Press, 1988), p. 68.

27. Cited in Richard K. Emmerson, *Antichrist in the Middle Ages: A Study of Medieval Apocalypticism, Art, and Literature* (Seattle: University of Washington Press, 1981), p. 64.

28. Cited in Walter K. Price, *The Coming Antichrist* (Chicago: Moody Press, 1974), p. 32.

29. The following material on Adso's *Letter on the Origin and Life of the Antichrist* comes from Bernard McGinn's *Visions of the End*, pp. 82–87.

30. Ibid., p. 84.

31. Emmerson, *Antichrist in the Middle Ages*.

32. McGinn, *Visions of the End*, p. 32.

33. Cited in McGinn, *Visions of the End*, p. 138. Other analyses of Joachim's thought can be found in Marjorie Reeves, *The Influence of Prophecy in the Later Middle Ages: A Study in Joachimism* (Oxford: Clarendon Press, 1969); Bernard McGinn, *The Calabrian Abbot: Joachim of Fiore in the History of Western Thought* (New York: Macmillan, 1985); and Norman Cohn, *The Pursuit of the Millennium* (London: Secker and Warburg, 1957).

34. Cited in McGinn, *Visions of the End*, p. 175.

35. Ibid.

36. Ibid., p. 263.

37. Martin Luther, cited in Christopher Hill, *Antichrist in Seventeenth-Century England* (Oxford: Oxford University Press, 1971), p. 5.

38. See Hill, *Antichrist in Seventeenth-Century England*; Paul Christianson, *Reformers and Babylon: English Apocalyptic Visions from the Reformation to the Eve of the Civil War* (Toronto: University of Toronto Press, 1978); Katherine Firth, *The Apocalyptic Tradition* (New York: Oxford University Press, 1979); and Bryan W. Ball, *A Great Expectation: Eschatological Thought in English Protestantism to 1660* (Oxford: Oxford University Press, 1966).

39. Hill, *Antichrist in Seventeenth-Century England*, p. 44.

40. John Nayler, cited in Hill, *Antichrist in Seventeenth-Century England*, p. 2.

Chapter 2. Thwarting the Errand

1. John Bale, *Image of Both Churches*, cited in Thomas Brown, "The Image of the Beast: Anti-Papal Rhetoric in Colonial America," in *Conspiracy: The Fear of Subversion in American History*, ed. Richard Curry and Thomas Brown (New York: Holt, Rinehart and Winston, 1972), p. 4.

2. Ibid.

3. See William Haller, "John Foxe and the Puritan Revolution," in *The Seventeenth Century: Studies in the History of English Thought and Literature from Bacon to Pope*, ed. Richard F. Jones et al. (Stanford, CA: Stanford University Press, 1951), p. 122.

4. John Foxe, cited in Brown, "The Image of the Beast," p. 5.

5. Peter Gay, *A Loss of Mastery* (Berkeley and Los Angeles: University of California Press, 1966), p. 16.

6. Christopher Hill, *Antichrist in Seventeenth-Century England* (Oxford: Oxford University Press, 1971), p. 167.

7. William Bradford, *Of Plimouth Plantation* (Boston, 1901), p. 102.

8. Ibid.

9. A brilliant assessment of Danforth's sermon appears in Perry Miller's *Errand into the Wilderness* (Cambridge, MA: Harvard University Press, 1956), pp. 1–15.

10. See Sacvan Bercovitch's extended analysis of Puritan rhetoric and his engaging reinterpretation of Perry Miller's assessments in his *The American Jeremiad* (Madison: University of Wisconsin Press, 1978).

11. See J. F. Jameson, ed., *Johnson's Wonder-Working Providence* (New York, 1910) pp. 23, 25.

12. Cotton Mather, *Magnalia Christi Americana* (1702), ed. Thomas Robbins (Hartford, 1853), vol. 2, p. 579.

13. Cotton Mather, cited in Winthrop S. Hudson, *Religion in America* (New York: Scribner, 1973), p. 100.

14. Increase Mather, cited in William W. Sweet, *Religion in Colonial America* (New York: Scribner, 1951), p. 2.

15. Bradford, *Of Plimouth Plantation*, p. 110.

16. See Hudson, *Religon in America*, p. 20.

17. John Winthrop, quoted in Perry Miller, ed., *The American Puritans* (Garden City, NY: Doubleday, 1956), p. 82.

18. John Winthrop, quoted in Miller, *Errand into the Wilderness*, p. 6.

19. Miller, *Errand into the Wilderness*, p. 6.

20. See David Hall's *Worlds of Wonder, Days of Judgment: Popular Religious Belief in Early New England* (New York: Knopf, 1989), p. 91.

21. Ibid.

22. Ibid.

23. Increase Mather, quoted in Brown, "The Image of the Beast," p. 7.

24. Bradford, *Of Plimouth Plantation*, quoted in Lois P. Zamora, "The Myth of Apocalypse and the American Literary Imagination," in *The Apocalyptic Vision*

in America: Interdisciplinary Essays on Myth and Culture, ed. Lois P. Zamora (Bowling Green, OH: Bowling Green University Popular Press, 1982), p. 102.

25. Accounts of the cultural confrontations between the Native Americans and the early European settlers can be found in James Axtell's *The European and the Indian* (New York: Oxford University Press, 1981), *Imagining the Other: The First Encounters in North America* (Washington, DC: American Historical Association, 1991), and *After Columbus: Essays in the Ethnohistory of Colonial North America* (New York: Oxford University Press, 1988); Alden T. Vaughan, *New England Frontier: Puritans and Indians, 1620–1675* (Boston: Little, Brown, 1965); and Richard Slotkin, *Regeneration Through Violence: The Mythology of the American Frontier, 1600–1860* (Middletown, CT: Wesleyan University Press, 1973).

26. William Bradford, quoted in Vaughan, *New England Frontier,* p. 65.

27. Ibid.

28. Cotton Mather, *Magnalia Christi Americana,* vol. 1, p. 503.

29. Jonathan Edwards, "A History of the Work of Redemption," in *The Works of President Edwards* (London, 1817, reprinted in New York by Burt Franklin, 1968), p. 222.

30. Slotkin, *Regeneration Through Violence,* p. 73.

31. Vaughan, *New England Frontier,* p. 236.

32. Samuel Nowell, quoted in Richard Slotkin, *The Fatal Environment: The Myth of the Frontier in the Age of Industrialization, 1800–1890* (Middleton, CT: Wesleyan University Press, 1985), p. 57.

33. Ibid., p. 59.

34. See Vaughan, *New England Frontier,* p. 35.

35. Cotton Mather, quoted in Slotkin, *Regeneration Through Violence,* p. 120.

36. Ibid., p. 121.

37. Miller, *Errand into the Wilderness,* p. 143.

38. Cotton Mather, *Magnalia Christi Americana,* vol. 1, p. 454.

39. See Miller, *Errand into the Wilderness,* pp. 7–8.

40. Kai Erikson, *Wayward Puritans: A Study in the Sociology of Deviance* (New York: Wiley, 1966).

41. Ibid., p. 64.

42. Brief accounts of Roger Williams's life and controversial actions can be found in Winthrop Hudson's *Religion in America* or Sydney Ahlstrom's *A Religious History of the American People* (New Haven, CT: Yale University Press, 1972). A fuller account can be found in Clark Gilpin's *The Millenarian Piety of Roger Williams* (Chicago: University of Chicago Press, 1979). Finally, a discussion of the apocalyptic rhetoric surrounding Williams's debates with the New England authorities can be found in Brown's "The Image of the Beast."

43. See Brown, "The Image of the Beast," p. 8.

44. The most lively and illuminating discussion of Anne Hutchinson's disputes with the New England authorities can be found in Kai Erikson's *Wayward Puritans.* Much of the following account of Hutchinson's attempts to "thwart the New England errand" comes from Erikson's crisp analysis. Other accounts of the Hutchinsion episode include those by Edmund S. Morgan, *The Puritan Dilemma* (Boston: Little, Brown, 1958); David Hall, ed., *The Antinomian Controversy, 1636–1638: A Documentary History* (Middletown, CT: Wesleyan University Press, 1968); and William Stoever, *"A Faire and Easie Way to Heaven":*

Covenant Theology and Antinomianism in Early Massachusetts (Middletown, CT: Wesleyan University Press, 1978).

45. Quoted in Erikson, *Wayward Puritans*, p. 94.

46. Ibid., p. 101.

47. Lyle Kohler, in *A Search for Power* (Urbana: University of Illinois Press, 1980), contends that the hysterical seizures precipitating the Salem witchcraft episode were based on sexual and gender hostility. John Demos's "Underlying Themes in the Witchcraft of Seventeenth-Century New England," *American Historical Review* 75 (1970): 1311–26, suggests that the underlying cause was generational conflict. Richard Slotkin, in *Regeneration Through Violence*, argues that demonic possession was a parody of the experience of captivity by the Indians. Linda Caporeal, in "Ergotism: The Satan Loosed in Salem?" *Science*, (April 2, 1976, pp. 21–26, hypothesizes that a fungus infestation of rye bread produced the seizures and hallucinations that spawned the whole witchcraft episode. Readers might also wish to consult David Thomas Konig's *Law and Society in Puritan Massachusetts* (Chapel Hill: University of North Carolina Press, 1979) for his interpretation of how witchcraft enabled "opponents of the law" to find avenues for gaining extralegal power.

48. Paul Boyer and Stephen Nissenbaum, *Salem Possessed: The Social Origins of Witchcraft* (Cambridge, MA: Harvard University Press, 1974). Much of my discussion of Salem witchcraft follows their excellent account of the social drama enacted in the witchcraft trials.

49. Ibid., p. 103.

50. Ibid., p. 170.

51. Ibid., p. 174.

52. Cotton Mather, *The Wonders of the Invisible World* (Boston: 1692, reprinted Mount Vernon, NY: Peter Pauper Press, 1950), p. 6.

53. Ibid., p. 14.

54. Ibid.

55. Ibid., p. 15.

56. Ibid., p. 59.

57. See John Cotton, *The Churches Resurrection* (London: Printed by R. O. and G. D. for Henry Overton, 1642), *The Pouring out of the Seven Vials* (London: Printed by R. S. for Henry Overton, 1642), and *An Exposition upon the Thirteenth Chapter of the Revelation* (London: Printed for Livewel Chapman, 1655); Thomas Shepard, *The Parable of the Ten Virgins Opened and Applied* (London: Printed by J. H. for John Rothwell and Samuel Thomson, 1660); Ephraim Huit, *The Whole Prophecie of Daniel Explained* (London: Printed for H. Overton, 1644); William Aspinwall, *A Brief Descripton of the Fifth Monarch, of Kingdome That Shortly Is to Come into the World* (London: Printed by M. Simmons, 1673); and Thomas Parker, *The Visions and Prophecies of Daniel Expounded* (London: Printed for E. Paxton, 1646).

58. See Michael Wiggelsworth, "God's Controversy with New England," in *God's New Israel*, ed. Conrad Cherry (Englewood Cliffs, NJ: Prentice-Hall, 1971), pp. 44–54, and "The Day of Doom; or, a Poetical Description of the Great and Last Judgment," reprinted by Kenneth B. Murdock, ed. (New York: Spiral Press, 1929), and also reprinted in an abridged version in *The Norton Anthology of American Literature*, ed. Nina Baym, Ronald Gottesman, Laurence Holland, Francis Murphy, Hershel Parker, William Pritchard, and David Kalstone (New York: Norton, 1985), pp. 119–138.

59. Robert Middlekauff, *The Mathers: Three Generations of Puritan Intellectuals, 1596–1728* (New York: Oxford University Press, 1971); and Kenneth Silverman, *The Life and Times of Cotton Mather* (New York: Harper & Row, 1984).

60. Increase Mather, *Kometographia, Or a Discourse Concerning Comets* (Boston, 1683).

61. Increase Mather, *A Discourse Concerning the Danger of Apostasy* (Boston, 1679) and *An Essay for the Recording of Illustrious Providences* (Boston: 1684).

62. Middlekauff, *The Mathers*, p. 154.

63. Ibid., p. 326. See also Silverman, *The Life and Times of Cotton Mather*, p. 93.

64. Middlekauff, *The Mathers*, p. 320.

65. Among the period's millennial literature that Mather most copiously studied was that by Joseph Mede, *The Key of the Revelation* (London, 1643); William Whiston, *An Essay on the Revelation of Saint John* (Cambridge, 1706); and Pierre Jurieu, *The Accomplishment of the Scripture Prophecies* (London, 1687).

66. Middlekauff, *The Mathers*, p. 341.

67. Perhaps the best single work on Edwards's thought is Perry Miller's *Jonathan Edwards* (New York: W. Sloane, 1949). A reliable biography is Ola E. Winslow's *Jonathan Edwards, 1703–1758* (New York: Macmillan, 1940). Edwards's influential role in shaping American religious thought is well described in Sydney Ahlstrom's *A Religious History of the American People* and William Clebsch's *American Religious Thought* (Chicago: University of Chicago Press, 1973).

68. Edwards's apocalyptic writings have been collected, along with a fine introductory essay, in John E. Smith, ed., *The Works of Jonathan Edwards*, 5 vols. (New Haven, CT: Yale University Press, 1957–1977), vol. 5: *Apocalyptic Writings*, ed. Stephen J. Stein (1977). See also "A History of the Work of Redemption" in *The Works of President Edwards*, vol. 5.

69. Edwards, *Apocalyptic Writings*, p. 120.

70. Edwards, "A History of the Work of Redemption," p. 207.

71. Edwards, *Apocalyptic Writings*, p. 125.

72. Edwards, "A History of the Work of Redemption," p. 220.

73. Ibid., p. 224.

74. Ibid., p. 327.

75. Edwards, *Apocalyptic Writings*, p. 136.

76. The best accounts of role of apocalyptic rhetoric in shaping the "revolutionary ideology" that undergird the American Revolution are Ruth Bloch's *Visionary Republic: Millennial Themes in American Thought, 1756–1800* (Cambridge: Cambridge University Press, 1985); and Nathan Hatch's *The Sacred Cause of Liberty: Republican Thought and the Millennium in Revolutionary New England* (New Haven, CT: Yale University Press, 1977). See also Stephen Stein, "An Apocalyptic Rationale for the American Revolution," *Early American Literature* 9 (1975): 211–225; and John C. Heald, "Apocalyptic Rhetoric: Agents of Antichrist from the French to the British," *Today's Speech*, Spring 1975, pp. 33–37.

77. Nathaniel Appleton, "Sermon Delivered October 9" (Portsmouth, NH, 1760), pp. 26, 36.

78. Aaron Burr, "Sermon Before the Synod of New York," cited in Bloch, *Visionary Republic*, p. 39.

79. Robert Smith, *A Wheel in the Middle of a Wheel* (Philadelphia, 1759), p. 55.

80. Eli Forbes, *God the Strength and Salvation of His People* (Boston, 1761), p. 9.

81. Hatch, *The Sacred Cause of Liberty*, p. 46.

82. Samuel Cooper, quoted in Hatch, *Sacred Liberty*, p. 46.

83. James Cogsell, *God, the Pious Soldier's Strength and Instructor*, quoted in Hatch, *Sacred Liberty*, p. 47.

84. See Bloch, *Visionary Republic*, pp. 60–63.

85. Scholarly works on the religious roots of the American Revolutionary War and American patriotism include William McLoughlin's "The Role of Religion in the Revolution: Liberty of Conscience and Cultural Cohesion in the New Nation," in *Essays on the American Revolution*, ed. Stephen G. Kurtz and James Hutson (Chapel Hill: University of North Carolina Press, 1973); Conrad Cherry, ed., *God's New Israel: Religious Interpretations of American Destiny* (Englewood Cliffs, NJ: Prentice-Hall, 1971); Catherine L. Albanese, *Sons of the Fathers: The Civil Religion of the American Revolution* (Philadelphia: Temple University Press, 1976); Cedric B. Cowing, *The Great Awakening and the American Revolution* (Chicago: University of Chicago Press, 1971); and Jerald Brauer, ed., *Religion and the American Revolution* (Philadelphia: Fortress Press, 1976).

86. Anonymous, *A Discourse, Adressed to the Sons of Liberty, at a Solemn Assembly, near Liberty-Tree, in Boston* (Providence, RI, 1766), quoted in Bloch, *Visionary Republic*, p. 48.

87. *Maryland Journal and Baltimore Advertiser*, July 17, 1776, quoted in Bloch, *Visionary Republic*, p. 56.

88. Anonymous, *Concerning the Number of the Beast* (n.p., 1777), quoted in Bloch, *Visionary Republic*, p. 56.

89. Samuel West, *A Sermon Preached Before the Honorable Council* (Boston, 1776), quoted in Hatch, *Sacred Cause of Liberty*, p. 55.

90. Elisha Fish, *A Discourse Delivered at Worcester, March 28th, 1775* (Worcester, MA, 1775), quoted in Bloch, *Visionary Republic*, p. 79.

91. For more thorough explanations of American "civil religion," see Sidney Mead, *The Nation with the Soul of a Church* (New York: Harper & Row, 1975); Robert Bellah, Civil Religion in America," in *Religion in America*, ed. Robert Bellah and William McLoughlin (Boston: Beacon Press, 1968); and Russell E. Richey and Donald G. Jones, eds., *American Civil Religion* (New York: Harper & Row, 1974).

92. George Duffield, *A Sermon Preached in the Third Presbyterian Church* (Philadelphia, 1784), quoted in Hatch, *Sacred Cause of Liberty*, p. 22.

Chapter 3. Impediments to Christian Commonwealth

1. Samuel West, *A Sermon Preached Before the Honorable Council* (Boston, 1776), p. 57.

2. An insightful account of the dilemma faced by early Americans as they sought to reconcile their desire to build the nation around a fairly specific set of religious–moral convictions while adhering to principles of toleration and democracy can be found in Randolph A. Roth, *The Democratic Dilemma: Religion, Reform and the Social Order in the Connecticut River Valley of Vermont, 1791–1850* (Cambridge: Cambridge University Press, 1987).

3. Nicholas Street, "A Sermon Preached at East Haven, Connecticut,

April, 1777," in *God's New Israel: Religious Interpretations of American Destiny*, ed. Conrad Cherry (Englewood Cliffs, NJ: Prentice-Hall, 1971), p. 69.

4. Nathan Strong, *Political Instruction from the Prophecies of God's Word* (New York: G. Forman, 1799), p. 9.

5. Joseph Lathrop, *A Sermon on the Dangers of the Times* (Springfield, MA, 1798), p. 7.

6. Jedidiah Morse, *A Sermon, Delivered at the New North Church in Boston* (Boston, 1798), p. 26.

7. Timothy Dwight, *The Duty of Americans at the Present Crisis* (New Haven, CT, 1798), p. 12.

8. Anonymous, *Characteristics in the Prophecies* (New York, 1798), p. 19.

9. David Tappan, *Christian Thankfulness Explained and Enforced* (Boston, 1795).

10. Abraham Cummings, cited in Ruth Bloch, *Visionary Republic: Millennial Themes in American Thought, 1756–1800* (Cambridge: Cambridge University Press, 1985), p. 205.

11. William Symmes, *A Sermon Preached Before His Honor Thomas Cushing* (Boston, 1785).

12. Timothy Dwight, *The Nature and Danger of Infidel Philosophy* (New Haven, CT, 1798), p. 89.

13. Nathan William, cited in Nathan Hatch, *The Sacred Cause of Liberty: Republican Thought and the Millennium in Revolutionary New England* (New Haven, CT: Yale University Press, 1977), p. 168.

14. Hatch, *Sacred Cause of Liberty*, p. 169.

15. David Osgood, *The Devil Let Loose* (Boston, 1799), p. 8.

16. Timothy Dwight, cited in Hatch, *Sacred Cause of Liberty*, p. 169.

17. Ethan Smith, *A Dissertation on the Prophecies Relative to Antichrist and the Last Times* (Charlestown, MA: Samuel T. Armstrong, 1811), p. 97.

18. Winthrop S. Hudson, *Religion in America* (New York: Scribner, 1973), pp. 134–164.

19. See Samuel Hopkins, *System of Doctrines*, in *American Christianity: An Historical Interpretation with Representative Documents*, ed. H. Shelton Smith, Robert T. Handy, and Lefferts A. Loetscher, 2 vols. (New York: Scribner, 1960–1963), vol. 1, pp. 539–545.

20. Mark Hopkins, cited in Hudson, *Religion in America*, p. 152.

21. Timothy Dwight, *Sermon Delivered in Boston, September 16, 1813, Before the American Board of Commissioners for Foreign Missions* (Boston, 1813), pp. 25, 19.

22. Horace Bushnell, *Barbarism the First Danger* (New York: American Home Missionary Society, 1847).

23. Robert Wiebe, *The Search for Order* (New York: Hill & Wang, 1967), p. 4.

24. Helpful overviews of Freemasonry include those by Bobby J. Demott, *Freemasonry in American Culture and Society* (Lanham, MA: University Press of America, 1986); Bernard Fay, *Revolution and Freemasonry, 1680–1800* (Boston: Little, Brown, 1935); Lynn Dumenil, *Freemasonry and American Culture, 1800–1930* (Princeton, NJ: Princeton University Press, 1984); and Stephen Knight, *The Brotherhood: The Secret World of the Freemasons* (Briarcliff Manor, NY: Stein & Day, 1984). For information concerning the Antimasonry movement, see

Lorman Ratner, *Antimasonry: The Crusade and the Party* (Englewood Cliffs, NJ: Prentice-Hall, 1969); Vernon Stauffer, *New England and the Bavarian Illuminati* (New York: Russell & Russell, 1918); and Roth, *Democratic Dilemma*.

25. Roth, *Democratic Dilemma*, p. 140.

26. Stauffer, *New England and the Bavarian Illuminati*, p. 64.

27. Morse, *A Sermon, Delivered at the New North Church in Boston*, p. 25.

28. Ibid., p. 21.

29. David Bernard, *Light on Masonry*, cited in Richard Hofstadter, *The Paranoid Style in American Politics* (New York: Knopf, 1965), p. 17.

30. Dwight, *Duty of Americans in the Present Crisis*, p. 15.

31. W. J. Rorabaugh, *The Alcoholic Republic* (New York: Oxford University Press, 1979), p. 9.

32. Cotton Mather, cited in John Allen Krout, *The Origins of Prohibition* (New York: Knopf, 1923), p. 53.

33. Rorabaugh, *The Alcoholic Republic*, p. 210.

34. Lyman Beecher, *Six Sermons on the Nature, Occasions, Signs, Evils, and Remedy of Intemperance* (New York: American Tract Society, 1827), p. 93.

35. The Grange, cited in Norman H. Clark, *The Dry Years: Prohibition and Social Change in Washington* (Seattle: University of Washington Press, 1965), p. 17.

36. Clark, *The Dry Years*.

37. Sydney Ahlstrom provides an overview of the connection between abolition and nineteenth-century American religion in his chapter "Slavery, Disunion, and the Churches," in his *A Religious History of the American People* (New Haven, CT: Yale University Press, 1972), pp. 648–670.

38. Roth, *Democratic Dilemma*, p. 80. See also David Brion Davis, "Some Themes of Countersubversion: An Analysis of Anti-Masonic, Anti-Catholic, and Anti-Mormon Literature," *Mississippi Valley Historical Review*, September 1960, pp. 205–224.

39. James H. Moorhead, *American Apocalypse: Yankee Protestants and the Civil War, 1860–1869* (New Haven, CT: Yale University Press, 1978), pp. 109–112.

40. Michael Baxter, cited in Moorhead, *American Apocalypse*, p. 57.

41. L. S. Weed, *Christian Advocate and Journal*, November 20, 1862, p. 59.

42. Hollis Read, *The Coming Crisis of the World; or, the Great Battle and the Golden Age* (Columbus, 1861), p. 157.

43. See Ernest Tuveson, *Redeemer Nation: The Idea of America's Millennial Role* (Chicago: University of Chicago Press, 1966), pp. 193–195.

44. *Christ in the Army: A Selection of Sketches of the Work of the U.S. Christian Commission*, cited in Moorhead, *American Apocalypse*, pp. 76–77 (italics added).

45. See "Civil War and National Destiny," in *God's New Israel*, ed. Cherry, pp. 155–210; and William A. Cebsch, "Christian Interpretation of the Civil War," *Church History*, June, 1961, pp. 212–222.

46. James W. Silver, *Confederate Morale and Church Propaganda* (New York: Norton, 1967).

47. Albert B. Morse, cited in Silver, *Confederate Morale*, p. 77.

48. Thomas Smyth, cited in Silver, *Confederate Morale*, p. 30.

49. Benjamin Palmer and Thomas Atkinson, cited in Silver, *Confederate Morale*, p. 27.

50. Excerpted from Julia Ward Howe, "The Battle Hymn," first published in the *Atlantic Monthly* 9 (1862): 145.

51. Tuveson, *Redeemer Nation*, p. 200.

52. E. O. Wilson, *Sociobiology* (Cambridge, MA: Belknap Press, 1975), pp. 564–565.

53. Garrett Hardin, "Population Skeletons in the Environmental Closet," *Bulletin of the Atomic Scientists*, June 1972, p. 39.

54. Sources on Judaism's early history in America include Ruth Gay, *Jews in America: A Short History* (New York: Basic Books, 1965); Nathan Glazer, *American Judaism* (Chicago: University of Chicago Press, 1957); Oscar Handlin, *Adventure in Freedom: Three Hundred Years of Jewish Life in America* (New York: McGraw-Hill, 1954); Irving Marlin, *Jews and Americans* (Carbondale: Southern Illinois University Press, 1965); and Charles Sherman, *The Jew Within American Society* (Detroit: Wayne State University Press, 1961).

55. Benjamin Rush, cited in Morton Borden, *Jews, Turks, and Infidels* (Chapel Hill: University of North Carolina Press, 1984), p. 5.

56. Rev. David Caldwell, cited in Borden, *Jews, Turks, and Infidels*, p. 11.

57. Rev. Henry Muhlenberg, cited in Borden, *Jews, Turks and Infidels*, p. 4.

58. Rev. D. X. Junkin, cited in Borden, *Jews, Turks, and Infidels*, p. 60.

59. See John Higham, *Strangers in the Land: Patterns of American Nativism, 1860–1925* (New Brunswick, NJ: Rutgers University Press, 1955), p. 16.

60. Helpful overviews of early Catholic history in the United States can be found in John Tracy Ellis, *Catholics in Colonial America* (Baltimore: Helicon Press, 1965); and Ahlstom, *Religious History of the American People*, pp. 540–568.

61. Lyman Beecher, *A Plea for the West*, 2nd ed. (Cincinnati: Truman & Smith, 1834).

62. Ray Allen Billingston, *The Protestant Crusade, 1800–1860: A Study of the Origins of American Nativism* (Gloucester, MA: Peter Smith, 1963), pp. 70–71.

63. Maria Monk, cited in Billingston, *Protestant Crusade*, p. 99.

64. Billingston, *Protestant Crusade*, p. 386.

65. See Donald Kinzer, *An Episode in Anti-Catholicism: The American Protective Association* (Seattle: University of Washington Press, 1964).

66. Cited in ibid., p. 49.

67. David Brion Davis, ed., *The Fear of Conspiracy* (Ithaca, NY: Cornell University Press, 1971), p. 11.

68. Josiah Strong, *Our Country: Its Possible Future and Present Crisis* (New York, 1885), p. 30.

69. See Ernest Sandeen, "Millerism," in *The Rise of Adventism*, ed. Edwin S. Gaustad (New York: Harper & Row, 1974), p. 109 (italics added).

70. Daniel H. Ludlow, ed., *Encyclopedia of Mormonism*, 3 vols. (New York: Macmillan, 1991), vol. 1, p. 44.

71. Ibid., p. 45.

72. There is no shortage of scholarship on the Millerites. One of the earliest works is Clara Endicott Sears's *Days of Delusion: A Strange Bit of History* (Boston: Houghton Mifflin, 1924). As her title suggests, Sears unapologetically treated the Millerites as irrational fanatics and may well have perpetuated unfounded rumors concerning the movement's "deluded" expectation of the Second Coming. Francis D. Nichol, a Seventh-Day Adventist minister, responded to Sears's volume with his own partisan *The Midnight Cry: A Defense of the Character and Conduct of William Miller and the Millerites, Who Mistakenly Believed That the Second Coming of Christ Would Take Place in the Year 1844* (Wash-

ington, DC: Review and Herald, 1944). Among the most helpful of the subsequent histories are those by Ruth Alden Doan, *The Miller Heresy, Millennialism, and American Culture* (Philadelphia: Temple University Press, 1987); David L. Rowe, *Thunder and Trumpets: Millerites and Dissenting Religion in Upstate New York, 1800–1850* (Chico, CA: Scholars Press, 1985); Gaustad, ed., *The Rise of Adventism*; and Ronald L. Numbers and Jonathan M. Butler, eds., *The Disappointed: Millerism and Millenarianism in the Nineteenth Century* (Bloomington: Indiana University Press, 1987).

73. For a more extensive discussion of the system that Miller used for Bible interpretation, see Wayne R. Judd, "William Miller: Disappointed Prophet," in *The Disappointed*, ed. Numbers and Butler, pp. 20–21.

74. David Ludlum, *Social Ferment in Vermont, 1791–1850* (New York: Columbia University Press, 1939), p. 251.

75. David L. Rowe cautions us that there is no empirical evidence to sustain the claim that those who affiliated with the Millerite movement were economically deprived. "Though they were not notably poor in the things of this world, as a group they certainly felt spiritually deprived—separated from God, yearning for the peace and joy of the millennium, eagerly anticipating release from the pain and troubles of this world." See his essay, "Millerites," in *The Disappointed*, ed. Numbers and Butler, pp. 1–16.

76. Ruth Alden Doan, "Millerism and Evangelical Culture" in *The Disappointed*, ed. Numbers and Butler, p. 127.

77. See Ronald L. Numbers and Janet S. Numbers, "Millerism and Madness: A Study of 'Religious Insanity' in Nineteenth-Century America," in *The Disappointed*, ed. Numbers and Butler, pp. 92–118.

78. Charles Fitch, *Come out of Her, My People: A Sermon* (Rochester, NY: J. V. Himes, 1843), p. 9.

79. Ibid., p. 5.

80. Ibid., p. 13.

81. Ibid., p. 15.

82. David T. Arthur, "Millerism," in *The Rise of Adventism*, ed. Gaustad, p. 171.

83. Discussions of the various Millerite reactions to the "Great Disappointment" can be found in *The Disappointed*, ed. Numbers and Butler, especially Wayne R. Judd's essay, "William Miller: Disappointed Prophet," pp. 17–35.

84. Ellen Gould White, *Selected Messages*, 3 vols. (Mountain View, CA: Pacific Press, 1962), vol. 3, p. 402.

85. Timothy Smith, *Revivalism and Social Reform in Mid-Nineteenth-Century America* (New York: Harper & Row, 1957), p. 236.

86. Eric Hoffer, *The True Believer* (New York: Harper & Bros., 1953), p. 89.

Chapter 4. The Battle Against Modernism

1. Excellent accounts of "modernism" and the liberal tradition in American Protestantism can be found in William R. Hutchison, *The Modernist Impulse in American Protestantism* (Cambridge, MA: Harvard University Press, 1976); and Martin E. Marty, *The Irony of It All: 1893–1919* (Chicago: University of Chicago Press, 1986).

2. See the excellent account of G. Stanley Hall's abandonment of the

ministry for a career in psychology in Dorothy Ross's *G. Stanley Hall: The Psychologist as Prophet* (Chicago: University of Chicago Press, 1972); and James Mark Baldwin's autobiographical entry in *A History of Psychology in Autobiography*, ed. E. G. Boring and G. Lindzey (New York: Appleton-Century-Crofts, 1967).

3. William G. McLoughlin, *Revivals, Awakenings, and Reform* (Chicago: University of Chicago Press, 1978). p. 152.

4. See Robert C. Fuller, *Americans and the Unconscious* (New York: Oxford University Press, 1986).

5. John Fiske, *Through Nature to God* (New York: Houghton Mifflin, 1899), p. 191.

6. Lyman Abbott, *The Theology of an Evolutionist* (New York: Outlook Company, 1925), p. 8.

7. Lyman Abbott, *Reminiscences* (Boston: Houghton Mifflin, 1915), p. 462.

8. James J. King, "The Present Condition of New York City Above Fourteenth Street, 1888," in *The Church and the City*, ed. Robert D. Cross (Indianapolis: Bobbs-Merrill, 1967), p. 30.

9. Ibid.

10. Robert Wiebe, *The Search for Order* (New York: Hill & Wang, 1967), p. 12.

11. G. T. Gaston, *Pentecostal Evangel*, October 12, 1929, p. 6.

12. *Pentecostal Evangel*, cited in Marty, *The Irony of it All*, p. 239.

13. Henry Parsons, "The Present Age and Development of Antichrist," in *Second Coming of Christ: Premillennial Essays of the Prophetic Conference, Held in the Church of the Holy Trinity, New York City, Oct. 30–Nov. 1, 1879*, ed. Nathaniel West (Chicago: Fleming H. Revell, 1879), p. 208.

14. Ibid., p. 210.

15. Samuel J. Andrews, *Christianity and Antichristianity in Their Final Conflict* (Chicago: Bible Institute Colportage Association, 1937).

16. Ibid., p. 46.

17. See Leon Festinger, *A Theory of Cognitive Dissonance* (Stanford, CA: Stanford University Press, 1957); and Leon Festinger, Henry Riecken, and Stanley Schacter, *When Prophecy Fails* (Minneapolis: University of Minnesota Press, 1956). Although Festinger's theory was challenged by D. J. Bem in his "Self-Perception: An Alternative Interpretation of Cognitive Dissonance Phenomena, *Psychological Review* 74 (1967): 183–200, it has shown considerable versatility, resilience, and predictive ability, as demonstrated in C. Kiesler and M. Pallak, "Arousal Properties of Dissonance Manipulations," *Psychological Bulletin* 83 (1976): 1014–1025; R. Fazio, M. Zanna, and J. Cooper, "Dissonance and Self-Perception: An Integrative View of Each Theory's Proper Domain of Application," *Journal of Experimental Social Psychology* 13 (1977): 464–479; and R. Croyle and J. Cooper, "Dissonance Arousal: Physiological Evidence," *Journal of Personality and Social Psychology* 45 (1983): 782–791.

18. Andrews, *Christianity and Anti-Christianity*, p. 178.

19. Ibid., p. 200.

20. Ibid., p. 183.

21. Ibid., p. 265.

22. Ibid., pp. 235, 236.

23. William B. Riley, *The Menace of Modernism* (New York: Christian Alliance Publishing, 1917), p. 33.

24. Ibid., p. 35.

25. For an account of the Straton–Potter debate, see C. Allyn Russell, *Voices of American Fundamentalism* (Philadelphia: Westminster Press, 1976), pp. 66–75.

26. Ibid., p. 73.

27. Curtis Lee Law, "Convention Side Lights," *Watchman-Examiner*, July 1, 1920, p. 3.

28. The two most authoritative accounts of the history and doctrinal heritage of contemporary fundamentalism are by George M. Marsden, *Fundamentalism and American Culture: The Shaping of Twentieth-Century Evangelicalism, 1870–1925* (New York: Oxford University Press, 1980); and Ernest R. Sandeen, *The Roots of Fundamentalism: British and American Millenarianism, 1800–1930* (Chicago: University of Chicago Press, 1970). Sandeen argues that premillennial theology was the organizing principle and historical force that gave rise to twentieth-century fundamentalism. Marsden concurs with Sandeen insofar as fundamentalism is viewed theologically but maintains that fundamentalism is also a social and cultural movement and for this reason must be interpreted in broader contexts. Other helpful discussions of the origins of American Protestant fundamentalism are Nancy T. Ammerman's essay "North American Protestant Fundamentalism," in *Fundamentalisms Observed*, ed. Martin E. Marty and Scott Appleby (Chicago: University of Chicago Press, 1991), pp. 1–65, Timothy Weber's *Living in the Shadow of the Second Coming* (New York: Oxford University Press, 1979); and Paul Boyer's *When Time Shall Be No More: Prophecy Belief in Modern American Culture* (Cambridge, MA: Belknap Press, 1992).

29. See the discussion of dispensationalism in Weber, *Living in the Shadow*, pp. 16–17; Marty, *The Irony of It All*, p. 220; and Sandeen, *Roots of Fundamentalism*, p. 62.

30. C. I. Scofield, ed., *The Scofield Reference Bible* (New York: Oxford University Press, 1917), p. 5.

31. C. I. Scofield, *Rightly Dividing the Word of Truth* (Oakland, CA: Western Book and Tract Company, n.d.), p. 18.

32. Marty, *The Irony of It All*, p. 221.

33. Eli Reece, *How Far Can a Premillennialist Pastor Cooperate with Social Service Programs*, cited in Weber, *Living in the Shadow*, pp. 93–94.

34. Nancy Ammerman, "North American Protestant Fundamentalism," p. 17.

35. Robert Cameron, cited in Sandeen, *Roots of Fundamentalism*, p. 212.

36. See William McLoughlin, *Modern Revivalism: Charles Grandison Finney to Billy Graham* (New York: Ronald Press, 1959); and Marsden's "D. L. Moody and a New American Evangelism," in his *Fundamentalism and American Culture*, pp. 32–39.

37. A discussion of Moody's appropriation of Darby's dispensationalism can be found in James F. Findlay's *Dwight L. Moody: American Evangelist 1837–1899* (Chicago: University of Chicago Press, 1969).

38. See Dwight L. Moody, "The Second Coming of Christ," in *The Best of D. L. Moody: Sixteen Sermons by the Great Evangelist*, ed. Wilbur M. Smith (Chicago: Moody Press, 1971), pp. 187–195.

39. A thorough discussion of the origin and doctrinal positions of *The Fundamentals* can be found in Sandeen, *Roots of Fundamentalism*, pp. 188–207.

40. *Scofield Reference Bible*, pp. 1227, 1250.

41. Ibid., p. 914.

42. Ibid., p. 918.

43. Ibid., pp. 1342–43.

44. Helpful summaries of modern end-times scenarios can be found in Weber, *Living in the Shadow*, pp. 106–108; and William Martin's "Waiting for the End," *Atlantic Monthly*, June 1982, pp. 31–37.

45. Marsden, *Fundamentalism and American Culture*, p. 204.

46. Ibid., p. 205.

47. William Blackstone, *Jesus Is Coming* (Chicago: Fleming H. Revell, 1908), p. 110.

48. Riley, *Menace of Modernism*, p. 100.

49. An example of the anti-Russellite sentiment found in premillennial literature is Jesse Forrest Silver's *The Lord's Return: Seen in History and in Scripture as Pre-Millennial and Imminent* (Chicago: Fleming H. Revell, 1914).

50. William McLoughlin, *Billy Sunday Was His Real Name* (Chicago: University of Chicago Press, 1955), p. 296.

Chapter 5. Crusades of Hate

1. David S. Kennedy, *The Presbyterian*, cited in George M. Marsden, *Fundamentalism and American Culture* (New York: Oxford University Press, 1980), p. 159.

2. Martin E. Marty and R. Scott Appleby, "Conclusion," in *Fundamentalisms Observed*, ed. Martin E. Marty and R. Scott Appleby (Chicago: University of Chicago Press, 1991), p. 820.

3. Ibid., pp. 820, 821.

4. John Higham's *Strangers in the Land: Patterns of American Nativism, 1860–1925* (New Brunswick, NJ: Rutgers University Press, 1955) is the classic study of nativistic thought in the United States. An excellent survey of American nativism, including a helpful bibliography, can be found in David A. Gerber's entry, "Nativism, Anti-Catholicism, and Anti-Semitism" in *Encyclopedia of American Social History*, ed. Mary Kupiec Cayton, Elliott J. Gorn, and Peter W. Williams, 3 vols. (New York: Scribner, 1993), vol. 3, pp. 2101–14.

5. See David Brion Davis, ed., *The Fear of Conspiracy* (Ithaca, NY: Cornell University Press, 1971); and Richard Curry and Thomas Brown, eds., *Conspiracy: The Fear of Subversion in American History* (New York: Holt, Rinehart and Winston, 1972).

6. Richard Hofstadter, *The Paranoid Strain in American Politics* (New York: Knopf, 1965), p. 29.

7. Ibid., p. 31.

8. Several excellent works chronicle the religious demagoguery of the Christian far right: Ralph Lord Roy, *Apostles of Discord: A Study of Organized Bigotry and Disruption of the Fringes of Protestantism* (Boston: Beacon Press, 1953); Leo Ribuffo, *The Old Christian Right: The Protestant Far Right from the Great Depression to the Cold War* (Philadelphia: Temple University Press, 1983); Erling Jarstad, *The Politics of Doomsday: Fundamentalists of the Far Right* (Nashville: Abingdon Press, 1970); Gary K. Clabaugh, *Thunder on the Right: The Protestant Fundamentalists* (Chicago: Nelson-Hall, 1974); and Leo Lowenthal and Norbert

Guterman, *Prophets of Deceit: A Study of the Techniques of the American Agitator* (New York: Harper & Bros., 1949).

9. Sydney Ahlstrom, *A Religious History of American People* (New Haven, CT: Yale University Press, 1972), p. 927.

10. Gerald L. K. Smith, *The Cross and the Flag*, June 1948, p. 2.

11. Carl McIntire, cited in Roy, *Apostles of Discord*, p. 212.

12. See Shelley Tennenbaum, "The Jews," in *Encyclopedia of American Social History*, vol. 2, pp. 769–782, for an overview of American Jewish social history and a helpful bibliography.

13. Gerald B. Winrod, *Antichrist and the Tribe of Dan* (Wichita, KS: Defender Publications, 1936), p. 8.

14. Henry Parsons, "The Present Age and Development of Antichrist," in *Second Coming of Christ*, ed. Nathaniel West (Chicago: Fleming H. Revell, 1879), p. 208.

15. Winrod, *Antichrist and the Tribe of Dan*, p. 8.

16. Gerald Winrod, *The Jewish Assault on Christianity* (Wichita, KS: Defender Publications, 1935).

17. Winrod, *Antichrist and the Tribe of Dan*, p. 13.

18. Ibid., p. 24.

19. Ibid., p. 25.

20. *Defender Magazine*, August 1952, p. 16.

21. Winrod, *Antichrist and the Tribe of Dan*, p. 30.

22. The Protocols of the Elders of Zion, cited in Dwight Wilson, *Armageddon Now! The Premillenarian Response to Russia and Israel Since 1917* (Grand Rapids, MI: Baker Book House, 1977), p. 75.

23. Arno Gaebelein, "Current Events," *Our Hope*, Austust 1922, p. 103.

24. Charles C. Cook, "The International Jew," *The King's Business*, November 1921, p. 1087.

25. Gerald Winrod, *Mussolini's Place in Prophecy* (Wichita, KS: Defender Publications, 1933), p. 22.

26. Ibid.

27. Ibid., p. 24.

28. Winrod, *Antichrist and the Tribe of Dan*, p. 30.

29. Ibid., p. 7.

30. Arno C. Gaebelein, *Meat in Due Season: Sermons, Discourses, and Expositions of the Word of Prophecy* (New York: Arno C. Gaebelein, n.d.), p. 150.

31. C. Winrod, *Antichrist and the Tribe of Dan*, p. 19.

32. David Rausch, in his *Zionism Within Early American Fundamentalism, 1878–1918: A Convergence of Two Traditions* (New York: Edwin Mellen Press, 1979), argues for a positive assessment of fundamentalists' support of Israel and Jewish heritage. Rausch may be correct in drawing attention to the complexities of fundamentalists' attitudes toward Jews, but he surely ignores the condescension, patronizing, and even blatant anti-Semitism displayed by leading fundamentalist spokespersons. For a more balanced assessment, see Yaakov Ariel, *On Behalf of Israel: American Fundamentalist Attitudes Toward Jews, Judaism, and Zionism, 1865–1945* (Brooklyn, NY: Carlson Publishing, 1991); Paul Boyer, *When Time Shall Be No More: Prophecy Belief in Modern American Culture* (Cambridge, MA: Belknap Press, 1992), pp. 181–224; Martin E. Marty, *The Irony*

of It All, 1893–1919 (Chicago: University of Chicago Press, 1986), pp. 228–231; and Wilson, *Armageddon Now.*

33. Dave Hunt, *Global Peace and the Rise of Antichrist* (Eugene, OR: Harvest House, 1990), p. 34.

34. Arthur E. Bloomfield, *How to Recognize the Antichrist* (Minneapolis: Bethany Fellowship, 1975), pp. 130–139.

35. It might be noted that overt references to racial hatred are strikingly absent from American premillennial literature. This is not to say, however, that those drawn to premillennialism are in any way immune from the kinds of racial prejudice that are common in American society. When blacks moved northward and urbanward in large numbers between 1880 and 1920, so too did racial anxieties. These decades marked the zenith of antiblack rhetoric in American history. Some of this inflamatory rhetoric was couched in religious terms, since white Anglo-Saxon Protestants had long viewed themselves as specially selected by God to spread democracy and true gospel faith throughout the world. For example, the director of the Anglo-Saxon Christian Association, Rev. H. M. Greene, maintained that the civil rights movement was being instigated by "oversexed people" who want "to intrude cohabitation upon God's country." Segregation, according to Greene, is "a God-given civil right, and unalienable right." Cited in Roy, *Apostles of Discord*, p. 107. Baptist minister Evall G. Johnston similarly linked racism with divine commandment when he bestowed Christian sanction on the Klan. Johnston declared "that the white race is still superior to the Negro race. . . . The Negro is black because he was cursed by the Almighty God, and that curse will never be lifted." Ibid., p. 125.

It is often difficult to discern whether racial concerns are obliquely connected with premillennial fears about the methods that the Antichrist might use to spread chaos and disorder throughout the country. Even Billy Graham, whose high-profile ministry has necessitated avoidance of inflamatory rhetoric, linked the cause of civil rights with the Antichrist's bid for world domination. In the long list of the "flames out of control" in these end-times, Graham linked "the race problem" with Communism, uncontrolled science, atheism, and pornography as among the positive proofs that the earth is a planet in rebellion. Deploring racism, Graham declared that the only hope for an end to the race problem is for every person on earth to have a vital personal experience of Jesus Christ. Acknowledging that such a mass conversion of both blacks and whites is unlikely in our time, he warned that "the racial tensions will increase, racial demands will become more militant, a great deal of blood will be shed. The race problem could become another flame out of control." Billy Graham, *World Aflame* (Garden City, NY: Doubleday, 1965), p. 8. As Graham's rendering of the prophetic significance of African Americans' "racial demands" indicates, it is often difficult to be certain about the extent to which race is implicitly associated with contemporary discussions of the end times.

36. Higham, *Strangers in the Land.*

37. Parsons, "Present Age and Development of Antichrist," p. 214.

38. Gaebelein, *Meat in Due Season*, p. 171.

39. I. M. Haldeman, cited in Wilson, *Armageddon Now!* p. 54.

40. See David M. Chalmers, *Hooded Americanism: The First Century of the Ku Klux Klan 1865–1965* (Garden City, NY: Doubleday, 1965).

41. Hiram Wesley Evans, "The Klan's Fight for Americanism," in *Conspiracy: The Fear of Subversion in American History*, ed. Curry and Brown, p. 166.

42. Ibid., p. 168.

43. Scholarly discussions of anti-Catholicism in modern Protestant fundamentalism can be found in both Roy's *Apostles of Discord* and Ribuffo's *The Old Christian Right*.

44. David Webber, *Countdown for Antichrist* (Oklahoma City: Southwest Radio Church, 1976).

45. Noah Hutchings, "The Vatican Connection," *Gospel Truth*, April 1984, p. 4.

46. John Ankenberg and John Weldon, *One World: Bible Prophecy and the New World Order* (Chicago: Moody Press, 1991), p. 19.

47. Peter Lalonde, *One World Under Antichrist* (Eugene, OR: Harvest House, 1991), p. 62.

48. See Dave Hunt's discussion, "Emperors and Popes," in his *Global Peace and the Rise of Antichrist*, pp. 99–111. The quotation is from p. 111.

49. The narrative in this section explaining the history of union and socialist movements in the United States relies on two helpful essays in the *Encyclopedia of American Social History*: John Jentz's "Labor: The Gilded Age Through the 1920s," vol. 2, pp. 1459–74; and Paul M. Buhle's "Socialist and Communist Movements," vol. 3, pp. 2251–68.

50. Helpful starting points for a survey of labor and unionization in American history are Foster R. Dulles and Melvyhn Dubofsky, *Labor in America: A History* 2nd rev. ed. (Arlington Heights, IL: Harlan Davidson,1984); David Gordon, Richard Edwards, and Michael Reich, *Segmented Work, Divided Workers: The Historical Transformation of Labor in the United States* (Cambridge: Cambridge University Press, 1982); and David Montgomery, *The Fall of the House of Labor: The Workplace, the State and American Labor Activism, 1865–1925* (Cambridge: Cambridge University Press,1987). Histories of American socialism include those by Donald Drew Egbert and Stow Persons, *Socialism and American Life*, 2 vols. (Princeton, NJ: Princeton University Press,1952); Daniel Bell, *Marxian Socialism in the United States* (Princeton, NJ: Princeton University Press, 1967); and Paul Buhle, *Marxism in the United States* (New York: Verso, 1987).

51. Seymour Martin Lipset, "The Radical Right: A Problem for American Diplomacy," *British Journal of Sociology*, June 1955, pp. 176–201.

52. Gaebelein, *Meat in Due Season*, p. 155.

53. Albert Sims, *The Approach of Antichrist* (Toronto: A. Sims, n.d.), p. 10.

54. Charles Hudson, *America in Danger*, July 3, 1938, p. 1.

55. Arno Gaebelein, "Current Events," *Our Hope*, July 1912, p. 49.

56. See Boyer, *When Time Shall Be No More*, p. 107.

57. In *Reasoning from the Scriptures* (Brooklyn, NY: Watch Tower Bible and Tract Society, 1985), the Jehovah's Witnesses adhere closely to 1 and 2 John in explaining that Antichrist means "against or instead of Christ. The term applies to all who deny what the Bible says about Jesus Christ, all who oppose his Kingdom, and all who mistreat his followers" (p. 32). A similar treatment of the term can be found in *Insight on the Scriptures*, 2 vols. (Brooklyn, NY: Watchtower Bible and Tract Society, 1988), vol. 1, pp. 115–116.

58. Billy James Hargis, quoted in John Redekop, *The American Far Right* (Grand Rapids, MI: Eerdmans, 1969), p. 79.

59. See, for example, Parsons, "Present Age and Development of Anti-christ" (1879), and Samuel J. Andrews, *Christianity and Anti-Christianity in Their Final Conflict* (Chicago: Bible Institute Colportage Association, 1898).

60. Arno Gaebelein, quoted in Boyer, *When Time Shall Be No More*, p. 107.

61. Citation from Donald S. Strong, *Organized Anti-Semitism in America: The Rise of Group Prejudice During the Decade 1930–40* (Westport, CT: Greenwood Press, 1941), p. 55.

62. Gerald Winrod, *The NRA in Prophecy and A Discussion of Beast Worship* (Wichita, KS: Defender Publishers, 1933).

63. Ibid., p. 12.

64. Marsden, ed. *Fundamentalism in American Culture*, p. 147.

65. R. Laurence Moore, *Religious Outsiders and the Making of America* (New York: Oxford University Press, 1986), p. 148.

66. C. I. Scofield, *The Scofield Reference Bible* (New York: Oxford University Press, 1967), p. 881.

67. Hal Lindsey, *The Late Great Planet Earth* (Grand Rapids, MI: Zondervan, 1970), p. 60.

68. Paul Boyer's discussion, "Russia and Prophecy in the Cold War," in his *When Time Shall Be No More* is an excellent starting point for further study of this topic. So, too, are Dwight Wilson's *Armageddon Now!*; Grace Halsell's *Prophecy and Politics: Militant Evangelists on the Road to Nuclear War* (Westport, CT: Lawrence Hill, 1986); and Erling Jarstad's *Politics of Doomsday*.

69. Gerald Winrod, *The United States and Russia in Prophecy and the Red Horse of the Apocalypse* (Wichita, KS: Defender Publishers, 1933), p. 32.

70. Cited in Boyer, *When Time Shall Be No More*, p. 157.

71. See Dan Gilbert, *The Red Terror and Bible Prophecy* (Grand Rapids, MI: Zondervan, 1944); Louis Bauman, *Russian Events in the Light of Bible Prophecy* (New York: Fleming H. Revell, 1942); Thomas S. McCall and Zola Levitt, *Coming Russian Invasion of Israel* (Chicago: Moody Press, 1987); and William Goetz, *Apocalypse Next!* (Cathedral City, CA: Horizon Books, 1981).

72. See Hal Lindsey, *The 1980s: Countdown to Armageddon* (New York: Bantam Books, 1980); and John F. Walvoord, *Armageddon, Oil and the Middle East Crisis* (Grand Rapids, MI: Zondervan, 1974). An excellent discussion of the rhetorical uses of apocalyptic language in the shaping of Cold War ideology can be found in Stephen O'Leary's *Arguing the Apocalypse* (New York: Oxford University Press, 1994), pp. 147–194.

73. Charles Taylor, *Bible Prophecy News*, July 1985, cited in O'Leary, *Arguing the Apocalypse*, p. 190.

74. O. R. Palmer, "Christ and Antichrist in Russia," *Moody Monthly*, October 1923, p. 59.

75. Howard E. Kershner, quoted in Ralph Lord Roy, *Apostles of Discord*, p. 295.

76. Billy James Hargis, *Communist America . . . Must It Be?* (Tulsa: Christian Crusade, 1960), p. 7.

77. Ibid., p. 54.

78. See William Alnor's chapter, "Pinning the Tail on Antichrist" in his *Soothsayers of the Second Advent* (Old Tappan, NJ: Fleming H. Revell, 1989).

79. See Robert Faid, *Gorbachev! Has the Real Antichrist Come?* (Tulsa: Victory House, 1988).

80. Winrod, *Antichrist and the Tribe of Dan*, p. 25.

81. David Webber and Noah W. Hutchings, *Countdown for Antichrist* (Oklahoma City: Southwest Radio Church, 1984), p. 121. See also Raymond Cox's "Will the Real Antichrist Please Stand Up," *Eternity*, May 1974, pp. 15–17. In interviews with William Alnor, both Webber and Hutchings conceded that they may have been in error in identifying Kissinger with the Antichrist. Hutchings told Alnor that he pleads "guilty to Henry Kissinger because I wrote an article pointing out the parallels. . . . I didn't say he was the Antichrist; I just said there were similarities." Webber similarly remarked, "I don't think it's out of line to speculate about personalities (being the Antichrist). A lot of people were interested in Henry Kissinger because of his international peace activities. The fact is that a mathematical formula calculates his name to add up to 666. . . . Actually most of the time I suggested that Henry Kissinger might be a forerunner of Antichrist because of his peace-keeping abilities. I never did think he was the Antichrist." See Alnor's *Soothsayers of the Second Advent*, pp. 115, 117.

82. Lindsey, *The 1980s: Countdown to Armageddon*, p. 149.

83. Lindsey, *The Late Great Planet Earth*, p. 173.

84. Hunt, *Global Peace and the Rise of Antichrist*.

85. Dan Betzer, *The Beast: A Novel of the Future World Dictator* (Lafayette, LA: Prescott Press, 1985), cited in Boyer, *When Time Shall Be No More*, p. 145.

86. James Robison, cited in Halsell, *Prophecy and Politics*, p. 15.

87. Halsell, *Prophecy and Politics*, p. 45. Halsell's chapter entitled "Reagan: Arming for a Real Armageddon" is a fascinating summary of Reagan's apocalyptic understanding of international politics.

88. Winrod, *The NRA in Prophecy*, p. 45.

89. See the discussions of "Gog and Glasnost" and "Apocalyptic Portents in a Post-Cold War World" in Paul Boyer's *When Time Shall Be No More*, pp. 176–200, 325–339.

90. Walvoord, *Armageddon, Oil, and the Middle East Crisis*.

91. Lindsey, *The 1980s: Countdown to Armageddon*, pp. 51–63.

92. Mary Stewart Relfe, cited in William Alnor's *Soothsayers of the Second Advent*, p. 24. For more on the identification of Spain's King Juan Carlos II as the Antichrist, see Charles Taylor, *Those Who Remain* (Huntington Beach, CA: Today in Bible Prophecy, 1980), and *Get All Excited—Jesus Is Coming Soon!* (Redondo Beach, CA: Today in Bible Prophecy, 1974).

93. See Paul Boyer's discussion, "Apocalyptic Portents in a Post-Cold War World," in his *When Time Shall Be No More*, pp. 325–340.

94. Wim Malgo, *Russia's Last Invasion* (Columbia, SC: Midnight Call, 1980), cited in Boyer, *When Time Shall Be No More*, p. 327.

95. *Gospel Truth*, July 1981, cited in Alnor, *Soothsayers of the Second Advent*, p. 22.

96. James McKeever, "The Muslims Have Declared War," *End-Times News Digest*, April 1989, p. 10, cited in Boyer, *When Time Shall Be No More*, p. 327.

97. See Boyer, *When Time Shall Be No More*, p. 330.

98. See John Ankenberg and John Weldon's discussion, "Islam, Idol Worship, and the Black Stone," in their *One World*; Grant Jeffrey's *Messiah: War in the Middle East and the Road to Armageddon* (Toronto: Frontier Research Publications, 1991); or Chuck Smith's *The Last Days, the Middle East and the Book of Revelation* (Grand Rapids, MI: Church Books, 1991). In his *World News and Bible*

Prophecy (Wheaton, IL: Tyndale House, 1993), Charles Dyer suggests that Iraq may still emerge as the prophesied Babylon and that Saddam Hussein may thus still turn out to be the beast of Revelation (p. 155).

99. See Dwight Wilson, *Armageddon Now!* pp. 81–85.

100. Winrod, *Mussolini's Place in Prophecy*, p. 28.

101. James McAlister, "Startling Signs of the Times," *Evangel*, July 10, 1920, cited in Wilson, *Armageddon Now!*, p. 81.

102. French E. Oliver, "The League of Nations," *The King's Business*, October 11, 1920, p. 926.

103. See W. Percy Hicks, "Proposed Revival of the Old Roman Empire," *Evangel*, March 29, 1926, p. 4; and I. R. Wall, "Christ and Antichrist," *The King's Business*, November 20, 1929, p. 524.

104. Wilbur M. Smith, "How Antichrist Will Rule," *Moody Monthly*, February 1948, p. 399.

105. Louis Bauman, "The Russian Bear Prowls Forth to His Doom," *The King's Business*, September 1950, p. 15.

106. Gerald L. K. Smith, quoted in Ralph Lord Ray, *Apostles of Discord*, p. 59.

107. Cited in Roy, *Apostles of Discord*, p. 11.

108. See Claybaugh, *Thunder on the Right*, p. 129.

109. Hargis, *Communist America*, p. 131. See also Tim LaHaye, *The Beginning of the End* (Wheaton, IL: Tyndale House, 1972), p. 159.

110. Winrod, *The NRA in Prophecy*, p. 11.

111. J. Harold Smith, quoted by James Rorty, "J. Harold Smith and the Dogs of Sin," *Harper's Magazine*, August 1949, p. 72.

112. An excellent discussion of the American Council of Churches' ultra-fundamentalism can be found in Jarstad, *The Politics of Doomsday*. The quotation is from p. 35.

113. Gerald L. K. Smith, "Editorial," *The Cross and the Flag*, March 1948, p. 2.

Chapter 6. Camouflaged Conspirators

1. Hal Lindsey, *The Late Great Planet Earth* (Grand Rapids, MI: Zondervan, 1970), p. 69.

2. Hal Lindsey, *The 1980s: Countdown to Armageddon* (New York: Bantam Books, 1981), p. 106.

3. Pat Robertson, *700 Club Newsletter*, February–March 1980, reprinted in *All in the Name of the Bible*, ed. Harsan Haddad and Donald Wagner (Brattleboro, VT: Amana Books, 1986), p. 121.

4. Charles Taylor, *Get All Excited—Jesus Is Coming Soon!* (Redondo Beach, CA: Today in Bible Prophecy, 1974), p. 26 (italics in original).

5. Peter Lalonde, *One World Under Antichrist* (Eugene, OR: Harvest House, 1991), p. 173.

6. Although I believe that every literary work is influenced by the author's social, cultural, and psychological setting, some writings on the Antichrist are relatively free from polemics that are extrinsic to textual history. A few treatises on the Antichrist produced in recent decades that stick fairly closely to scriptural exegesis are Arthur Bloomfield's *How to Recognize the Antichrist* (Minneapolis: Bethany Fellowship, 1975); Walter K. Price's *The Coming Anti-*

christ (Chicago: Moody Press, 1974); and the republication of P. Huchede's *History of Antichrist* (Rockford, IL: Tan Books, 1968).

7. Sigmund Freud, *Totem and Taboo* (London: Routledge & Kegan Paul, 1950). This is what the noted literary theorist Northrop Frye had in mind when he observed that apocalyptic writings constitute "the categories of reality in the forms of human desire." See Northrop Frye, *Anatomy of Criticism* (Princeton, NJ: Princeton University Press, 1957).

8. Richard Hofstadter, *The Paranoid Style in American Politics* (New York: Knopf, 1965), p. 32.

9. Malcolm Muggeridge, foreword to Vincent Miceli's *The Antichrist* (West Hanover, MA: Christopher Publishing, 1981), p. 7 (italics added).

10. Ibid., p. 11.

11. Ibid., p. 161.

12. Hal Lindsey, cited in Stephen O'Leary, *Arguing the Apocalypse* (New York: Oxford University Press, 1994), pp. 143–144.

13. Lindsey, *The Late Great Planet Earth*, p. vii.

14. Ibid., p. 97.

15. Ibid., p. 92.

16. Ibid., p. 100.

17. Tim LaHaye, *The Beginning of the End* (Wheaton, IL: Tindale House, 1972), p. 136.

18. Alan Peshkin, *God's Choice: The Total World of a Fundamentalist School* (Chicago: University of Chicago Press, 1986), p. 6.

19. Susan Rose, *Keeping Them out of the Hands of Satan* (New York: Routledge, Chapman and Hill, 1988), p. xiv.

20. A. C. Janney, cited in Peshkin, *God's Choice*, p. 36.

21. Rose, *Keeping Them out of the Hands of Satan*, p. 16.

22. Tim LaHaye, *The Battle for the Mind* (Old Tappan, NJ: Fleming H. Revell, 1980), p. 9.

23. Ernest Angley, cited in Paul Boyer, *When Time Shall Be No More* (Cambridge, MA: Belknap Press, 1992), p. 282.

24. Lalonde, *One World Under Antichrist*, p. 204.

25. Ibid., pp. 144–146.

26. Lindsey, *The Late Great Planet Earth*, p. 97.

27. Paul Boyer provides a brief, but illustrative, overview of end-time motifs in the lyrics of rock songs. He draws particular attention the Sex Pistols' 1976 song "Anarchy in the U.K." which opens with the line, "I am the Antichrist." The well-known group Genesis produced a song in 1972 entitled "Apocalypse, in 9/8" that chillingly proclaimed:

> With the guards of Magog, swarming around
> The Pied Piper takes his children underground.
> The dragon's coming out of the sea,
> and the shimmering head of wisdom looking at me.
> . . . . .
> 666 is no longer alone,
> He's getting out the marrow in your backbone,
> And the seven trumpets blowing sweet rock and roll,
> Gonna blow right down inside your soul.

Another 1972 album produced by a group called Aphrodite's Child was entitled 666 and included such songs as "The Beast," "The Seventh Seal," and "The Four Horsemen." See Boyer, *When Time Shall Be No More*, pp. 8–10.

28. Miceli, *The Antichrist*, p. 230.

29. David Noebel, cited in Gary K. Cabaugh, *Thunder on the Right* (Chicago: Nelson-Hall, 1974), p. 127 (italics in original).

30. Ibid. (italics in original).

31. Jacob Aranza, *Backward Masking Unmasked* (Shreveport, LA: Huntington House, 1983), p. 7. Readers might also wish to consult the feature issue on rock music in *Fundamentalist Journal*, February 1986, which maintains that "heavy metal groups overtly demonstrate the spirit of antichrist and rebellion that so often permeates today's hard rock scence" (p. 19).

32. Colin Deal, *Christ Returns by 1988* (Rutherford College, NC: Colin Deal, 1979), p. 81.

33. Miceli, *The Antichrist*, p. 169.

34. Ibid., p. 231.

35. Readers interested in pursuing the connections between biblical and modern secular forms of apocalyptic thinking should consult Saul Friedlander, Gerald Holton, Leo Marx, and Eugene Skolnokoff, eds., *Visions of Apocalypse* (New York: Holmes & Meier, 1985).

36. Peter Malone, *Movie Christs and Antichrists* (New York: Crossroads Press, 1990).

37. W. Warren Wagar, *Terminal Visions: The Literature of the Last Things* (Bloomington: Indiana University Press, 1982).

38. Ibid., p. 76.

39. Mary Stewart Relfe, *The New Money System 666* (Montgomery, AL: Ministries, 1982), p. i.

40. David Webber and Noah Hutchings, *Computers and the Beast of Revelation* (Shreveport, LA: Huntington House, 1986), p. 69.

41. Ibid., p. 12.

42. Lalonde, *One World Under Antichrist*, p. 229.

43. Southwestern Radio Church, cited in William Alnor, *Soothsayers of the Second Advent* (Old Tappan, NJ: Fleming H. Revell, 1989), p. 74.

44. Deal, *Christ Returns by 1988*, p. 86.

45. *Awakeners' Newsletter* (c. 1979), cited in Alnor, *Soothsayers of the Second Advent*, p. 76.

46. Emil Gaverluk and Patrick Fisher, *Fiber Optics: The Eye of the Antichrist* (Oklahoma City: Southwestern Radio Church, 1979), cited in Alnor, *Soothsayers of the Second Advent*, p. 93.

47. Mary Stewart Relfe, *When Your Money Fails . . . The "666 System" Is Here* (Montgomery, AL: Ministries, 1981), p. 134.

48. David Webber and Noah Hutchings, *Apocalyptic Signs in the Heavens* (Oklahoma City: Southwestern Radio Church, 1979), p. 44. Not to be outdone, Colin Deal also offered prophetic rumination on the significance of UFOS. Deal was finally unclear, however, as to whether UFOS are angelic manifestations, as Billy Graham hinted in his *Angels: God's Secret Agents* (Dallas: Word Publications, 1986), or whether they were manifestations of occult or demonic powers. See Deal's *Christ Returns by 1988*.

49. Dave Hunt, *Global Peace and the Rise of Antichrist* (Eugene, OR: Harvest House, 1990), p. 5.

50. Ibid., p. 93.

51. Ibid., p. 94.

52. *Awakeners Newsletter*, cited in Alnor, *Soothsayers of the Second Advent*, p. 79.

53. Webber and Hutchings, *Computers and the Beast of Revelation*, p. 129.

54. Charles Taylor, cited in Alnor, *Soothsayers of the Second Advent*, p. 78.

55. Relfe, *The New Money System 666*, p. 121.

56. Ibid., p. 207.

57. Billy Graham, *World Aflame* (Garden City, NY: Doubleday, 1965), p. 167.

58. Miceli, *The Antichrist*, p. 167.

59. Ibid., p. 194.

60. Lindsey, *The Late Great Planet Earth*, p. 117.

61. O'Leary, *Arguing the Apocalypse*, p. 162.

62. Charles Fitch, *Come out of Her, My People: A Sermon* (Rochester, NY: J. V. Himes, 1843), p. 9 (see Chapter 3, n. 78). Also cited in O'Leary, *Arguing the Apocalypse*, p. 162.

63. Lindsey, *The Late Great Planet Earth*, pp. 104–105.

64. Constance Cumbey, *The Hidden Dangers of the Rainbow* (Shreveport, LA: Huntington House, 1983), p. i.

65. Scholarly assessments of the New Age movement can be found in Catherine Albanese's "Religion and the American Experience," *Church History*, September 1988, pp. 337–351, and her *Nature Religion in America* (Chicago: University of Chicago Press, 1992); William McLoughlin's discussion of the "Fourth Great Awakening" in American religious thought in his *Revivals, Awakenings and Reform* (Chicago: University of Chicago Press, 1978); Duncan S. Ferguson, ed., *New Age Spirituality* (Louisville, KY: John Knox/Westminster Press, 1993); and Antoine Faivre and Jacob Needleman, eds., *Modern Esoteric Spirituality* (New York: Crossroads Press, 1992).

66. Constance Cumbey, *A Planned Deception* (East Detroit, MI: Pointe Publications, 1985), p. 13.

67. Ibid., p. 146.

68. Hunt, *Global Peace and the Rise of Antichrist*, p. 164.

69. See, for example, the ecological essayist Wendell Berry's *A Continuous Harmony* (New York: Harvest/Harcourt Brace Jovanovich, 1972), in which he maintains that the greatest disaster of human history from an ecological point of view "is one that happened to or within religion: that is, the conceptual division between the holy and the world, the excerpting of the Creator from the creation." To Berry's way of thinking, Western monotheism elevates God so far beyond earth that it becomes possible to worship God while hating God's creation: "If God was not in the world, then obviously the world was a thing of inferior importance, or of no importance at all . . . a man [can] aspire to heaven with his mind and his heart while destroying the earth and his fellow men, with his hands" (pp. 6–7).

70. Hunt, *Global Peace and the Rise of Antichrist*, p. 166.

71. Ibid.

72. Ibid., p. 269.

Epilogue. Interpreting the Obsession

1. Norman Cohn, *The Pursuit of the Millennium* (London: Secker and War-burg, 1957), p. 309.

2. See, for example, Kenelm Burridge's *New Heaven New Earth: A Study of Millenarian Activities* (Oxford: Basil Blackwell, 1969).

3. Michael Barkun, *Disaster and the Millennium* (New Haven, CT: Yale University Press, 1974).

4. David Aberle, "A Note on Relative Deprivation Theory as Applied to Millenarian and Other Cult Movements," in *Millennial Dreams in Action: Studies in Revolutionary Movements*, ed. Sylvia Thrupp (New York: Schocken Books, 1970).

5. Robert Jay Lifton, "The Image of the End of the World: A Psycho-historical View," in *Visions of Apocalypse: End or Rebirth*, ed. Saul Friedlander, Gerald Horton, Leo Marx, and Eugene Sklnikoff (New York: Holmes & Meier, 1985), pp. 151–170.

6. Charles B. Strozier, *Apocalypse: On the Psychology of Fundamentalism in America* (Boston: Beacon Press, 1994), p. 251.

7. Ibid., p. 252.

8. Ibid.

9. Stephen O'Leary, *Arguing the Apocalypse* (New York: Oxford University Press, 1994), p. 34.

10. I have applied pragmatism and functional analysis more systematically to the study of religion in both my *Religion and the Life Cycle* (Philadelphia: Fortress Press, 1988), and *Ecology of Care* (Louisville: Westminster Press, 1991).

11. William James, "What Pragmatism Means," in his *Pragmatism* (Indianapolis: Hackett, 1981), p. 38.

12. William James, "The Moral Philosopher and the Moral Life," in his *The Will to Believe* (New York: Dover, 1956), p. 210.

13. Garrett Hardin, "Population Skeletons in the Environmental Closet," *Bulletin of the Atomic Scientists*, June 1972, p. 39.

14. Peter Homans, *Jung in Context* (Chicago: University of Chicago Press), p. 174.

15. Paul Pruyser, *A Dynamic Psychology of Religion* (New York: Harper & Row, 1976), p. 159.

16. W. Warren Wagar, *Terminal Visions* (Bloomington: Indiana University Press, 1982), p. 66 (italics added).

17. Melanie Klein, *The Psycho-Analysis of Children* (London: Hogarth Press, 1930), p. 170. See also the relevant discussions in Jay R. Greenberg and Stephen Mitchell, *Object Relations in Psychoanalytic Theory* (Cambridge, MA: Harvard University Press, 1983); and Harry Guntrip, *Psychoanalytic Theory, Therapy, and the Self* (New York: Basic Books, 1971).

Index